ΕΥΡΙΠΙΔΟΥ ΕΚΑΒΗ.

THE

HECUBA OF EURIPIDES.

Pitt Press Series.

ΕΥΡΙΠΙΔΟΥ ΕΚΑΒΗ.

THE

HECUBA OF EURIPIDES

WITH INTRODUCTION AND NOTES

BY

W. S. HADLEY M.A.

FELLOW OF PEMBROKE COLLEGE, CAMBRIDGE.

EDITED FOR THE SYNDICS OF THE UNIVERSITY PRESS.

CAMBRIDGE:

AT THE UNIVERSITY PRESS.

1894

CAMBRIDGE UNIVERSITY PRESS
Cambridge, New York, Melbourne, Madrid, Cape Town,
Singapore, São Paulo, Delhi, Tokyo, Mexico City

Cambridge University Press
The Edinburgh Building, Cambridge CB2 8RU, UK

Published in the United States of America by
Cambridge University Press, New York

www.cambridge.org
Information on this title: www.cambridge.org/9781107601406

First published 1894
First paperback edition 2011

A catalogue record for this publication is available from the British Library

ISBN 978-1-107-60140-6 Paperback

PREFACE.

THE text of this edition of the Hecuba is in the main
that of Prinz (Leipsic 1883), but, where difficulties
occur, I have to the best of my ability endeavoured to
weigh the evidence independently, and if I have been led
to adopt conclusions other than his, I have written the
text in conformity with my own views. Happily, in the
Hecuba, textual difficulties are comparatively few, and,
when we do meet with them, our task is more frequently
to decide between the retention and the excision of lines
which have stirred the somewhat easily roused suspicions of
susceptible editors than to restore the mangled tradition of
warring families of battered manuscripts. In dealing with
the former class of questions, I have throughout inclined to
a conservative view, partly on the narrower ground of lack
of cogency in the destructive criticism applied to particular
passages, partly on the general principle that such a method
of criticism is a dangerous weapon in any save the most
experienced and skilful hands.

As the Hecuba is a play which is usually read at an
early stage of acquaintance with the Greek language, I have
been careful to exclude from the explanatory commentary
all discussions of the text, but have subjoined a brief notice

of the manuscripts and the more important variants and conjectures, with short critical remarks on some passages, for the use of any who return to Euripides when a little further advanced on the path of scholarship. Of such unfortunately the number is but small, and apart from a limited circle of enthusiastic admirers, the poet's audience is mainly confined to those who use his plays as the painful but necessary exercise-ground of syntax, and whose recollections, so far from being appreciative, are apt to be tinged with a certain bitterness and even scorn.

In writing the commentary, I have consulted the editions of Porson, Pflugk-Wecklein, Paley and many others of the numberless scholars who have edited or illustrated Euripides: but I have endeavoured to form an independent judgment on each question before referring to the notes of others, in the belief that a fresh point of view is more likely to be attained by an editor, who does not at once fly to the assistance of his predecessors, when wishing to explain a difficulty or illustrate a view. I have read with great pleasure the translation of the Hecuba by Mr Way, a translation which will I hope become as widely known as it deserves. The grammars to which I have referred are those of Hadley (Macmillan, 1884) and Thompson (*A Syntax of Attic Greek*, Rivingtons, 1883). Finally my warmest thanks are due to Mr R. A. Neil, who has read all the proof-sheets and has assisted me throughout with valuable suggestions and criticism. I am indebted also to Mr L. Whibley for much kind help.

TABLE OF CONTENTS.

INTRODUCTION.

THE date of the production of the Hecuba is not certain, but from two pieces of internal evidence we may attribute it approximately to the year 425 B.C.: line 173 of the Hecuba is parodied by Aristophanes in the 'Clouds' (l. 1165), which was performed B.C. 423, and in line 462 reference is made to the recent re-establishment by the Athenians of the Delia in B.C. 426[1]. The subject of the play seems to have been taken from one of the non-Homeric legends of the epic cycle, contained possibly in the 'Ιλίου πέρσις of Arctinus of Miletus, an early poet of the eighth century B.C. If we accept B.C. 425 as the date of its production, Euripides was then a man of 55, and had been prominently before the public for 30 years, though of his extant dramas only four or five probably are of earlier date than the Hecuba.

Modern estimates of the tragedy have been mostly unfavourable, the objection urged against it being the apparent want of unity in the plot: the points raised in this criticism are in themselves interesting, and at the same time important, as affecting our appreciation of the play: I accordingly propose to devote a short time to their consideration. Is there then in the Hecuba a unity of design and a coherence of parts? The answer to this question I take to be affirmative: there is a unity of design which awakens what may be termed a collective interest, by bringing into line actions and events, which, though at first sight unconnected, yet by reference to some common centre become parts of a coherent whole: the effect thus

[1] Cf. note on line 456.

produced within the compass of a single play is comparable to that brought about on a larger scale by the older trilogy. The true unity to be sought for is the unity of the objective impression on ourselves, an answering echo of the unity of conception in the poet's mind, an effect beyond the reach of mere calculating workmanship and defying analysis. This trilogy *in petto* may be regarded as an experiment made by the youngest of the three great tragedians at a time perhaps when novelty alike of construction and of treatment was as much desired by the Athenian audiences as it was in accord with the poet's own standpoint and method, wherein in some ways he differed so widely from his two distinguished rivals. The central interest, which creates the unity of the Hecuba, is the character of the heroine, and the study of her change from submission to ferocity under the influence of the events represented in the play, events in themselves unconnected save by fortuitous turns of the plot, which nevertheless by their influence on the development of the leading character acquire an intimate co-relation with each other. The separate episodes of Polyxena, Polydorus[1], and Polymestor all serve in turn to bring out and illustrate the workings of Hecuba's broken but indomitable heart.

In the first act Hecuba overcome with grief is an entirely pathetic character: the blows she has received are severe indeed but inflicted legitimately by gods and open enemies. Her dispute with Odysseus, though during the altercation she calls attention to the meanness of his conduct in neglecting to repay past benefits, is couched in no fierce spirit of invective, and it is with the faint hope of kindling in his heart a shame which may lead him to relent, that she recalls to his memory the days of his distress. So at the end, when swooning with agony, she has no words of cursing save for Helen, guilty cause of all the bloodshed of the war: while the sympathetic bearing of Talthybius and his account of the honour paid by the Greeks to the heroism of Polyxena, help to assuage the proud mother's grief, and her mood becomes one almost of acquiescence in

[1] By the episode of Polydorus I mean that part of the play which deals with the discovery of his death.

the inevitable, finding vent in the utterance of sad reflections on the uncertainty of human happiness.

In the second episode how great the change ! The calamity which forms its subject is the same, the loss of a loved child : harder of course to bear as crowning a series of similar bereavements, but not so overwhelming in its intensity as to alter the very nature of one inured to woes as Hecuba by this time was. Further the blow was not entirely unanticipated[1]. It is not the loss itself that transforms the mood of submission to one of vindictive fury : it is the circumstances of the tragedy : the death of the daughter amid the respectful admiration of her unwilling slayers, victim of a fate, cruel indeed, but nowise dishonourable, is a stately albeit touching scene : how different the picture of the son, sea-tost, unburied, disfigured by gaping wounds ; victim of the cupidity of one who professed himself a friend, but has proved a murderer and a breaker of the troth of hospitality. In the former case Hecuba could sadly acquiesce, bowing her head to Heaven's stroke, and meekly longing for the relief which death will some day bring even to her : but now she has one darling object to achieve, before the accomplishment of which death would be premature, she must take vengeance on the murderer, who, not in accordance with Heaven's will, but in despite of its most holy teaching, has wrought the death of a hapless boy entrusted to his charge in the sacred name of hospitality, amid every circumstance of shame and outrage, and crowned his infamy by refusing that burial, which alone could open the gates of a future life of honour in the nether world. What a contrast this to the passing of the daughter amid the sad praises even of her enemies and the generous desire of every Greek both high and low to dignify the descent of their heroic victim to the realms of Hades.

The second act has seen the sorrow-laden woman, submissive to the blows of fate, change to the implacable avenger of a foully slaughtered son : the third act portrays

---

[1] Cf. ll. 73, 429.

the vengeance, a vengeance horrible enough to stifle for the
moment our pity for Hecuba, and our loathing for her
victim, till we remember the hideous crime the fruits of which
he now is reaping. A Greek audience would not forget that
Polymestor is a barbarian, and that conduct which would be
revolting if employed against a Hellene, is capable of palliation
when directed against the brutal Thracian, who has no reverence
for the will of the gods, or the rights of his fellow men.   In
Hecuba's veins too runs the same Eastern blood, passionate and
vindictive, that had throbbed in Medea's breast, which can
bear with fortitude the chances of life, the anger of gods or
triumph of an open foe, but which pursues to the death the
betrayer of honour or the traitor to a trust.

That the Hecuba is not a drama of episode, but a drama of
character illustrated by episode, may I think fairly be main-
tained. Hecuba is the central figure which supplies unity to all
the incidents grouped around it, and it is the influence of these
incidents on her character which the poet would have us consider.   It is not a play wherein the several characters of the
actors, by their mutual and necessary action and reaction,
conspire to bring about a certain result, but rather an object
lesson in character, a study of a particular mind as affected
by varying circumstances. Assuming this as the central idea
of the play, there is no reason why the poet should not
elaborate the subdivisions and paint with a firm hand the
subordinate characters: this he has done, and with such
success that the reader in admiration of detached parts is in
danger of losing sight of the meaning of the whole.   Polyxena,
for instance, is so beautiful a creation, that one cannot avoid
the feeling that, when she passes from the stage, she takes our
thoughts and our interest with her, and leaves the play the
poorer. The mad ravings of Polymestor and the details of
his undoing are so realistic, that it is on them that we fix our
attention, and for the moment become forgetful of the element
in the play which they are designed to illustrate, not to efface.
It is only when we remember that the character of Hecuba herself
supplies the poet with his theme, that we can grasp the real

unity of a drama, which by reason of the beauty and the vigour of its separate scenes, has been roughly criticized as being not one play, but two. At the same time the adroitness of the transitions, or rather of the coupling together of the episodes, shows that Euripides was not unaware of the risk he ran of criticism on this ground. The discovery of the body of Polydorus, around whom centres the interest of the second act, by the very attendant sent to fetch water for the last sad rites due to the body of Polyxena, the heroine of the first episode, is extremely skilful; while the mention of Hecuba's twofold terror inspired by her dream prepares the spectators for a double catastrophe, quite apart from the preliminary sketch of the action supplied by the poet in the prologue.

In this play the prologue is of the ordinary Euripidean style and is open to the same attack and admits of the same defence as others of its class. The themes of tragedy, or at least the main features of those themes, were all well known to every Athenian audience. Homer and the Cyclic poets had been ransacked for their heroes, and audiences of the early and middle fifth century knew as well what would happen to Ajax or to Oedipus, as we know that Richard III. will die on Bosworth Field and Wolsey deplore the ingratitude of his king. So long as justness of sentiment, or illustration of the ways of gods to men, the drawing of types of character or the tracing out of fate, were felt to be the main objects of the tragedian, no prologue was required : it was not the tale, but the telling of it, that men looked to : but when Euripides claimed sympathy for very men and women, when gods and heroes descended, like Socrates' Philosophy, from heaven to earth, treading the same paths, pained by the same pains and rejoicing with the same joy, as the thronging crowds who felt the kinship of their suffering, then the old situations, the thread-bare plots, had lost their charm; new incidents, fresh developments must be discovered to be the vehicle of the new sympathy, and the explanatory prologue became a necessity as real for those days, as a play-bill is for ours.

Another point for which Euripides has had to bear the

brunt of much unfavourable criticism, the frequency of ἐπι-
δείξεις—of the forensic displays so dear to him and doubtless
to his audiences also, receives illustration in this play. Hecuba
in the agony of supplication for her daughter, Polymestor newly
robbed of sight and children, do not forget the rules of pleading.
To us there is something strangely cold in these precise
measured echoes of the courts : but theatre and court were
different then ; as the Athenian theatre was more restrained
than our modern stage, so the Athenian dicastery with its huge
and irresponsible jury of men even then ever looking for some
new thing, was more open to passionate appeals, than a bench of
twelve men controlled by a skilled expounder of the laws. It is
not for us to grumble : a poet, especially a dramatic poet, cannot
be unaffected by the tastes of those whom he wishes to touch
and influence : Shakspere puns, but he is Shakspere still, and if
Euripides at times employed a method which was to the taste
of his public, why should an age, not without literary vices of
its own, abuse him for it ? The same defence may be offered
to the charge, justly enough brought against him, of sometimes
philosophizing off the point and out of season : ideas with the
dulness of 2000 years' repetition on them now, were bright
once : bright enough to delight, perhaps to dazzle, audiences,
which even we cannot call uncritical. Defects they may be,
but defects sometimes reveal the touch of a human hand, just
as the irregularities of a Persian rug, the waywardness of a
piece of beaten iron, attract us more than the four-squareness
of the productions of steam and rule.

Of the merits of the play it is a pleasant task to speak.
Euripides' conception and drawing of the character of Hecuba
have been already touched upon, but much remains to praise.
In our poet's gallery of noble women none holds a higher place
than Polyxena ; not Alcestis, not Macaria. Patience, tender-
ness, purity, fortitude, noblest qualities of womanhood, elevated
with the indefinable dignity conferred on virtue by high birth,
are united in the character of the virgin princess, who appears
but for one brief scene upon the stage, speaks little, yet leaves
us filled with a sense of having been in converse with one

of the noblest creations of dramatic literature. To convey such an impression in so short a time, to paint such a portrait in a few strokes, is surely the work of a master, and argues too the existence of an ideal in the creator's mind, earnest, pervading, pure, which by its presence could enable him to draw so quickly and so well. We have but to remember this to dismiss at once the idle theories of Euripides' hate for women, theories which owe their existence to heedless reasoning from random lines divorced from their context and considered without reference to the character in whose mouth they are placed, or the occasion on which they are uttered. In Odysseus Euripides has drawn an able man of the world, of a type on which we may well imagine many a busy ambitious Athenian would have wished to fashion himself: destitute of that οἶκτος, which Thucydides' Cleon declared to be ἀρχῇ ἀσυμφορώτατος, yet not ruffianly : plausible of speech, quick of action, shrewd, patient, determined : by his side Agamemnon, king of men, becomes insignificant and lacks the dignity which his great position calls for : much as he wishes, he dares not aid Hecuba in her vengeance, lest the army should misunderstand his action : the captive queen fears not to taunt him with his lack of liberty, and though he does not waver in the trial scene, but gives sentence in the Trojan's favour and approves her deed, yet he effects no strong impression ; he fails to make the reader feel that he is in the presence of a leader of men, and one is inclined to ascribe to the petulance of a weak nature his outburst of offended pride at the conclusion of the play, when he orders the wretched Thracian's exposure on a desert island as a punishment for his presumption in foretelling troubles in his home. Well drawn too is the character of Talthybius ; most courteous of heralds, he must fulfil his task, albeit it pains him to add to the woes of one, Trojan though she be, whose misery makes him doubt the goodness, nay the existence, of the gods : tenderly almost does he tell the weeping mother the story of her child's brave death, giving what comfort may be given. There is one more picture, which by its dark colouring serves to bring into relief the other portraits which the poet

draws : the savage Thracian, faithless and covetous, who spoils
and slays the fatherless child, and deepens the guilt of fraud
and murder by that to the ancient world unpardonable crime, vio-
lation of the rights of hospitality, is an addition to the character-
studies of the play, sombre indeed but effective, and serves to
mark most clearly the exclusive feeling of the Greek, that barbarous and brutal were synonymous : strictly, of course, Hecuba
is barbarous too, but the long and evenly-balanced struggle
between Greeks and Trojans which formed the theme of the
Hellene's bible, had raised the latter to equality with their
conquerors. The choral odes remain for mention : although,
in accordance with the practice of Euripides, they are of the
nature of detached lyrics, yet they are directly suggested by and
in accordance with the development of the action of the play :
many and exquisite as are the choral songs scattered over his
works, Euripides has never, in my judgment, given a finer
example of his power than in that ode in which the captive
women describe the fatal security, the surprise and carnage of
the last night of Troy. In it he seems to have caught the
inspiration of that romantic school, of which it is not too much
to say he was the unconscious and unrecognized forerunner.

That the verdict of antiquity was favourable to the play is
proved by the number of translations and imitations of it from
Ennius onward. Echoes of it are found in Catullus and Pro-
pertius, in Virgil and Ovid : the latter poet may indeed almost
be reckoned as a translator (cf. Metam. xiii. 407 sqq.), though
Seneca has borrowed but little from it in his Troades. With
the Phoenissae and Orestes, it formed the favourite reading book
in the later Byzantine schools. The Hecuba was one of the
first Greek plays translated by the French humanist Lazare de
Baïf, while Erasmus put it into Latin, and the Venetian Luigi
Dolce published an Italian version. Hamlet's player tells the
story of the 'mobled queen,' and the sorrows of Hecuba became
a phrase. One need not mention the imitations of the French
classic drama, the exhausting Polyxènes of Pradon, of Lafosse,
of Chateaubrun, save to introduce the profound comment of
M. Patin, whose concluding words sum up for us the lessons of

the Attic theatre. "Je ne crois pas qu'on parvienne jamais à nous faire prendre en patience les calmes et contemplatifs développements de la tragédie grecque. Ce qu'il faut lui demander, ce ne sont pas ses sujets, ni la forme de ses drames, les uns usés et l'autre incompatible avec l'allure actuelle de notre imagination : c'est, s'il se peut, ce secret que nous cherchons encore, *d'être variés, mais sans bigarrure et sans disparate; vrais, mais d'une vérité choisie; simples, mais avec simplicité.*"

ARGUMENT.

First Episode.

THE scene is laid on the shore of the Thracian Chersonese, whither the Greek host had crossed after the fall of Troy. The fleet is delayed there by contrary winds.

1—58. Prologue spoken by the ghost of Polydorus; he describes his own murder by Polymestor, king of the district where the action takes place, who coveted the treasure which had been committed to him by Priam in trust for Polydorus. He also describes how the ghost of Achilles has appeared and claimed his sister Polyxena as a victim, to be slaughtered at his tomb, prophetically adding that the sacrifice will be carried out. He relates that he has appeared in a vision to his mother Hecuba, who

59—97 appears supported by some fellow captives: she describes the ominous dream, which has driven her forth filled with forebodings for the fate of her two children.

98—176. The chorus of Trojan captive women enter and announce to Hecuba the decision of the Greek generals to sacrifice Polyxena at the tomb of Achilles. Hecuba breaks into lamentation and summons her ill-fated daughter, who,

177—215 on hearing her doom, gives all her pity to the mother who will be left alone, but utters no complaint for herself.

216—331. Odysseus arrives with a formal announcement of the decree. Hecuba appeals to him for a return of the kindness she had once shown him in·his need, and begs him to plead for her daughter, now her only stay and comfort. Odysseus, though acknowledging his obligation, refuses to do more than guarantee Hecuba's own personal safety, and urges the bad effect, which neglect to do honour to brave warriors after death produces, as a justification of his sternness.

332—381. Hecuba, seeing her own efforts fruitless, bids Polyxena plead her own cause. Odysseus is a father and may relent before a child's petition. Polyxena however expresses her more than willingness to die, contrasting her probable lot, if allowed to live, with what had once been her reasonable expectations as the daughter of a king.

382—443. Hecuba, to no purpose, offers her own life in exchange, and Polyxena, entreating her mother to submit to fate, takes an affecting leave of her, and follows Odysseus to her doom. Hecuba swoons and falls senseless to the ground, with a final imprecation on Helen, the cause of all her misery. A break in the action occurs here, which is marked

444—483 by a choral ode, in which the captive women speculate on the probable scene of their slavery, closing with a brief lament over their fallen country.

484—628. The herald Talthybius arrives, and after questioning the existence of gods who can permit such sorrows as Hecuba's to be, bids her tend the burial of her child. To Hecuba's request for particulars of the sacrifice, he replies by giving a touching account of the heroic maiden's last moments and of the admiring pity of the Greeks for her noble fortitude. The mother's grief is lightened by the recital of her daughter's glorious death, and she begs that orders may be given that the corpse shall not be disturbed, and that she may be permitted to render the last sad offices, as well as a captive may, to her daughter's remains. Thus ends the first episode.

Second Episode.

629—656. After a brief ode, tracing all their misery to Paris' fatal arbitrament on Ida, the chorus

657—722 are met by an attendant, who has been to fetch water for the funeral rites of Polyxena; she enquires for Hecuba, and after brief preface displays to her the body of her murdered son Polydorus, which she has discovered when on her quest for lustral water: the horror-stricken mother with her lamentations mingles curses on the faithless Thracian, whom she recognizes as the author of the crime.

723—904. Agamemnon appears, enquiring the cause of Hecuba's delay in carrying out the funeral rites of Polyxena, but seeing the corpse of Polydorus demands an explanation of this fresh catastrophe: after brief consultation with herself, Hecuba decides to tell Agamemnon all, and to beg his help in a scheme of vengeance she has planned. She does so, appealing to him as the vicegerent of the gods, whom Polymestor has outraged by his heinous breach of their most holy laws: in pathetic tones too she pleads for his pity, urging even his love for Cassandra as a ground for acceding to her request. Agamemnon professes his sympathy, and would willingly he says help her, but that the army counts the Thracian their friend, and her an enemy. Hecuba, half scornful of his timidity, asks that if he will not actively assist her, he will tacitly permit her to carry out herself a plan of vengeance. He consents and wishes her success.

905—951. The interval between this act and the next is filled by the chorus, who sing a most beautiful ode descriptive of the last night of Troy: how in false security the warrior was stretched in careless sleep, his wife lingering over her preparations for repose, when the war-cry of the Greeks was heard in the city, and in a moment all was carnage and destruction.

Third Episode.

952—1022. Polymestor, in response to a summons of Hecuba, appears with his two infant sons: she has, she says, a secret to reveal to him, the place of concealment of the treasure of the Trojan kings: also she would entrust to him some valuables which she has saved from Troy, and which she keeps concealed in the apartments of the captive women: let him dismiss his guards, and accompany her within, bringing his children to share the secret of the treasure, in case anything should happen to himself. He falls into the trap,

1023—1108 and, after a short choral ode of triumph, he is heard within screaming in agony, and after a few moments appears on the stage, blinded and mad with fury, breathing fierce threats of vengeance on the tigresses who have robbed him at once of sight and children.

1109—1295. Agamemnon, hearing the uproar, comes to learn its cause: Polymestor appeals to him, and gives a graphic description of the women's onset. he admits his murder of Polydorus, but assigns plausible and, as he thinks, satisfactory reasons for it: Hecuba answers, exposing the falseness of his pretences and showing that avarice was the only spring of his action. After a violent invective, she makes a final appeal to Agamemnon, who gives judgment in her favour: whereupon the baffled Thracian bewails his lot, but finds some little satisfaction in prophesying for Hecuba a violent and shameful end, for Agamemnon a faithless wife and cruel death. Enraged at his presumption, the Grecian leader orders him to be cast upon a desert island, while the captive women are bidden to return to their quarters, and prepare for their sad voyage to Greece and slavery.

ΕΥΡΙΠΙΔΟΥ ΕΚΑΒΗ.

TA TOY ΔΡΑΜΑΤΟΣ ΠΡΟΣΩΠΑ.

———

ΠΟΛΥΔΩΡΟΥ ΕΙΔΩΛΟΝ.
ΕΚΑΒΗ.
ΧΟΡΟΣ ΑΙΧΜΑΛΩΤΙΔΩΝ ΓΥΝΑΙΚΩΝ.
ΠΟΛΥΞΕΝΗ.
ΟΔΥΣΣΕΥΣ.
ΤΑΛΘΥΒΙΟΣ.
ΘΕΡΑΠΑΙΝΑ.
ΑΓΑΜΕΜΝΩΝ.
ΠΟΛΥΜΗΣΤΩΡ ΚΑΙ ΟΙ ΠΑΙΔΕΣ ΑΥΤΟΥ.

ΠΟΛΥΔΩΡΟΥ ΕΙΔΩΛΟΝ.

Ἥκω νεκρῶν κευθμῶνα καὶ σκότου πύλας
λιπών, ἵν᾽ Ἅιδης χωρὶς ᾤκισται θεῶν,
Πολύδωρος, Ἑκάβης παῖς γεγὼς τῆς Κισσέως
Πριάμου τε πατρός, ὅς μ᾽, ἐπεὶ Φρυγῶν πόλιν
κίνδυνος ἔσχε δορὶ πεσεῖν Ἑλληνικῷ,   5
δείσας ὑπεξέπεμψε Τρωικῆς χθονὸς
Πολυμήστορος πρὸς δῶμα Θρηκίου ξένου,
ὃς τήνδ᾽ ἀρίστην Χερσονησίαν πλάκα
σπείρει, φίλιππον λαὸν εὐθύνων δορί.
πολὺν δὲ σὺν ἐμοὶ χρυσὸν ἐκπέμπει λάθρᾳ   10
πατήρ, ἵν᾽, εἴ ποτ᾽ Ἰλίου τείχη πέσοι,
τοῖς ζῶσιν εἴη παισὶ μὴ σπάνις βίου.
νεώτατος δ᾽ ἦ Πριαμιδῶν, ὃ καί με γῆς
ὑπεξέπεμψεν· οὔτε γὰρ φέρειν ὅπλα
οὔτ᾽ ἔγχος οἷός τ᾽ ἦ νέῳ βραχίονι.   15
ἕως μὲν οὖν γῆς ὄρθ᾽ ἔκειθ᾽ ὁρίσματα
πύργοι τ᾽ ἄθραυστοι Τρωικῆς ἦσαν χθονὸς
Ἕκτωρ τ᾽ ἀδελφὸς οὑμὸς ηὐτύχει δορί,
καλῶς παρ᾽ ἀνδρὶ Θρηκὶ πατρῴῳ ξένῳ
τροφαῖσιν ὥς τις πτόρθος ηὐξόμην τάλας.   20
ἐπεὶ δὲ Τροία θ᾽ Ἕκτορός τ᾽ ἀπόλλυται
ψυχὴ πατρῴα θ᾽ ἑστία κατεσκάφη,

αὐτὸς δὲ βωμῷ πρὸς θεοδμήτῳ πίτνει
σφαγεὶς Ἀχιλλέως παιδὸς ἐκ μιαιφόνου,
κτείνει με χρυσοῦ τὸν ταλαίπωρον χάριν 25
ξένος πατρῷος καὶ κτανὼν ἐς οἶδμ᾽ ἁλὸς
μεθῆχ᾽, ἵν᾽ αὐτὸς χρυσὸν ἐν δόμοις ἔχῃ.
κεῖμαι δ᾽ ἐπ᾽ ἀκταῖς, ἄλλοτ᾽ ἐν πόντου σάλῳ,
πολλοῖς διαύλοις κυμάτων φορούμενος,
ἄκλαυτος ἄταφος· νῦν δ᾽ ὑπὲρ μητρὸς φίλης 30
Ἑκάβης ἀΐσσω, σῶμ᾽ ἐρημώσας ἐμόν,
τριταῖον ἤδη φέγγος αἰωρούμενος,
ὅσονπερ ἐν γῇ τῇδε Χερσονησίᾳ
μήτηρ ἐμὴ δύστηνος ἐκ Τροίας πάρα.
πάντες δ᾽ Ἀχαιοὶ ναῦς ἔχοντες ἥσυχοι 35
θάσσουσ᾽ ἐπ᾽ ἀκταῖς τῆσδε Θρῃκίας χθονός·
ὁ Πηλέως γὰρ παῖς ὑπὲρ τύμβου φανεὶς
κατέσχ᾽ Ἀχιλλεὺς πᾶν στράτευμ᾽ Ἑλληνικόν,
πρὸς οἶκον εὐθύνοντας ἐναλίαν πλάτην·
αἰτεῖ δ᾽ ἀδελφὴν τὴν ἐμὴν Πολυξένην 40
τύμβῳ φίλον πρόσφαγμα καὶ γέρας λαβεῖν.
καὶ τεύξεται τοῦδ᾽ οὐδ᾽ ἀδώρητος φίλων
ἔσται πρὸς ἀνδρῶν· ἡ πεπρωμένη δ᾽ ἄγει
θανεῖν ἀδελφὴν τῷδ᾽ ἐμὴν ἐν ἤματι.
δυοῖν δὲ παίδοιν δύο νεκρὼ κατόψεται 45
μήτηρ, ἐμοῦ τε τῆς τε δυστήνου κόρης.
φανήσομαι γάρ, ὡς τάφου τλήμων τύχω,
δούλης ποδῶν πάροιθεν ἐν κλυδωνίῳ.
τοὺς γὰρ κάτω σθένοντας ἐξῃτησάμην
τύμβου κυρῆσαι κἀς χέρας μητρὸς πεσεῖν. 50
τοὐμὸν μὲν οὖν ὅσονπερ ἤθελον τυχεῖν
ἔσται· γεραιᾷ δ᾽ ἐκποδὼν χωρήσομαι
Ἑκάβῃ· περᾷ γὰρ ἥδ᾽ ὑπὸ σκηνῆς πόδα

Ἀγαμέμνονος, φάντασμα δειμαίνουσ᾽ ἐμόν.
φεῦ·
ὦ μῆτερ ἥτις ἐκ τυραννικῶν δόμων   55
δούλειον ἦμαρ εἶδες, ὡς πράσσεις κακῶς
ὅσονπερ εὖ ποτ᾽. ἀντισηκώσας δέ σε
φθείρει θεῶν τις τῆς πάροιθ᾽ εὐπραξίας.

ΕΚΑΒΗ.

ἄγετ᾽, ὦ παῖδες, τὴν γραῦν πρὸ δόμων,
ἄγετ᾽ ὀρθοῦσαι τὴν ὁμόδουλον,   60
Τρῳάδες, ὑμῖν, πρόσθε δ᾽ ἄνασσαν.
λάβετε φέρετε πέμπετ᾽ ἀείρετέ μου
γεραιᾶς χειρὸς προσλαζύμεναι·
κἀγὼ σκολιῷ σκίπωνι χερὸς   65
διερειδομένα σπεύσω βραδύπουν
ἤλυσιν ἄρθρων προτιθεῖσα.
ὦ στεροπὰ Διός, ὦ σκοτία νύξ,
τί ποτ᾽ αἴρομαι ἔννυχος οὕτω
δείμασι φάσμασιν; ὦ πότνια χθών,   70
μελανοπτερύγων μῆτερ ὀνείρων,
ἀποπέμπομαι ἔννυχον ὄψιν,
ἣν περὶ παιδὸς ἐμοῦ τοῦ σῳζομένου κατὰ Θρήκην
ἀμφὶ Πολυξείνης τε φίλης θυγατρὸς δι᾽ ὀνείρων
φοβερὰν ἐδάην.   76
ὦ χθόνιοι θεοί, σώσατε παῖδ᾽ ἐμόν,
ὃς μόνος οἴκων ἄγκυρ᾽ ἀμῶν   80
τὴν χιονώδη Θρήκην κατέχει
ξείνου πατρίου φυλακαῖσιν.
ἔσται τι νέον,
ἥξει τι μέλος γοερὸν γοεραῖς.
οὔποτ᾽ ἐμὰ φρὴν ὧδ᾽ ἀλίαστος   85

φρίσσει ταρβεῖ.
ποῦ ποτε θείαν Ἑλένου ψυχὰν
καὶ Κασάνδραν ἐσίδω, Τρῳάδες,
ὥς μοι κρίνωσιν ὀνείρους;
εἶδον γὰρ βαλιὰν ἔλαφον λύκου αἵμονι χαλᾷ 90
σφαζομέναν, ἀπ᾽ ἐμῶν γονάτων σπασθεῖσαν ἀ-
νοίκτως.
καὶ τόδε δεῖμά μοι·
ἦλθ᾽ ὑπὲρ ἄκρας τύμβου κορυφᾶς
φάντασμ᾽ Ἀχιλέως· ᾔτει δὲ γέρας
τῶν πολυμόχθων τινὰ Τρωιάδων.   95
ἀπ᾽ ἐμᾶς, ἀπ᾽ ἐμᾶς οὖν τόδε παιδὸς
πέμψατε, δαίμονες, ἱκετεύω.

ΧΟΡΟΣ.

Εκάβη, σπουδῇ πρός σ᾽ ἐλιάσθην
τὰς δεσποσύνους σκηνὰς προλιποῦσ᾽,
ἵν᾽ ἐκληρώθην καὶ προσετάχθην   100
δούλη, πόλεως ἀπελαυνομένη
τῆς Ἰλιάδος, λόγχης αἰχμῇ
δοριθήρατος πρὸς Ἀχαιῶν,
οὐδὲν παθέων ἀποκουφίζουσ᾽,
ἀλλ᾽ ἀγγελίας βάρος ἀραμένη   105
μέγα σοί τε, γύναι, κῆρυξ ἀχέων.
ἐν γὰρ Ἀχαιῶν πλήρει ξυνόδῳ
λέγεται δόξαι σὴν παῖδ᾽ Ἀχιλεῖ
σφάγιον θέσθαι· τύμβου δ᾽ ἐπιβὰς
οἶσθ᾽ ὅτε χρυσέοις ἐφάνη σὺν ὅπλοις,   110
τὰς ποντοπόρους δ᾽ ἔσχε σχεδίας
λαίφη προτόνοις ἐπερειδομένας,

τάδε θωΰσσων·
ποῖ δή, Δαναοί, τὸν ἐμὸν τύμβον
στέλλεσθ᾽ ἀγέραστον ἀφέντες;   115
πολλῆς δ᾽ ἔριδος ξυνέπαισε κλύδων,
δόξα δ᾽ ἐχώρει δίχ᾽ ἀν᾽ Ἑλλήνων
στρατὸν αἰχμητήν, τοῖς μὲν διδόναι
τύμβῳ σφάγιον, τοῖς δ᾽ οὐχὶ δοκοῦν.
ἦν δὲ τὸ μὲν σὸν σπεύδων ἀγαθὸν   120
τῆς μαντιπόλου Βάκχης ἀνέχων
λέκτρ᾽ Ἀγαμέμνων·
τὼ Θησείδα δ᾽, ὄζω Ἀθηνῶν,
δισσῶν μύθων ῥήτορες ἦσαν·
γνώμῃ δὲ μιᾷ συνεχωρείτην,   125
τὸν Ἀχίλλειον τύμβον στεφανοῦν
αἵματι χλωρῷ, τὰ δὲ Κασάνδρας
λέκτρ᾽ οὐκ ἐφάτην τῆς Ἀχιλείας
πρόσθεν θήσειν ποτὲ λόγχης.
σπουδαὶ δὲ λόγων κατατεινομένων   130
ἦσαν ἴσαι πως, πρὶν ὁ ποικιλόφρων
κόπις ἡδυλόγος δημοχαριστὴς
Λαερτιάδης πείθει στρατιὰν
μὴ τὸν ἄριστον Δαναῶν πάντων
δούλων σφαγίων εἵνεκ᾽ ἀπωθεῖν,   135
μηδέ τιν᾽ εἰπεῖν παρὰ Περσεφόνῃ
στάντα φθιμένων
ὡς ἀχάριστοι Δαναοὶ Δαναοῖς
τοῖς οἰχομένοις ὑπὲρ Ἑλλήνων
Τροίας πεδίων ἀπέβησαν.   140
ἥξει δ᾽ Ὀδυσεὺς ὅσον οὐκ ἤδη,
πῶλον ἀφέλξων σῶν ἀπὸ μαστῶν
ἔκ τε γεραιᾶς χερὸς ὁρμήσων.

ἀλλ᾽ ἴθι ναούς, ἴθι πρὸς βωμούς,
ἵζ᾽ Ἀγαμέμνονος ἱκέτις γονάτων,   145
κήρυσσε θεοὺς τούς τ᾽ οὐρανίδας
τούς θ᾽ ὑπὸ γαῖαν.
ἢ γάρ σε λιταὶ διακωλύσουσ᾽
ὀρφανὸν εἶναι παιδὸς μελέας,
ἢ δεῖ σ᾽ ἐπιδεῖν τύμβου προπετῆ   150
φοινισσομένην αἵματι παρθένον
ἐκ χρυσοφόρου
δειρῆς νασμῷ μελαναυγεῖ.

ΕΚ.   οἲ ᾽γὼ μελέα, τί ποτ᾽ ἀπύσω;
       ποίαν ἀχώ, ποῖον ὀδυρμόν;   155
       δειλαία δειλαίου γήρως,
       δουλείας τᾶς οὐ τλατᾶς,
       τᾶς οὐ φερτᾶς· ὤμοι μοι.
       τίς ἀμύνει μοι; ποία γέννα,
       ποία δὲ πόλις;   160
       φροῦδος πρέσβυς, φροῦδοι παῖδες.
       ποίαν ἢ ταύταν ἢ κείναν
       στείχω; ποῖ δ᾽ ἥσω; ποῦ τις θεῶν
       ἢ δαίμων νῷν ἐπαρωγός;
       ὦ κάκ᾽ ἐνεγκοῦσαι Τρωάδες, ὦ   165
       κάκ᾽ ἐνεγκοῦσαι
       πήματ᾽, ἀπωλέσατ᾽ ὠλέσατ᾽· οὐκέτι μοι βίος
       ἀγαστὸς ἐν φάει.
       ὦ τλάμων ἄγησαί μοι
       πούς, ἄγησαι τᾷ γραίᾳ   170
       πρὸς τάνδ᾽ αὐλάν· ὦ τέκνον, ὦ παῖ
       δυστανοτάτας ματέρος, ἔξελθ᾽
       ἔξελθ᾽ οἴκων· ἄιε ματέρος
       αὐδάν, ὦ τέκνον, ὡς εἰδῇς

οἵαν οἵαν ἀίω φάμαν 175
περὶ σᾶς ψυχᾶς.

ΠΟΛΥΞΕΝΗ.

ἰώ,
μᾶτερ μᾶτερ, τί βοᾷς; τί νέον
καρύξασ' οἴκων μ' ὥστ' ὄρνιν
θάμβει τῷδ' ἐξέπταξας;
ΕΚ. οἴμοι, τέκνον. 180
ΠΟΛΥΞ. τί με δυσφημεῖς; φροίμιά μοι κακά.
ΕΚ. αἰαῖ, σᾶς ψυχᾶς.
ΠΟΛΥΞ. ἐξαύδα, μὴ κρύψῃς δαρόν.
δειμαίνω δειμαίνω, μᾶτερ,
τί ποτ' ἀναστένεις. 185
ΕΚ. τέκνον τέκνον μελέας ματρός.
ΠΟΛΥΞ. τί τόδ' ἀγγέλλεις;
ΕΚ. σφάξαι σ' Ἀργείων κοινὰ
συντείνει πρὸς τύμβον γνώμα
Πηλείδᾳ γέννᾳ. 190
ΠΟΛΥΞ. οἴμοι, μᾶτερ, πῶς φθέγγει
ἀμέγαρτα κακῶν; μάνυσόν μοι
μάνυσον, μᾶτερ.
ΕΚ. αὐδῶ, παῖ, δυσφάμους φάμας·
ἀγγέλλουσ' Ἀργείων δόξαι 195
ψήφῳ τᾶς σᾶς περί μοι ψυχᾶς.
ΠΟΛΥΞ. ὦ δεινὰ παθοῦσ', ὦ παντλάμων,
ὦ δυστάνου μᾶτερ βιοτᾶς,
οἵαν οἵαν αὖ σοι λώβαν
ἐχθίσταν ἀρρήταν τ' 200
ὦρσέν τις δαίμων;
οὐκέτι σοι παῖς ἅδ' οὐκέτι δὴ

γήρᾳ δειλαίῳ δειλαία
συνδουλεύσω.
σκύμνον γάρ μ' ὥστ' οὐριθρέπταν,   205
μόσχον δειλαία δειλαίαν
εἰσόψει χειρὸς ἀναρπαστὰν
σᾶς ἄπο λαιμότομόν τ' Ἀΐδᾳ
γᾶς ὑποπεμπομέναν σκότον, ἔνθα νεκρῶν μέτα
τάλαινα κείσομαι.   210
καὶ σοῦ μέν, μᾶτερ, δυστάνου
κλαίω πανδύρτοις θρήνοις,
τὸν ἐμὸν δὲ βίον, λώβαν λύμαν τ',
οὐ μετακλαίομαι, ἀλλὰ θανεῖν μοι
ξυντυχία κρείσσων ἐκύρησεν.   215

ΧΟ. καὶ μὴν Ὀδυσσεὺς ἔρχεται σπουδῇ ποδός,
Ἑκάβη, νέον τι πρὸς σὲ σημανῶν ἔπος.

ΟΔΥΣΣΕΥΣ.

γύναι, δοκῶ μέν σ' εἰδέναι γνώμην στρατοῦ
ψῆφόν τε τὴν κρανθεῖσαν· ἀλλ' ὅμως φράσω.
ἔδοξ' Ἀχαιοῖς παῖδα σὴν Πολυξένην   220
σφάξαι πρὸς ὀρθὸν χῶμ' Ἀχιλλείου τάφου.
ἡμᾶς δὲ πομποὺς καὶ κομιστῆρας κόρης
τάσσουσιν εἶναι· θύματος δ' ἐπιστάτης
ἱερεύς τ' ἐπέστη τοῦδε παῖς Ἀχιλλέως.
οἶσθ' οὖν ὃ δρᾶσον; μήτ' ἀποσπασθῇς βίᾳ   225
μήτ' ἐς χερῶν ἅμιλλαν ἐξέλθῃς ἐμοί·
γίγνωσκε δ' ἀλκὴν καὶ παρουσίαν κακῶν
τῶν σῶν. σοφόν τοι κἀν κακοῖς ἃ δεῖ φρονεῖν.

ΕΚ. αἰαῖ· παρέστηχ', ὡς ἔοικ', ἀγὼν μέγας,
πλήρης στεναγμῶν οὐδὲ δακρύων κενός.   230
κἄγωγ' ἄρ' οὐκ ἔθνησκον οὗ με χρῆν θανεῖν,

οὐδ' ὤλεσέν με Ζεύς, τρέφει δ', ὅπως ὁρῶ
κακῶν κάκ' ἄλλα μεῖζον' ἡ τάλαιν' ἐγώ.
εἰ δ' ἔστι τοῖς δούλοισι τοὺς ἐλευθέρους
μὴ λυπρὰ μηδὲ καρδίας δηκτήρια   235
ἐξιστορῆσαι, σοὶ μὲν εἰρῆσθαι χρεών,
ἡμᾶς δ' ἀκοῦσαι τοὺς ἐρωτῶντας τάδε.
ΟΔ. ἔξεστ', ἐρώτα· τοῦ χρόνου γὰρ οὐ φθονῶ.
ΕΚ. οἶσθ' ἡνίκ' ἦλθες Ἰλίου κατάσκοπος,
δυσχλαινίᾳ τ' ἄμορφος, ὀμμάτων τ' ἄπο   240
φόνου σταλαγμοὶ σὴν κατέσταζον γένυν;
ΟΔ. οἶδ'· οὐ γὰρ ἄκρας καρδίας ἔψαυσέ μου.
ΕΚ. ἔγνω δέ σ' Ἑλένη, καὶ μόνῃ κατεῖπ' ἐμοί;
ΟΔ. μεμνήμεθ' ἐς κίνδυνον ἐλθόντες μέγαν.
ΕΚ. ἦψω δὲ γονάτων τῶν ἐμῶν ταπεινὸς ὤν;   245
ΟΔ. ὥστ' ἐνθανεῖν γε σοῖς πέπλοισι χεῖρ' ἐμήν.
ΕΚ. τί δῆτ' ἔλεξας, δοῦλος ὢν ἐμὸς τότε;
ΟΔ. πολλῶν λόγων εὑρήμαθ', ὥστε μὴ θανεῖν.
ΕΚ. ἔσωσα δῆτά σ', ἐξέπεμψά τε χθονός;
ΟΔ. ὥστ' εἰσορᾶν γε φέγγος ἡλίου τόδε.   250
ΕΚ. οὔκουν κακύνει τοῖσδε τοῖς βουλεύμασιν,
ὃς ἐξ ἐμοῦ μὲν ἔπαθες οἷα φῂς παθεῖν,
δρᾷς δ' οὐδὲν ἡμᾶς εὖ, κακῶς δ' ὅσον δύνῃ;
ἀχάριστον ὑμῶν σπέρμ', ὅσοι δημηγόρους
ζηλοῦτε τιμάς· μηδὲ γιγνώσκοισθέ μοι,   255
οἳ τοὺς φίλους βλάπτοντες οὐ φροντίζετε,
ἢν τοῖσι πολλοῖς πρὸς χάριν λέγητέ τι.
ἀτὰρ τί δὴ σόφισμα τοῦθ' ἡγούμενοι
ἐς τήνδε παῖδα ψῆφον ὥρισαν φόνου;   259
πότερα τὸ χρῆν σφ' ἐπήγαγ' ἀνθρωποσφαγεῖν
πρὸς τύμβον, ἔνθα βουθυτεῖν μᾶλλον πρέπει;
ἢ τοὺς κτανόντας ἀνταποκτεῖναι θέλων

ἐς τήνδ' Ἀχιλλεὺς ἐνδίκως τείνει φόνον;
ἀλλ' οὐδὲν αὐτὸν ἥδε γ' εἴργασται κακόν.
Ἑλένην νιν αἰτεῖν χρῆν τάφῳ προσφάγματα·
κείνη γὰρ ὤλεσέν νιν ἐς Τροίαν τ' ἄγει.   266
εἰ δ' αἰχμάλωτον χρή τιν' ἔκκριτον θανεῖν
κάλλει θ' ὑπερφέρουσαν, οὐχ ἡμῶν τόδε·
ἡ Τυνδαρὶς γὰρ εἶδος ἐκπρεπεστάτη,
ἀδικοῦσά θ' ἡμῶν οὐδὲν ἧσσον ηὑρέθη.   270
τῷ μὲν δικαίῳ τόνδ' ἁμιλλῶμαι λόγον·
ἃ δ' ἀντιδοῦναι δεῖ σ' ἀπαιτούσης ἐμοῦ,
ἄκουσον. ἧψω τῆς ἐμῆς, ὡς φής, χερὸς
καὶ τῆσδε γραίας προσπίτνων παρηΐδος·
ἀνθάπτομαί σου τῶνδε τῶν αὐτῶν ἐγώ,   275
χάριν τ' ἀπαιτῶ τὴν τόθ' ἱκετεύω τέ σε,
μή μου τὸ τέκνον ἐκ χερῶν ἀποσπάσῃς,
μηδὲ κτάνητε· τῶν τεθνηκότων ἅλις.   278
ἥδ' ἀντὶ πολλῶν ἐστί μοι παραψυχή,   280
πόλις τιθήνη βάκτρον ἡγεμὼν ὁδοῦ.
οὐ τοὺς κρατοῦντας χρὴ κρατεῖν ἃ μὴ χρεών,
οὐδ' εὐτυχοῦντας εὖ δοκεῖν πράξειν ἀεί.
κἀγὼ γὰρ ἦ ποτ', ἀλλὰ νῦν οὐκ εἴμ' ἔτι,
τὸν πάντα δ' ὄλβον ἦμαρ ἕν μ' ἀφείλετο.   285
ἀλλ', ὦ φίλον γένειον, αἰδέσθητί με,
οἴκτιρον· ἐλθὼν δ' εἰς Ἀχαιϊκὸν στρατὸν
παρηγόρησον, ὡς ἀποκτείνειν φθόνος
γυναῖκας, ἃς τὸ πρῶτον οὐκ ἐκτείνατε
βωμῶν ἀποσπάσαντες, ἀλλ' ᾠκτίρατε.   290
νόμος δ' ἐν ὑμῖν τοῖς τ' ἐλευθέροις ἴσος
καὶ τοῖσι δούλοις αἵματος κεῖται πέρι.
τὸ δ' ἀξίωμα, κἂν κακῶς λέγῃς, τὸ σὸν
πείσει λόγος γὰρ ἔκ τ' ἀδοξούντων ἰὼν

κἀκ τῶν δοκούντων αὐτὸς οὐ ταὐτὸν σθένει.

ΧΟ. οὐκ ἔστιν οὕτω στερρὸς ἀνθρώπου φύσις, 296
ἥτις γόων σῶν καὶ μακρῶν ὀδυρμάτων
κλύουσα θρήνους οὐκ ἂν ἐκβάλοι δάκρυ.

ΟΔ. Ἑκάβη, διδάσκου μηδὲ τῷ θυμουμένῳ
τὸν εὖ λέγοντα δυσμενῆ ποιοῦ φρενί. 300
ἐγὼ τὸ μὲν σὸν σῶμ' ὑφ' οὗπερ ηὐτύχουν
σῴζειν ἕτοιμός εἰμι, κοὐκ ἄλλως λέγω·
ἃ δ' εἶπον εἰς ἅπαντας οὐκ ἀρνήσομαι,
Τροίας ἁλούσης ἀνδρὶ τῷ πρώτῳ στρατοῦ
σὴν παῖδα δοῦναι σφάγιον ἐξαιτουμένῳ. 305
ἐν τῷδε γὰρ κάμνουσιν αἱ πολλαὶ πόλεις,
ὅταν τις ἐσθλὸς καὶ πρόθυμος ὢν ἀνὴρ
μηδὲν φέρηται τῶν κακιόνων πλέον.
ἡμῖν δ' Ἀχιλλεὺς ἄξιος τιμῆς, γύναι,
θανὼν ὑπὲρ γῆς Ἑλλάδος κάλλιστ' ἀνήρ. 310
οὔκουν τόδ' αἰσχρόν, εἰ βλέποντι μὲν φίλῳ
χρώμεσθ', ἐπεὶ δ' ὄλωλε, μὴ χρώμεσθ' ἔτι;
εἶεν· τί δῆτ' ἐρεῖ τις, ἤν τις αὖ φανῇ
στρατοῦ τ' ἄθροισις πολεμίων τ' ἀγωνία;
πότερα μαχούμεθ' ἢ φιλοψυχήσομεν, 315
τὸν κατθανόνθ' ὁρῶντες οὐ τιμώμενον;
καὶ μὴν ἔμοιγε ζῶντι μέν, καθ' ἡμέραν
κεἰ σμίκρ' ἔχοιμι, πάντ' ἂν ἀρκούντως ἔχοι·
τύμβον δὲ βουλοίμην ἂν ἀξιούμενον 319
τὸν ἐμὸν ὁρᾶσθαι· διὰ μακροῦ γὰρ ἡ χάρις.
εἰ δ' οἰκτρὰ πάσχειν φής, τάδ' ἀντάκουέ μου·
εἰσὶν παρ' ἡμῖν οὐδὲν ἧσσον ἄθλιαι
γραῖαι γυναῖκες ἠδὲ πρεσβῦται σέθεν,
νύμφαι τ' ἀρίστων νυμφίων τητώμεναι,
ὧν ἥδε κεύθει σώματ' Ἰδαία κόνις. 325

τόλμα τάδ'· ἡμεῖς δ', εἰ κακῶς νομίζομεν
τιμᾶν τὸν ἐσθλόν, ἀμαθίαν ὀφλήσομεν·
οἱ βάρβαροι δὲ μήτε τοὺς φίλους φίλους
ἡγεῖσθε μήτε τοὺς καλῶς τεθνηκότας
θαυμάζεθ', ὡς ἂν ἡ μὲν Ἑλλὰς εὐτυχῇ,   330
ὑμεῖς δ' ἔχηθ' ὅμοια τοῖς βουλεύμασιν.

ΧΟ. αἰαῖ· τὸ δοῦλον ὡς κακὸν πέφυκ' ἀεὶ
τολμᾷ θ' ἃ μὴ χρή, τῇ βίᾳ νικώμενον.

ΕΚ. ὦ θύγατερ, οὑμοὶ μὲν λόγοι πρὸς αἰθέρα
φροῦδοι μάτην ῥιφθέντες ἀμφὶ σοῦ φόνου·   335
σὺ δ', εἴ τι μείζω δύναμιν ἢ μήτηρ ἔχεις,
σπούδαζε πάσας ὥστ' ἀηδόνος στόμα
φθογγὰς ἱεῖσα, μὴ στερηθῆναι βίου.
πρόσπιπτε δ' οἰκτρῶς τοῦδ' Ὀδυσσέως γόνυ
καὶ πεῖθ'. ἔχεις δὲ πρόφασιν· ἔστι γὰρ τέκνα
καὶ τῷδε, τὴν σὴν ὥστ' ἐποικτῖραι τύχην.   341

ΠΟΛΥΞ. ὁρῶ σ', Ὀδυσσεῦ, δεξιὰν ὑφ' εἵματος
κρύπτοντα χεῖρα καὶ πρόσωπον ἔμπαλιν
στρέφοντα, μή σου προσθίγω γενειάδος.
θάρσει· πέφευγας τὸν ἐμὸν ἱκέσιον Δία·   345
ὡς ἕψομαί γε τοῦ τ' ἀναγκαίου χάριν
θανεῖν τε χρήζουσ'· εἰ δὲ μὴ βουλήσομαι,
κακὴ φανοῦμαι καὶ φιλόψυχος γυνή.
τί γάρ με δεῖ ζῆν; ᾗ πατὴρ μὲν ἦν ἄναξ
Φρυγῶν ἁπάντων· τοῦτό μοι πρῶτον βίου·   350
ἔπειτ' ἐθρέφθην ἐλπίδων καλῶν ὕπο
βασιλεῦσι νύμφη, ζῆλον οὐ σμικρὸν γάμων
ἔχουσ', ὅτου δῶμ' ἑστίαν τ' ἀφίξομαι·
δέσποινα δ' ἡ δύστηνος Ἰδαίαισιν ἡ
γυναιξὶ παρθένοις τ' ἀπόβλεπτος μέτα,   355
ἴση θεοῖσι πλὴν τὸ κατθανεῖν μόνον·

νῦν δ᾽ εἰμὶ δούλη. πρῶτα μέν με τοὔνομα
θανεῖν ἐρᾶν τίθησιν οὐκ εἰωθὸς ὄν·
ἔπειτ᾽ ἴσως ἂν δεσποτῶν ὠμῶν φρένας
τύχοιμ᾽ ἄν, ὅστις ἀργύρου μ᾽ ὠνήσεται,   360
τὴν Ἕκτορός τε χἀτέρων πολλῶν κάσιν,
προσθεὶς δ᾽ ἀνάγκην σιτοποιὸν ἐν δόμοις,
σαίρειν, τε δῶμα κερκίσιν τ᾽ ἐφεστάναι
λυπρὰν ἄγουσαν ἡμέραν μ᾽ ἀναγκάσει·
λέχη δὲ τἀμὰ δοῦλος ὠνητός ποθεν   365
χρανεῖ, τυράννων πρόσθεν ἠξιωμένα.
οὐ δῆτ᾽· ἀφίημ᾽ ὀμμάτων ἐλευθέρων
φέγγος τόδ᾽, Ἅιδῃ προστιθεῖσ᾽ ἐμὸν δέμας.
ἄγ᾽ οὖν μ᾽, Ὀδυσσεῦ, καὶ διέργασαί μ᾽ ἄγων·
οὔτ᾽ ἐλπίδος γὰρ οὔτε του δόξης ὁρῶ   370
θάρσος παρ᾽ ἡμῖν ὥς ποτ᾽ εὖ πρᾶξαί με χρή.
μῆτερ, σὺ δ᾽ ἡμῖν μηδὲν ἐμποδὼν γένῃ,
λέγουσα μηδὲ δρῶσα· συμβούλου δέ μοι
θανεῖν πρὶν αἰσχρῶν μὴ κατ᾽ ἀξίαν τυχεῖν.
ὅστις γὰρ οὐκ εἴωθε γεύεσθαι κακῶν,   375
φέρει μέν, ἀλγεῖ δ᾽ αὐχέν᾽ ἐντιθεὶς ζυγῷ·
θανὼν δ᾽ ἂν εἴη μᾶλλον εὐτυχέστερος
ἢ ζῶν· τὸ γὰρ ζῆν μὴ καλῶς μέγας πόνος.
ΧΟ. δεινὸς χαρακτὴρ κἀπίσημος ἐν βροτοῖς
ἐσθλῶν γενέσθαι, κἀπὶ μεῖζον ἔρχεται   380
τῆς εὐγενείας ὄνομα τοῖσιν ἀξίοις.
ΕΚ. καλῶς μὲν εἶπας, θύγατερ, ἀλλὰ τῷ καλῷ
λύπη πρόσεστιν. εἰ δὲ δεῖ τῷ Πηλέως
χάριν γενέσθαι παιδὶ καὶ ψόγον φυγεῖν
ὑμᾶς, Ὀδυσσεῦ, τήνδε μὲν μὴ κτείνετε,   385
ἡμᾶς δ᾽ ἄγοντες πρὸς πυρὰν Ἀχιλλέως
κεντεῖτε, μὴ φείδεσθ᾽· ἐγὼ ᾽τεκον Πάριν,

ὃς παῖδα Θέτιδος ὤλεσεν τόξοις βαλών.

ΟΔ. οὐ σ᾽, ὦ γεραιά, κατθανεῖν Ἀχιλλέως
φάντασμ᾽ Ἀχαιούς, ἀλλὰ τήνδ᾽ ᾐτήσατο.   390

ΕΚ. ὑμεῖς δέ μ᾽ ἀλλὰ θυγατρὶ συμφονεύσατε,
καὶ δὶς τόσον πῶμ᾽ αἵματος γενήσεται
γαίᾳ νεκρῷ τε τῷ τάδ᾽ ἐξαιτουμένῳ.

ΟΔ. ἅλις κόρης σῆς θάνατος, οὐ προσοιστέος
ἄλλος πρὸς ἄλλῳ· μηδὲ τόνδ᾽ ὠφείλομεν.   395

ΕΚ. πολλή γ᾽ ἀνάγκη θυγατρὶ συνθανεῖν ἐμέ.

ΟΔ. πῶς; οὐ γὰρ οἶδα δεσπότας κεκτημένος.

ΕΚ. ὁποῖα κισσὸς δρυὸς ὅπως τῆσδ᾽ ἕξομαι.

ΟΔ. οὐκ, ἤν γε πείθῃ τοῖσι σοῦ σοφωτέροις.

ΕΚ. ὡς τῆσδ᾽ ἑκοῦσα παιδὸς οὐ μεθήσομαι.   400

ΟΔ. ἀλλ᾽ οὐδ᾽ ἐγὼ μὴν τήνδ᾽ ἄπειμ᾽ αὐτοῦ λιπών.

ΠΟΛΥΞ. μῆτερ, πιθοῦ μοι· καὶ σύ, παῖ Λαερτίου,
χάλα τοκεῦσιν εἰκότως θυμουμένοις,
σύ τ᾽, ὦ τάλαινα, τοῖς κρατοῦσι μὴ μάχου.
βούλει πεσεῖν πρὸς οὖδας ἑλκῶσαί τε σὸν   405
γέροντα χρῶτα πρὸς βίαν ὠθουμένη,
ἀσχημονῆσαί τ᾽ ἐκ νέου βραχίονος
σπασθεῖσ᾽, ἃ πείσει; μὴ σύ γ᾽· οὐ γὰρ ἄξιον.
ἀλλ᾽, ὦ φίλη μοι μῆτερ, ἡδίστην χέρα
δὸς καὶ παρειὰν προσβαλεῖν παρηίδι·   410
ὡς οὔποτ᾽ αὖθις, ἀλλὰ νῦν πανύστατον
ἀκτῖνα κύκλον θ᾽ ἡλίου προσόψομαι.
τέλος δέχει δὴ τῶν ἐμῶν προσφθεγμάτων.
ὦ μῆτερ, ὦ τεκοῦσ᾽, ἄπειμι δὴ κάτω.

ΕΚ. ὦ θύγατερ, ἡμεῖς δ᾽ ἐν φάει δουλεύσομεν.   415

ΠΟΛΥΞ. ἄνυμφος ἀνυμέναιος ὧν με χρῆν τυχεῖν.

ΕΚ. οἰκτρὰ σύ, τέκνον, ἀθλία δ᾽ ἐγὼ γυνή.

ΠΟΛΥΞ. ἐκεῖ δ᾽ ἐν Ἅιδου κείσομαι χωρὶς σέθεν.

ΕΚ. οἴμοι· τί δράσω; ποῖ τελευτήσω βίον;

ΠΟΛΤΞ. δούλη θανοῦμαι, πατρὸς οὖσ᾽ ἐλευθέρου. 420

ΕΚ. ἡμεῖς δὲ πεντήκοντά γ᾽ ἄμμοροι τέκνων.

ΠΟΛΤΞ. τί σοι πρὸς Ἕκτορ᾽ ἢ γέροντ᾽ εἴπω πόσιν;

ΕΚ. ἄγγελλε πασῶν ἀθλιωτάτην ἐμέ.

ΠΟΛΤΞ. ὦ στέρνα μαστοί θ᾽, οἵ μ᾽ ἐθρέψαθ᾽ ἡδέως.

ΕΚ. ὦ τῆς ἀώρου θύγατερ ἀθλία τύχης. 425

ΠΟΛΤΞ. χαῖρ᾽, ὦ τεκοῦσα, χαῖρε Κασάνδρα τ᾽ ἐμοί.

ΕΚ. χαίρουσιν ἄλλοι, μητρὶ δ᾽ οὐκ ἔστιν τόδε.

ΠΟΛΤΞ. ὅ τ᾽ ἐν φιλίπποις Θρῃξὶ Πολύδωρος κάσις.

ΕΚ. εἰ ζῇ γ᾽· ἀπιστῶ δ᾽· ὧδε πάντα δυστυχῶ.

ΠΟΛΤΞ. ζῇ καὶ θανούσης ὄμμα συγκλῄσει τὸ σόν. 430

ΕΚ. τέθνηκ᾽ ἔγωγε πρὶν θανεῖν κακῶν ὕπο.

ΠΟΛΤΞ. κόμιζ᾽, Ὀδυσσεῦ, μ᾽ ἀμφιθεὶς κάρᾳ πέ-
πλους·
ὡς πρὶν σφαγῆναί γ᾽ ἐκτέτηκα καρδίαν
θρήνοισι μητρὸς τήνδε τ᾽ ἐκτήκω γόοις.
ὦ φῶς· προσειπεῖν γὰρ σὸν ὄνομ᾽ ἔξεστί μοι, 435
μέτεστι δ᾽ οὐδὲν πλὴν ὅσον χρόνον ξίφους
βαίνω μεταξὺ καὶ πυρᾶς Ἀχιλλέως.

ΕΚ. οἳ 'γώ, προλείπω· λύεται δέ μου μέλη.
ὦ θύγατερ, ἅψαι μητρός, ἔκτεινον χέρα,
δός· μὴ λίπῃς μ᾽ ἄπαιδ᾽. ἀπωλόμην, φίλαι. 440
ὡς τὴν Λάκαιναν σύγγονον Διοσκόροιν
Ἑλένην ἴδοιμι· διὰ καλῶν γὰρ ὀμμάτων
αἴσχιστα Τροίαν εἷλε τὴν εὐδαίμονα.

ΧΟ. αὔρα, ποντιὰς αὔρα, στρ. α´.
ἅτε ποντοπόρους κομίζεις 445
θοὰς ἀκάτους ἐπ᾽ οἶδμα λίμνας,
ποῖ με τὰν μελέαν πορεύσεις;
τῷ δουλόσυνος πρὸς οἶκον

κτηθεῖσ' ἀφίξομαι;
ἢ Δωρίδος ὅρμον αἶας   450
ἢ Φθιάδος, ἔνθα τὸν
καλλίστων ὑδάτων πατέρα
φασὶν Ἀπιδανὸν πεδία λιπαίνειν;   454
ἢ νάσων, ἁλιήρει   ἀντ. α'.
κώπᾳ πεμπομέναν τάλαιναν,
οἰκτρὰν βιοτὰν ἔχουσαν οἴκοις,
ἔνθα πρωτόγονός τε φοῖνιξ
δάφνα θ' ἱεροὺς ἀνέσχε
πτόρθους Λατοῖ φίλᾳ   460
ὠδῖνος ἄγαλμα Δίας;
σὺν Δηλιάσιν τε κού-
ραισιν Ἀρτέμιδός τε θεᾶς
χρυσέαν ἄμπυκα τόξα τ' εὐλογήσω;   465
ἢ Παλλάδος ἐν πόλει   στρ. β'.
τᾶς καλλιδίφρου θεᾶς
ναίουσ' ἐν κροκέῳ πέπλῳ
ζεύξομαι ἆρα πώλους ἐν
δαιδαλέαισι ποικίλλουσ'   470
ἀνθοκρόκοισι πήναις,
ἢ Τιτάνων γενεὰν
τὰν Ζεὺς ἀμφιπύρῳ
κοιμίζει φλογμῷ Κρονίδας;   474
ὤμοι τεκέων ἐμῶν,   ἀντ. β'.
ὤμοι πατέρων, χθονός θ',
ἃ καπνῷ κατερείπεται
τυφομένα δορίκτητος
Ἀργείων· ἐγὼ δ' ἐν ξεί-
νᾳ χθονὶ δὴ κέκλημαι
δούλα, λιποῦσ' Ἀσίαν,   480

Εὐρώπας θεράπναν
ἀλλάξασ', Ἅιδα θαλάμους.

ΤΑΛΘΥΒΙΟΣ.

ποῦ τὴν ἄνασσαν δή ποτ' οὖσαν Ἰλίου
Ἑκάβην ἂν ἐξεύροιμι, Τρῳάδες κόραι; 485
ΧΟ. αὕτη πέλας σου νῶτ' ἔχουσ' ἐπὶ χθονί,
Ταλθύβιε, κεῖται ξυγκεκλημένη πέπλοις.
ΤΑ. ὦ Ζεῦ, τί λέξω; πότερά σ' ἀνθρώπους ὁρᾶν;
ἢ δόξαν ἄλλως τήνδε κεκτῆσθαι μάτην
ψευδῆ, δοκοῦντας δαιμόνων εἶναι γένος, 490
τύχην δὲ πάντα τὰν βροτοῖς ἐπισκοπεῖν;
οὐχ ἥδ' ἄνασσα τῶν πολυχρύσων Φρυγῶν,
οὐχ ἥδε Πριάμου τοῦ μέγ' ὀλβίου δάμαρ;
καὶ νῦν πόλις μὲν πᾶσ' ἀνέστηκεν δορί,
αὐτὴ δὲ δούλη γραῦς ἄπαις ἐπὶ χθονὶ 495
κεῖται κόνει φύρουσα δύστηνον κάρα.
φεῦ φεῦ. γέρων μέν εἰμ', ὅμως δέ μοι θανεῖν
εἴη πρὶν αἰσχρᾷ περιπεσεῖν τύχῃ τινί.
ἀνίστασ', ὦ δύστηνε, καὶ μετάρσιον
πλευρὰν ἔπαιρε καὶ τὸ πάλλευκον κάρα. 500
ΕΚ. ἔα· τίς οὗτος σῶμα τοὐμὸν οὐκ ἐᾷς
κεῖσθαι; τί κινεῖς μ' ὅστις εἶ λυπουμένην;
ΤΑ. Ταλθύβιος ἥκω, Δαναϊδῶν ὑπηρέτης,
Ἀγαμέμνονος πέμψαντος, ὦ γύναι, μέτα.
ΕΚ. ὦ φίλτατ', ἆρα κἄμ' ἐπισφάξαι τάφῳ 505
δοκοῦν Ἀχαιοῖς ἦλθες; ὡς φίλ' ἂν λέγοις.
σπεύδωμεν ἐγκονῶμεν· ἡγοῦ μοι, γέρον.
ΤΑ. σὴν παῖδα κατθανοῦσαν ὡς θάψῃς, γύναι,
ἥκω μεταστείχων σε· πέμπουσιν δέ με

2—2

δισσοί τ᾽ Ἀτρεῖδαι καὶ λεὼς Ἀχαιϊκός.   510

ΕΚ. οἴμοι, τί λέξεις; οὐκ ἄρ᾽ ὡς θανουμένους
μετῆλθες ἡμᾶς, ἀλλὰ σημανῶν κακά;
ὄλωλας, ὦ παῖ, μητρὸς ἁρπασθεῖσ᾽ ἄπο·
ἡμεῖς δ᾽ ἄτεκνοι τοὐπὶ σ᾽· ὦ τάλαιν᾽ ἐγώ.
πῶς καί νιν ἐξεπράξατ᾽; ἆρ᾽ αἰδούμενοι;   515
ἢ πρὸς τὸ δεινὸν ἤλθεθ᾽ ὡς ἐχθράν, γέρον,
κτείνοντες; εἰπὲ καίπερ οὐ λέξων φίλα.

ΤΑ. διπλᾶ με χρῄζεις δάκρυα κερδᾶναι, γύναι,
σῆς παιδὸς οἴκτῳ· νῦν τε γὰρ λέγων κακὰ
τέγξω τόδ᾽ ὄμμα, πρὸς τάφῳ θ᾽ ὅτ᾽ ὤλλυτο.   520
παρῆν μὲν ὄχλος πᾶς Ἀχαιϊκοῦ στρατοῦ
πλήρης πρὸ τύμβου σῆς κόρης ἐπὶ σφαγάς·
λαβὼν δ᾽ Ἀχιλλέως παῖς Πολυξένην χερὸς
ἔστησ᾽ ἐπ᾽ ἄκρου χώματος, πέλας δ᾽ ἐγώ·
λεκτοί τ᾽ Ἀχαιῶν ἔκκριτοι νεανίαι,   525
σκίρτημα μόσχου σῆς καθέξοντες χεροῖν,
ἕσποντο· πλῆρες δ᾽ ἐν χεροῖν λαβὼν δέπας
πάγχρυσον αἴρει χειρὶ παῖς Ἀχιλλέως
χοὰς θανόντι πατρί· σημαίνει δέ μοι
σιγὴν Ἀχαιῶν παντὶ κηρῦξαι στρατῷ.   530
κἀγὼ παραστὰς εἶπον ἐν μέσοις τάδε·
σιγᾶτ᾽, Ἀχαιοί, σῖγα πᾶς ἔστω λεώς,
σίγα σιώπα· νήνεμον δ᾽ ἔστησ᾽ ὄχλον.
ὁ δ᾽ εἶπεν· ὦ παῖ Πηλέως, πατὴρ δ᾽ ἐμός,
δέξαι χοάς μου τάσδε κηλητηρίους,   535
νεκρῶν ἀγωγούς· ἐλθὲ δ᾽, ὡς πίῃς μέλαν
κόρης ἀκραιφνὲς αἷμ᾽, ὅ σοι δωρούμεθα
στρατός τε κἀγώ· πρευμενὴς δ᾽ ἡμῖν γενοῦ
λῦσαί τε πρύμνας καὶ χαλινωτήρια
νεῶν δὸς ἡμῖν πρευμενοῦς τ᾽ ἀπ᾽ Ἰλίου   540

νόστου τυχόντας πάντας ἐς πάτραν μολεῖν.
τοσαῦτ' ἔλεξε, πᾶς δ' ἐπηύξατο στρατός.
εἶτ' ἀμφίχρυσον φάσγανον κώπης λαβὼν
ἐξεῖλκε κολεοῦ, λογάσι δ' Ἀργείων στρατοῦ
νεανίαις ἔνευσε παρθένον λαβεῖν. 545
ἣ δ', ὡς ἐφράσθη, τόνδ' ἐσήμηνεν λόγον·
ὦ τὴν ἐμὴν πέρσαντες Ἀργεῖοι πόλιν,
ἑκοῦσα θνῄσκω· μή τις ἅψηται χροὸς
τοὐμοῦ· παρέξω γὰρ δέρην εὐκαρδίως.
ἐλευθέραν δέ μ', ὡς ἐλευθέρα θάνω, 550
πρὸς θεῶν μεθέντες κτείνατ'· ἐν νεκροῖσι γὰρ
δούλη κεκλῆσθαι βασιλὶς οὖσ' αἰσχύνομαι.
λαοὶ δ' ἐπερρόθησαν, Ἀγαμέμνων τ' ἄναξ
εἶπεν μεθεῖναι παρθένον νεανίαις. 554
κἀπεὶ τόδ' εἰσήκουσε δεσποτῶν ἔπος, 557
λαβοῦσα πέπλους ἐξ ἄκρας ἐπωμίδος
ἔρρηξε λαγόνας εἰς μέσας παρ' ὀμφαλόν,
μαστούς τ' ἔδειξε στέρνα θ' ὡς ἀγάλματος 560
κάλλιστα, καὶ καθεῖσα πρὸς γαῖαν γόνυ
ἔλεξε πάντων τλημονέστατον λόγον·
ἰδού, τόδ', εἰ μὲν στέρνον, ὦ νεανία,
παίειν προθυμεῖ, παῖσον, εἰ δ' ὑπ' αὐχένα
χρῄζεις, πάρεστι λαιμὸς εὐτρεπὴς ὅδε. 565
ὃ δ' οὐ θέλων τε καὶ θέλων οἴκτῳ κόρης,
τέμνει σιδήρῳ πνεύματος διαρροάς·
κρουνοὶ δ' ἐχώρουν· ἣ δὲ καὶ θνῄσκουσ' ὅμως
πολλὴν πρόνοιαν εἶχεν εὐσχήμως πεσεῖν,
κρύπτουσ' ἃ κρύπτειν ὄμματ' ἀρσένων χρεών. 570
ἐπεὶ δ' ἀφῆκε πνεῦμα θανασίμῳ σφαγῇ,
οὐδεὶς τὸν αὐτὸν εἶχεν Ἀργείων πόνον·
ἀλλ' οἱ μὲν αὐτῶν τὴν θανοῦσαν ἐκ χερῶν

φύλλοις ἔβαλλον, οἱ δὲ πληροῦσιν πυρὰν
κορμοὺς φέροντες πευκίνους, ὁ δ᾽ οὐ φέρων   575
πρὸς τοῦ φέροντος τοιάδ᾽ ἤκουεν κακά·
ἔστηκας, ὦ κάκιστε, τῇ νεάνιδι
οὐ πέπλον οὐδὲ κόσμον ἐν χεροῖν ἔχων;
οὐκ εἶ τι δώσων τῇ περίσσ᾽ εὐκαρδίῳ
ψυχήν τ᾽ ἀρίστῃ; τοιάδ᾽ ἀμφὶ σῆς λέγω   580
παιδὸς θανούσης, εὐτεκνωτάτην δέ σε
πασῶν γυναικῶν δυστυχεστάτην θ᾽ ὁρῶ.

ΧΟ. δεινόν τι πῆμα Πριαμίδαις ἐπέζεσεν
πόλει τε τῇ μῇ θεῶν ἀναγκαῖον τόδε.

ΕΚ. ὦ θύγατερ, οὐκ οἶδ᾽ εἰς ὅ τι βλέψω κακῶν,   585
πολλῶν παρόντων· ἢν γὰρ ἅψωμαί τινος,
τόδ᾽ οὐκ ἐᾷ με, παρακαλεῖ δ᾽ ἐκεῖθεν αὖ
λύπη τις ἄλλη διάδοχος κακῶν κακοῖς.
καὶ νῦν τὸ μὲν σὸν ὥστε μὴ στένειν πάθος
οὐκ ἂν δυναίμην ἐξαλείψασθαι φρενός·   590
τὸ δ᾽ αὖ λίαν παρεῖλες ἀγγελθεῖσά μοι
γενναῖος. οὔκουν δεινόν, εἰ γῆ μὲν κακὴ
τυχοῦσα καιροῦ θεόθεν εὖ στάχυν φέρει,
χρηστὴ δ᾽ ἁμαρτοῦσ᾽ ὧν χρεὼν αὐτὴν τυχεῖν
κακὸν δίδωσι καρπόν, ἄνθρωποι δ᾽ ἀεὶ   595
ὁ μὲν πονηρὸς οὐδὲν ἄλλο πλὴν κακός,
ὁ δ᾽ ἐσθλὸς ἐσθλὸς οὐδὲ συμφορᾶς ὕπο
φύσιν διέφθειρ᾽, ἀλλὰ χρηστός ἐστ᾽ ἀεί;
ἆρ᾽ οἱ τεκόντες διαφέρουσιν ἢ τροφαί;
ἔχει γε μέντοι καὶ τὸ θρεφθῆναι καλῶς   600
δίδαξιν ἐσθλοῦ· τοῦτο δ᾽ ἤν τις εὖ μάθῃ,
οἶδεν τό γ᾽ αἰσχρόν, κανόνι τοῦ καλοῦ μαθών.
καὶ ταῦτα μὲν δὴ νοῦς ἐτόξευσεν μάτην·
σὺ δ᾽ ἐλθὲ καὶ σήμηνον Ἀργείοις τάδε,

μὴ θιγγάνειν μοι μηδέν’, ἀλλ’ εἴργειν ὄχλον 605
τῆς παιδός. ἔν τοι μυρίῳ στρατεύματι
ἀκόλαστος ὄχλος ναυτική τ’ ἀναρχία
κρείσσων πυρός, κακὸς δ’ ὁ μή τι δρῶν κακόν.
σὺ δ’ αὖ λαβοῦσα τεῦχος, ἀρχαία λάτρι,
βάψασ’ ἔνεγκε δεῦρο ποντίας ἁλός,   610
ὡς παῖδα λουτροῖς τοῖς πανυστάτοις ἐμὴν
νύμφην τ’ ἄνυμφον παρθένον τ’ ἀπάρθενον
λούσω προθῶμαί θ’, ὡς μὲν ἀξία, πόθεν;
οὐκ ἂν δυναίμην· ὡς δ’ ἔχω· τί γὰρ πάθω;
κόσμον τ’ ἀγείρασ’ αἰχμαλωτίδων πάρα,   615
αἵ μοι πάρεδροι τῶνδ’ ἔσω σκηνωμάτων
ναίουσιν, εἴ τις τοὺς νεωστὶ δεσπότας
λαθοῦσ’ ἔχει τι κλέμμα τῶν αὑτῆς δόμων.
ὦ σχήματ’ οἴκων, ὦ ποτ’ εὐτυχεῖς δόμοι,
ὦ πλεῖστ’ ἔχων κάλλιστά τ’, εὐτεκνώτατε   620
Πρίαμε, γεραιά θ’ ἥδ’ ἐγὼ μήτηρ τέκνων,
ὡς ἐς τὸ μηδὲν ἥκομεν, φρονήματος
τοῦ πρὶν στερέντες. εἶτα δῆτ’ ὀγκούμεθα
ὁ μέν τις ἡμῶν πλουσίοισι δώμασιν,
ὁ δ’ ἐν πολίταις τίμιος κεκλημένος.   625
τὰ δ’ οὐδέν· ἄλλως φροντίδων βουλεύματα
γλώσσης τε κόμποι. κεῖνος ὀλβιώτατος,
ὅτῳ κατ’ ἦμαρ τυγχάνει μηδὲν κακόν.
ΧΟ. ἐμοὶ χρῆν συμφοράν,   στρ.
ἐμοὶ χρῆν πημονὰν γενέσθαι,   630
Ἰδαίαν ὅτε πρῶτον ὕλαν
Ἀλέξανδρος εἰλατίναν
ἐτάμεθ’, ἅλιον ἐπ’ οἶδμα ναυστολήσων
Ἑλένας ἐπὶ λέκτρα, τὰν
καλλίσταν ὁ χρυσοφαὴς   635

Ἅλιος αὐγάζει.
πόνοι γὰρ καὶ πόνων   ἀντ.
ἀνάγκαι κρείσσονες κυκλοῦνται.
κοινὸν δ' ἐξ ἰδίας ἀνοίας   640
κακὸν τᾷ Σιμουντίδι γᾷ
ὀλέθριον ἔμολε συμφορά τ' ἀπ' ἄλλων.
ἐκρίθη δ' ἔρις, ἂν ἐν Ἴ-
δᾳ κρίνει τρισσὰς μακάρων   645
παῖδας ἀνὴρ βούτας,
ἐπὶ δορὶ καὶ φόνῳ καὶ ἐμῶν μελάθρων λώβα·
                                                              ἐπῳδ.
στένει δὲ καί τις ἀμφὶ τὸν εὔροον Εὐρώταν 650
Λάκαινα πολυδάκρυτος ἐν δόμοις κόρα,
πολιόν τ' ἐπὶ κρᾶτα μάτηρ
τέκνων θανόντων
τίθεται χέρα δρύπτεταί τε παρειάν,   655
δίαιμον ὄνυχα τιθεμένα σπαραγμοῖς.

ΘΕΡΑΠΑΙΝΑ.

γυναῖκες, Ἑκάβη ποῦ ποθ' ἡ παναθλία,
ἡ πάντα νικῶσ' ἄνδρα καὶ θῆλυν σπορὰν
κακοῖσιν; οὐδεὶς στέφανον ἀνθαιρήσεται.   660
ΧΟ. τί δ', ὦ τάλαινα σῆς κακογλώσσου βοῆς;
ὡς οὔποθ' εὕδει λυπρά σου κηρύγματα.
ΘΕ. Ἑκάβῃ φέρω τόδ' ἄλγος· ἐν κακοῖσι δὲ
οὐ ῥᾴδιον βροτοῖσιν εὐφημεῖν στόμα.
ΧΟ. καὶ μὴν περῶσα τυγχάνει δόμων ὕπερ   665
ἥδ', ἐς δὲ καιρὸν σοῖσι φαίνεται λόγοις.
ΘΕ. ὦ παντάλαινα κἄτι μᾶλλον ἢ λέγω,
δέσποιν', ὄλωλας κοὐκέτ' εἶ βλέπουσα φῶς,
ἄπαις ἄνανδρος ἄπολις ἐξεφθαρμένη·

ΕΚ. οὐ καινὸν εἶπας, εἰδόσιν δ᾽ ὠνείδισας. 670
ἀτὰρ τί νεκρὸν τόνδε μοι Πολυξένης
ἥκεις κομίζουσ᾽, ἧς ἀπηγγέλθη τάφος
πάντων Ἀχαιῶν διὰ χερὸς σπουδὴν ἔχειν;
ΘΕ. ἥδ᾽ οὐδὲν οἶδεν, ἀλλά μοι Πολυξένην
θρηνεῖ, νέων δὲ πημάτων οὐχ ἅπτεται. 675
ΕΚ. οἲ 'γὼ τάλαινα· μῶν τὸ βακχεῖον κάρα
τῆς θεσπιῳδοῦ δεῦρο Κασάνδρας φέρεις;
ΘΕ. ζῶσαν λέλακας, τὸν θανόντα δ᾽ οὐ στένεις
τόνδ᾽. ἀλλ᾽ ἄθρησον σῶμα γυμνωθὲν νεκροῦ,
εἴ σοι φανεῖται θαῦμα καὶ παρ᾽ ἐλπίδας. 680
ΕΚ. οἴμοι, βλέπω δὴ παῖδ᾽ ἐμὸν τεθνηκότα,
Πολύδωρον, ὅν μοι Θρῇξ ἔσῳζ᾽ οἴκοις ἀνήρ.
ἀπωλόμην δύστηνος, οὐκέτ᾽ εἰμὶ δή.
ὦ τέκνον τέκνον,
αἰαῖ, κατάρχομαι νόμον 685
βακχεῖον, ἐξ ἀλάστορος
ἀρτιμαθὴς κακῶν.
ΘΕ. ἔγνως γὰρ ἄτην παιδός, ὦ δύστηνε σύ;
ΕΚ. ἄπιστ᾽ ἄπιστα, καινὰ καινὰ δέρκομαι.
ἕτερα δ᾽ ἀφ᾽ ἑτέρων κακὰ κακῶν κυρεῖ· 690
οὐδέποτ᾽ ἀστένακτος ἀδάκρυτος ἁ-
μέρα ἐπισχήσει.
ΧΟ. δείν᾽, ὦ τάλαινα, δεινὰ πάσχομεν κακά.
ΕΚ. ὦ τέκνον τέκνον ταλαίνας ματρός, 695
τίνι μόρῳ θνῄσκεις, τίνι πότμῳ κεῖσαι;
πρὸς τίνος ἀνθρώπων;
ΘΕ. οὐκ οἶδ᾽. ἔπ᾽ ἀκταῖς νιν κυρῶ θαλασσίαις.
ΕΚ. ἔκβλητον, ἢ πέσημα φοινίου δορός,
ἐν ψαμάθῳ λευρᾷ; 700
ΘΕ. πόντου νιν ἐξήνεγκε πελάγιος κλύδων.

ΕΚ. ὤμοι, αἰαῖ, ἔμαθον ἐνύπνιον ὀμμάτων
    ἐμῶν ὄψιν, οὔ με παρέβα φά-
    σμα μελανόπτερον,   705
    ἃν εἰσεῖδον ἀμφί σ',
    ὦ τέκνον, οὐκέτ' ὄντα Διὸς ἐν φάει.
ΧΟ. τίς γάρ νιν ἔκτειν'; οἶσθ' ὀνειρόφρων φράσαι;
ΕΚ. ἐμὸς ἐμὸς ξένος, Θρήκιος ἱππότας,   710
    ἵν' ὁ γέρων πατὴρ ἔθετό νιν κρύψας.
ΧΟ. ὤμοι, τί λέξεις; χρυσὸν ὡς ἔχοι κτανών;
ΕΚ. ἄρρητ' ἀνωνόμαστα, θαυμάτων πέρα,
    οὐχ ὅσι' οὐδ' ἀνεκτά. ποῦ δίκα ξένων;   715
    ὦ κατάρατ' ἀνδρῶν, ὡς διεμοιράσω
    χρόα, σιδαρέῳ τεμὼν φασγάνῳ
    μέλεα τοῦδε παιδὸς οὐδ' ᾠκτίσω.   720
ΧΟ. ὦ τλῆμον, ὥς σε πολυπονωτάτην βροτῶν
    δαίμων ἔθηκεν ὅστις ἐστί σοι βαρύς.
    ἀλλ' εἰσορῶ γὰρ τοῦδε δεσπότου δέμας
    Ἀγαμέμνονος, τοὐνθένδε σιγῶμεν, φίλαι.   725

ΑΓΑΜΕΜΝΩΝ.

    Ἑκάβη, τί μέλλεις παῖδα σὴν κρύπτειν τάφῳ
    ἐλθοῦσ', ἐφ' οἷσπερ Ταλθύβιος ἤγγειλέ μοι
    μὴ θιγγάνειν σῆς μηδέν' Ἀργείων κόρης;
    ἡμεῖς μὲν οὖν ἐῶμεν οὐδὲ ψαύομεν·
    σὺ δὲ σχολάζεις, ὥστε θαυμάζειν ἐμέ.   730
    ἥκω δ' ἀποστελῶν σε· τἀκεῖθεν γὰρ εὖ
    πεπραγμέν' ἐστίν, εἴ τι τῶνδ' ἐστὶν καλῶς.
    ἔα· τίν' ἄνδρα τόνδ' ἐπὶ σκηναῖς ὁρῶ
    θανόντα Τρώων; οὐ γὰρ Ἀργεῖον πέπλοι
    δέμας περιπτύσσοντες ἀγγέλλουσί μοι.   735
ΕΚ. δύστην', ἐμαυτὴν γὰρ λέγω λέγουσα σέ,

Ἑκάβη, τί δράσω; πότερα προσπέσω γόνυ
Ἀγαμέμνονος τοῦδ' ἢ φέρω σιγῇ κακά;

ΑΓ. τί μοι προσώπῳ νῶτον ἐγκλίνασα σὸν
δύρει, τὸ πραχθὲν δ' οὐ λέγεις; τίς ἔσθ' ὅδε; 740

ΕΚ. ἀλλ', εἴ με δούλην πολεμίαν θ' ἡγούμενος
γονάτων ἀπώσαιτ', ἄλγος ἂν προσθείμεθ' ἄν.

ΑΓ. οὔτοι πέφυκα μάντις, ὥστε μὴ κλύων
ἐξιστορῆσαι σῶν ὁδὸν βουλευμάτων.

ΕΚ. ἆρ' ἐκλογίζομαί γε πρὸς τὸ δυσμενὲς 745
μᾶλλον φρένας τοῦδ', ὄντος οὐχὶ δυσμενοῦς;

ΑΓ. εἴ τοί με βούλει τῶνδε μηδὲν εἰδέναι,
ἐς ταὐτὸν ἥκεις· καὶ γὰρ οὐδ' ἐγὼ κλύειν.

ΕΚ. οὐκ ἂν δυναίμην τοῦδε τιμωρεῖν ἄτερ
τέκνοισι τοῖς ἐμοῖσι. τί στρέφω τάδε; 750
τολμᾶν ἀνάγκη, κἂν τύχω κἂν μὴ τύχω.
Ἀγάμεμνον, ἱκετεύω σε τῶνδε γουνάτων
καὶ σοῦ γενείου δεξιᾶς τ' εὐδαίμονος.

ΑΓ. τί χρῆμα μαστεύουσα; μῶν ἐλεύθερον
αἰῶνα θέσθαι; ῥᾴδιον γάρ ἐστί σοι. 755

ΕΚ. οὐ δῆτα· τοὺς κακοὺς δὲ τιμωρουμένη
αἰῶνα τὸν σύμπαντα δουλεύειν θέλω.

ΑΓ. καὶ δὴ τίν' ἡμᾶς εἰς ἐπάρκεσιν καλεῖς;

* * * * * *

ΕΚ. οὐδέν τι τούτων ὧν σὺ δοξάζεις, ἄναξ.
ὁρᾷς νεκρὸν τόνδ', οὗ καταστάζω δάκρυ; 760

ΑΓ. ὁρῶ· τὸ μέντοι μέλλον οὐκ ἔχω μαθεῖν.

ΕΚ. τοῦτόν ποτ' ἔτεκον κἄφερον ζώνης ὕπο.

ΑΓ. ἔστιν δὲ τίς σῶν οὗτος, ὦ τλῆμον, τέκνων;

ΕΚ. οὐ τῶν θανόντων Πριαμιδῶν ὑπ' Ἰλίῳ.

ΑΓ. ἦ γάρ τιν' ἄλλον ἔτεκες ἢ κείνους, γύναι; 765

ΕΚ. ἀνόνητά γ', ὡς ἔοικε, τόνδ' ὃν εἰσορᾷς.

ΑΓ.   ποῦ δ' ὢν ἐτύγχαν', ἡνίκ' ὤλλυτο πτόλις;
ΕΚ.   πατήρ νιν ἐξέπεμψεν ὀρρωδῶν θανεῖν.
ΑΓ.   ποῖ τῶν τότ' ὄντων χωρίσας τέκνων μόνον;
ΕΚ.   ἐς τήνδε χώραν, οὖπερ ηὑρέθη θανών.   770
ΑΓ.   πρὸς ἄνδρ' ὃς ἄρχει τῆσδε Πολυμήστωρ χθονός;
ΕΚ.   ἐνταῦθ' ἐπέμφθη πικροτάτου χρυσοῦ φύλαξ.
ΑΓ.   θνῄσκει δὲ πρὸς τοῦ καὶ τίνος πότμου τυχών;
ΕΚ.   τίνος δ' ὑπ' ἄλλου; Θρῇξ νιν ὤλεσε ξένος.
ΑΓ.   ὦ τλῆμον· ἦ που χρυσὸν ἠράσθη λαβεῖν;   775
ΕΚ.   τοιαῦτ', ἐπειδὴ ξυμφορὰν ἔγνω Φρυγῶν.
ΑΓ.   ηὗρες δὲ ποῦ νιν, ἢ τίς ἤνεγκεν νεκρόν;
ΕΚ.   ἥδ', ἐντυχοῦσα ποντίας ἀκτῆς ἔπι.
ΑΓ.   τοῦτον ματεύουσ' ἢ πονοῦσ' ἄλλον πόνον;
ΕΚ.   λούτρ' ᾤχετ' οἴσουσ' ἐξ ἁλὸς Πολυξένῃ.   780
ΑΓ.   κτανών νιν, ὡς ἔοικεν, ἐκβάλλει ξένος.
ΕΚ.   θαλασσόπλαγκτόν γ', ὧδε διατεμὼν χρόα.
ΑΓ.   ὦ σχετλία σὺ τῶν ἀμετρήτων πόνων.
ΕΚ.   ὄλωλα, κοὐδὲν λοιπόν, Ἀγάμεμνον, κακῶν.
ΑΓ.   φεῦ φεῦ· τίς οὕτω δυστυχὴς ἔφυ γυνή;   785
ΕΚ.   οὐκ ἔστιν, εἰ μὴ τὴν τύχην αὐτὴν λέγοις.
        ἀλλ' ὧνπερ εἵνεκ' ἀμφὶ σὸν πίπτω γόνυ
        ἄκουσον· εἰ μὲν ὅσιά σοι παθεῖν δοκῶ,
        στέργοιμ' ἄν· εἰ δὲ τοὐμπαλιν, σύ μοι γενοῦ
        τιμωρὸς ἀνδρὸς ἀνοσιωτάτου ξένου,   790
        ὃς οὔτε τοὺς γῆς νέρθεν οὔτε τοὺς ἄνω
        δείσας δέδρακεν ἔργον ἀνοσιώτατον·
        κοινῆς τραπέζης πολλάκις τυχὼν ἐμοὶ
        ξενίας τ' ἀριθμῷ πρῶτα τῶν ἐμῶν ξένων,
        τυχὼν δ' ὅσων δεῖ καὶ λαβὼν προμηθίαν   795
        ἔκτεινε, τύμβου δ', εἰ κτανεῖν ἐβούλετο,
        οὐκ ἠξίωσεν, ἀλλ' ἀφῆκε πόντιον.

ἡμεῖς μὲν οὖν δοῦλοί τε κἀσθενεῖς ἴσως·
ἀλλ' οἱ θεοὶ σθένουσι χὡ κείνων κρατῶν
νόμος· νόμῳ γὰρ τοὺς θεοὺς ἡγούμεθα   800
καὶ ζῶμεν ἄδικα καὶ δίκαι' ὡρισμένοι·
ὃς εἰς σ' ἀνελθὼν εἰ διαφθαρήσεται,
καὶ μὴ δίκην δώσουσιν οἵτινες ξένους
κτείνουσιν ἢ θεῶν ἱερὰ τολμῶσιν φέρειν,
οὐκ ἔστιν οὐδὲν τῶν ἐν ἀνθρώποις ἴσον.   805
ταῦτ' οὖν ἐν αἰσχρῷ θέμενος αἰδέσθητί με·
οἴκτιρον ἡμᾶς, ὡς γραφεύς τ' ἀποσταθεὶς
ἰδοῦ με κἀνάθρησον οἷ' ἔχω κακά.
τύραννος ἦ ποτ', ἀλλὰ νῦν δούλη σέθεν,
εὔπαις ποτ' οὖσα, νῦν δὲ γραῦς ἄπαις θ' ἅμα,   810
ἄπολις ἔρημος ἀθλιωτάτη βροτῶν.
οἴμοι τάλαινα, ποῖ μ' ὑπεξάγεις πόδα;
ἔοικα πράξειν οὐδέν· ὦ τάλαιν' ἐγώ.
τί δῆτα θνητοὶ τἄλλα μὲν μαθήματα
μοχθοῦμεν ὡς χρὴ πάντα καὶ μαστεύομεν,   815
πειθὼ δὲ τὴν τύραννον ἀνθρώποις μόνην
οὐδέν τι μᾶλλον ἐς τέλος σπουδάζομεν
μισθοὺς διδόντες μανθάνειν, ἵν' ἦν ποτὲ
πείθειν ἅ τις βούλοιτο τυγχάνειν θ' ἅμα;
τί οὖν ἔτ' ἄν τις ἐλπίσαι πράξειν καλῶς;   820
οἱ μὲν γὰρ ὄντες παῖδες οὐκέτ' εἰσί μοι,
αὐτὴ δ' ἐπ' αἰσχροῖς αἰχμάλωτος οἴχομαι·
καπνὸν δὲ πόλεως τόνδ' ὑπερθρῴσκονθ' ὁρῶ.
καὶ μὴν ἴσως μὲν τοῦ λόγου κενὸν τόδε,
Κύπριν προβάλλειν· ἀλλ' ὅμως εἰρήσεται·   825
πρὸς σοῖσι πλευροῖς παῖς ἐμὴ κοιμίζεται
ἡ φοιβάς, ἣν καλοῦσι Κασάνδραν Φρύγες.
ποῦ τὰς φίλας δῆτ' εὐφρόνας δείξεις, ἄναξ,

ἢ τῶν ἐν εὐνῇ φιλτάτων ἀσπασμάτων
χάριν τίν' ἕξει παῖς ἐμή, κείνης δ' ἐγώ;   830
ἄκουε δή νυν· τὸν θανόντα τόνδ' ὁρᾷς;   833
τοῦτον καλῶς δρῶν ὄντα κηδεστὴν σέθεν
δράσεις. ἑνός μοι μῦθος ἐνδεὴς ἔτι.   835
εἴ μοι γένοιτο φθόγγος ἐν βραχίοσι
καὶ χερσὶ καὶ κόμαισι καὶ ποδῶν βάσει
ἢ Δαιδάλου τέχναισιν ἢ θεῶν τινος,
ὡς πάνθ' ὁμαρτῇ σῶν ἔχοιτο γουνάτων
κλαίοντ' ἐπισκήπτοντα παντοίους λόγους.   840
ὦ δέσποτ', ὦ μέγιστον Ἕλλησιν φάος,
πιθοῦ, παράσχες χεῖρα τῇ πρεσβύτιδι
τιμωρόν, εἰ καὶ μηδέν ἐστιν, ἀλλ' ὅμως.
ἐσθλοῦ γὰρ ἀνδρὸς τῇ δίκῃ θ' ὑπηρετεῖν
καὶ τοὺς κακοὺς δρᾶν πανταχοῦ κακῶς ἀεί.   845
ΧΟ. δεινόν γε, θνητοῖς ὡς ἅπαντα συμπίτνει,
καὶ τῆς ἀνάγκης οἱ νόμοι διώρισαν,
φίλους τιθέντες τούς γε πολεμιωτάτους
ἐχθρούς τε τοὺς πρὶν εὐμενεῖς ποιούμενοι.
ΑΓ. ἔγωγε καὶ σὸν παῖδα καὶ τύχας σέθεν,   850
Ἑκάβη, δι' οἴκτου χεῖρά θ' ἱκεσίαν ἔχω
καὶ βούλομαι θεῶν θ' εἵνεκ' ἀνόσιον ξένον
καὶ τοῦ δικαίου τήνδε σοι δοῦναι δίκην,
εἴ πως φανείη γ' ὥστε σοί τ' ἔχειν καλῶς,
στρατῷ τε μὴ δόξαιμι Κασάνδρας χάριν   855
Θρῄκης ἄνακτι τόνδε βουλεῦσαι φόνον.
ἔστιν γὰρ ᾗ ταραγμὸς ἐμπέπτωκέ μοι·
τὸν ἄνδρα τοῦτον φίλιον ἡγεῖται στρατός,
τὸν κατθανόντα δ' ἐχθρόν· εἰ δ' ἐμοὶ φίλος
ὅδ' ἐστί, χωρὶς τοῦτο κοὐ κοινὸν στρατῷ.   860
πρὸς ταῦτα φρόντιζ'· ὡς θέλοντα μέν μ' ἔχεις

σοὶ ξυμπονῆσαι καὶ ταχὺν προσαρκέσαι,
βραδὺν δ', Ἀχαιοῖς εἰ διαβληθήσομαι.

ΕΚ. φεῦ.
οὐκ ἔστι θνητῶν ὅστις ἔστ' ἐλεύθερος·
ἢ χρημάτων γὰρ δοῦλός ἐστιν ἢ τύχης,   865
ἢ πλῆθος αὐτὸν πόλεος ἢ νόμων γραφαὶ
εἴργουσι χρῆσθαι μὴ κατὰ γνώμην τρόποις.
ἐπεὶ δὲ ταρβεῖς τῷ τ' ὄχλῳ πλέον νέμεις,
ἐγώ σε θήσω τοῦδ' ἐλεύθερον φόβου.
σύνισθι μὲν γάρ, ἤν τι βουλεύσω κακὸν   870
τῷ τόνδ' ἀποκτείναντι, συνδράσῃς δὲ μή.
ἢν δ' ἐξ Ἀχαιῶν θόρυβος ἢ 'πικουρία
πάσχοντος ἀνδρὸς Θρῃκὸς οἷα πείσεται
φανῇ τις, εἶργε μὴ δοκῶν ἐμὴν χάριν.
τὰ δ' ἄλλα θάρσει· πάντ' ἐγὼ θήσω καλῶς.   875

ΑΓ. πῶς οὖν; τί δράσεις; πότερα·φάσγανον χερὶ
λαβοῦσα γραίᾳ φῶτα βάρβαρον κτενεῖς,
ἢ φαρμάκοισιν, ἢ 'πικουρίᾳ τίνι;
τίς σοι ξυνέσται χείρ; πόθεν κτήσει φίλους;

ΕΚ. στέγαι κεκεύθασ' αἵδε Τρωάδων ὄχλον.   880

ΑΓ. τὰς αἰχμαλώτους εἶπας, Ἑλλήνων ἄγραν;

ΕΚ. ξὺν ταῖσδε τὸν ἐμὸν φονέα τιμωρήσομαι.

ΑΓ. καὶ πῶς γυναιξὶν ἀρσένων ἔσται κράτος;

ΕΚ. δεινὸν τὸ πλῆθος σὺν δόλῳ τε δύσμαχον.

ΑΓ. δεινόν· τὸ μέντοι θῆλυ μέμφομαι γένος.   885

ΕΚ. τί δ'; οὐ γυναῖκες εἷλον Αἰγύπτου τέκνα
καὶ Λῆμνον ἄρδην ἀρσένων ἐξῴκισαν;
ἀλλ' ὡς γενέσθω· τόνδε μὲν μέθες λόγον,
πέμψον δέ μοι τήνδ' ἀσφαλῶς διὰ στρατοῦ
γυναῖκα. καὶ σὺ Θρῃκὶ πλαθεῖσα ξένῳ   890
λέξον· καλεῖ σ' ἄνασσα δή ποτ' Ἰλίου

Ἑκάβη, σὸν οὐκ ἔλασσον ἢ κείνης χρέος,
καὶ παῖδας· ὡς δεῖ καὶ τέκν' εἰδέναι λόγους
τοὺς ἐξ ἐκείνης. τὸν δὲ τῆς νεοσφαγοῦς
Πολυξένης ἐπίσχες, Ἀγάμεμνον, τάφον, 895
ὡς τώδ' ἀδελφὼ πλησίον μιᾷ φλογί,
δισσὴ μέριμνα μητρί, κρυφθῆτον χθονί.

ΑΓ. ἔσται τάδ' οὕτω· καὶ γὰρ εἰ μὲν ἦν στρατῷ
πλοῦς, οὐκ ἂν εἶχον τήνδε σοι δοῦναι χάριν·
νῦν δ', οὐ γὰρ ἧσ' οὐρίας πνοὰς θεός, . 900
μένειν ἀνάγκη πλοῦν ὁρῶντας ἥσυχον.
γένοιτο δ' εὖ πως· πᾶσι γὰρ κοινὸν τόδε
ἰδίᾳ θ' ἑκάστῳ καὶ πόλει, τὸν μὲν κακὸν
κακόν τι πάσχειν, τὸν δὲ χρηστὸν εὐτυχεῖν·

ΧΟ. σὺ μέν, ὦ πατρὶς Ἰλιάς,   στρ. ά.
τῶν ἀπορθήτων πόλις οὐκέτι λέξει·   906
τοῖον Ἑλλάνων νέφος ἀμφί σε κρύπτει
δορὶ δὴ δορὶ πέρσαν.
ἀπὸ δὲ στεφάναν κέκαρσαι   910
πύργων, κατὰ δ' αἰθάλου
κηλῖδ' οἰκτροτάταν κέχρωσαι·
τάλαιν', οὐκέτι σ' ἐμβατεύσω.
μεσονύκτιος ὠλλύμαν,   ἀντ. ά.
ἦμος ἐκ δείπνων ὕπνος ἡδὺς ἐπ' ὄσσοις   915
σκίδναται, μολπᾶν δ' ἄπο καὶ χοροποιὸν
θυσίαν καταπαύσας
πόσις ἐν θαλάμοις ἔκειτο,
ξυστὸν δ' ἐπὶ πασσάλῳ,   920
ναύταν οὐκέθ' ὁρῶν ὅμιλον
Τροίαν Ἰλιάδ' ἐμβεβῶτα.
ἐγὼ δὲ πλόκαμον ἀναδέτοις   στρ. β'.
μίτραισιν ἐρρυθμιζόμαν

χρυσέων ἐνόπτρων 925
λεύσσουσ' ἀτέρμονας εἰς αὐγάς,
ἐπιδέμνιος ὡς πέσοιμ' ἐς εὐνάν.
ἀνὰ δὲ κέλαδος ἔμολε πόλιν·
κέλευμα δ' ἦν κατ' ἄστυ Τροίας τόδ'· ὦ
παῖδες Ἑλλάνων, πότε δὴ πότε τὰν 930
Ἰλιάδα σκοπιὰν
πέρσαντες ἥξετ' οἴκους;
λέχη δὲ φίλια μονόπεπλος   ἀντ. β'.
λιποῦσα, Δωρὶς ὡς κόρα,
σεμνὰν προσίζουσ' 935
οὐκ ἤνυσ' Ἄρτεμιν ἁ τλάμων·
ἄγομαι δὲ θανόντ' ἰδοῦσ' ἀκοίταν
τὸν ἐμὸν ἅλιον ἐπὶ πέλαγος,
πόλιν τ' ἀποσκοποῦσ', ἐπεὶ νόστιμον
ναῦς ἐκίνησεν πόδα καί μ' ἀπὸ γᾶς 940
ὥρισεν Ἰλιάδος·
τάλαιν' ἀπεῖπον ἄλγει,
τὰν τοῖν Διοσκόροιν Ἑλέναν κάσιν
Ἰδαῖόν τε βούταν   ἐπῳδ.
αἰνόπαριν κατάρᾳ 945
διδοῦσ', ἐπεί με γᾶς
ἐκ πατρίας ἀπώλεσεν
ἐξῴκισέν τ' οἴκων γάμος, οὐ γάμος,
ἀλλ' ἀλάστορός τις οἰζύς· 950
ἂν μήτε πέλαγος ἅλιον ἀπαγάγοι πάλιν,
μήτε πατρῷον ἵκοιτ' ἐς οἶκον.

ΠΟΛΥΜΗΣΤΩΡ.

ὦ φίλτατ' ἀνδρῶν Πρίαμε, φιλτάτη δὲ σύ,
Ἑκάβη, δακρύω σ' εἰσορῶν πόλιν τε σήν,

τήν τ' ἀρτίως θανοῦσαν ἔκγονον σέθεν.   955
φεῦ·
οὐκ ἔστιν οὐδὲν πιστόν, οὔτ' εὐδοξία
οὔτ' αὖ καλῶς πράσσοντα μὴ πράξειν κακῶς.
φύρουσι δ' αὐτὰ θεοὶ πάλιν τε καὶ πρόσω
ταραγμὸν ἐντιθέντες, ὡς ἀγνωσίᾳ
σέβωμεν αὐτούς· ἀλλὰ ταῦτα μὲν τί δεῖ   960
θρηνεῖν προκόπτοντ' οὐδὲν ἐς πρόσθεν κακῶν;
σὺ δ', εἴ τι μέμφει τῆς ἐμῆς ἀπουσίας,
σχές· τυγχάνω γὰρ ἐν μέσοις Θρῄκης ὅροις
ἀπών, ὅτ' ἦλθες δεῦρ'· ἐπεὶ δ' ἀφικόμην,
ἤδη πόδ' ἔξω δωμάτων αἴροντί μοι   965
ἐς ταὐτὸν ἥδε συμπίτνει δμωὶς σέθεν,
λέγουσα μύθους, ὧν κλύων ἀφικόμην.
ΕΚ. αἰσχύνομαί σε προσβλέπειν ἐναντίον,
Πολυμῆστορ, ἐν τοιοῖσδε κειμένη κακοῖς.
ὅτῳ γὰρ ὤφθην εὐτυχοῦσ', αἰδώς μ' ἔχει   970
ἐν τῷδε πότμῳ τυγχάνουσ' ἵν' εἰμὶ νῦν
κοὐκ ἂν δυναίμην προσβλέπειν ὀρθαῖς κόραις.
ἀλλ' αὐτὸ μὴ δύσνοιαν ἡγήσῃ σέθεν,
Πολυμῆστορ· ἄλλως δ' αἴτιόν τι καὶ νόμος,
γυναῖκας ἀνδρῶν μὴ βλέπειν ἐναντίον.   975
ΠΟΛΥΜ. καὶ θαῦμά γ' οὐδέν. ἀλλὰ τίς χρεία σ' ἐμοῦ;
τί χρῆμ' ἐπέμψω τὸν ἐμὸν ἐκ δόμων πόδα;
ΕΚ. ἴδιον ἐμαυτῆς δή τι πρὸς σὲ βούλομαι
καὶ παῖδας εἰπεῖν σούς· ὀπάονας δέ μοι
χωρὶς κέλευσον τῶνδ' ἀποστῆναι δόμων.   980
ΠΟΛΥΜ. χωρεῖτ'· ἐν ἀσφαλεῖ γὰρ ἥδ' ἐρημία.
φίλη μὲν εἶ σύ, προσφιλὲς δέ μοι τόδε
στράτευμ' Ἀχαιῶν. ἀλλὰ σημαίνειν σε χρὴν
τί χρὴ τὸν εὖ πράσσοντα μὴ πράσσουσιν εὖ

φίλοις ἐπαρκεῖν· ὡς ἕτοιμός εἰμ' ἐγώ. 985

ΕΚ. πρῶτον μὲν εἰπὲ παῖδ' ὃν ἐξ ἐμῆς χερὸς
Πολύδωρον ἔκ τε πατρὸς ἐν δόμοις ἔχεις,
εἰ ζῆ· τὰ δ' ἄλλα δεύτερόν σ' ἐρήσομαι.

ΠΟΛΥΜ. μάλιστα· τοὐκείνου μὲν εὐτυχεῖς μέρος.

ΕΚ. ὦ φίλταθ', ὡς εὖ κἀξίως σέθεν λέγεις. 990

ΠΟΛΥΜ. τί δῆτα βούλει δεύτερον μαθεῖν ἐμοῦ;

ΕΚ. εἰ τῆς τεκούσης τῆσδε μέμνηταί τί μου.

ΠΟΛΥΜ. καὶ δεῦρό γ' ὡς σὲ κρύφιος ἐζήτει μολεῖν.

ΕΚ. χρυσὸς δὲ σῶς ὃν ἦλθεν ἐκ Τροίας ἔχων; 994

ΠΟΛΥΜ. σῶς, ἐν δόμοις γε τοῖς ἐμοῖς φρουρούμενος.

ΕΚ. σῶσόν νυν αὐτὸν μηδ' ἔρα τῶν πλησίον.

ΠΟΛΥΜ. ἥκιστ'· ὀναίμην τοῦ παρόντος, ὦ γύναι.

ΕΚ. οἶσθ' οὖν ἃ λέξαι σοί τε καὶ παισὶν θέλω;

ΠΟΛΥΜ. οὐκ οἶδα· τῷ σῷ τοῦτο σημανεῖς λόγῳ.

ΕΚ. ἔστ', ὦ φιληθεὶς ὡς σὺ νῦν ἐμοὶ φιλεῖ, 1000

ΠΟΛΥΜ. τί χρῆμ' ὃ κἀμὲ καὶ τέκν' εἰδέναι χρεών;

ΕΚ. χρυσοῦ παλαιαὶ Πριαμιδῶν κατώρυχες.

ΠΟΛΥΜ. ταῦτ' ἔσθ' ἃ βούλει παιδὶ σημῆναι σέθεν;

ΕΚ. μάλιστα, διὰ σοῦ γ'· εἶ γὰρ εὐσεβὴς ἀνήρ.

ΠΟΛΥΜ. τί δῆτα τέκνων τῶνδε δεῖ παρουσίας; 1005

ΕΚ. ἄμεινον, ἢν σὺ κατθάνῃς, τούσδ' εἰδέναι.

ΠΟΛΥΜ. καλῶς ἔλεξας· τῇδε καὶ σοφώτερον.

ΕΚ. οἶσθ' οὖν 'Αθάνας 'Ιλίας ἵνα στέγαι;

ΠΟΛΥΜ. ἐνταῦθ' ὁ χρυσός ἐστι; σημεῖον δὲ τί;

ΕΚ. μέλαινα πέτρα γῆς ὑπερτέλλουσ' ἄνω. 1010

ΠΟΛΥΜ. ἔτ' οὖν τι βούλει τῶν ἐκεῖ φράζειν ἐμοί;

ΕΚ. σῶσαί σε χρήμαθ' οἷς συνεξῆλθον θέλω.

ΠΟΛΥΜ. ποῦ δῆτα; πέπλων ἐντός, ἢ κρύψασ' ἔχεις;

ΕΚ. σκύλων ἐν ὄχλῳ ταῖσδε σῴζεται στέγαις. 1014

ΠΟΛΥΜ. ποῦ δ'; αἵδ' 'Αχαιῶν ναύλοχοι περιπτυχαί.

ΕΚ.   ἰδίᾳ γυναικῶν αἰχμαλωτίδων στέγαι.
ΠΟΛΥΜ.   τἄνδον δὲ πιστὰ κἀρσένων ἐρημία;
ΕΚ.   οὐδεὶς Ἀχαιῶν ἔνδον, ἀλλ' ἡμεῖς μόναι.
      ἀλλ' ἕρπ' ἐς οἴκους· καὶ γὰρ Ἀργεῖοι νεῶν
      λῦσαι ποθοῦσιν οἴκαδ' ἐκ Τροίας πόδα·   1020
      ὡς πάντα πράξας ὧν σε δεῖ στείχῃς πάλιν
      ξὺν παισὶν οὗπερ τὸν ἐμὸν ᾤκισας γόνον.
ΧΟ.   οὔπω δέδωκας, ἀλλ' ἴσως δώσεις δίκην·
      ἀλίμενόν τις ὡς εἰς ἄντλον πεσὼν   1025
      λέχριος ἐκπεσεῖ φίλας καρδίας,
      ἀμέρσας βίον. τὸ γὰρ ὑπέγγυον
      δίκᾳ καὶ θεοῖσιν οὐ συμπίτνει,   1030
      ὀλέθριον ὀλέθριον κακόν.
      ψεύσει σ' ὁδοῦ τῆσδ' ἐλπὶς ἥ σ' ἐπήγαγεν
      θανάσιμον πρὸς Ἅιδαν, ὦ τάλας·
      ἀπολέμῳ δὲ χειρὶ λείψεις βίον.   1034
ΠΟΛΥΜ.   ὤμοι, τυφλοῦμαι φέγγος ὀμμάτων τάλας.
ΧΟ.   ἠκούσατ' ἀνδρὸς Θρῃκὸς οἰμωγήν, φίλαι;
ΠΟΛΥΜ.   ὤμοι μάλ' αὖθις, τέκνα, δυστήνου σφαγῆς.
ΧΟ.   φίλαι, πέπρακται καίν' ἔσω δόμων κακά.
ΠΟΛΥΜ.   ἀλλ' οὔτι μὴ φύγητε λαιψηρῷ ποδί.
      βάλλων γὰρ οἴκων τῶνδ' ἀναρρήξω μυχούς·   1040
      ἰδού, βαρείας χειρὸς ὁρμᾶται βέλος.
ΧΟ.   βούλεσθ' ἐπεσπέσωμεν; ὡς ἀκμὴ καλεῖ
      Ἑκάβῃ παρεῖναι Τρῳάσιν τε συμμάχους.
ΕΚ.   ἄρασσε, φείδου μηδέν, ἐκβάλλων πύλας·
      οὐ γάρ ποτ' ὄμμα λαμπρὸν ἐνθήσεις κόραις,   1045
      οὐ παῖδας ὄψει ζῶντας οὓς ἔκτειν' ἐγώ.
ΧΟ.   ἦ γὰρ καθεῖλες Θρῆκα καὶ κρατεῖς ξένου,
      δέσποινα, καὶ δέδρακας οἷάπερ λέγεις;
ΕΚ.   ὄψει νιν αὐτίκ' ὄντα δωμάτων πάρος

τυφλὸν τυφλῷ στείχοντα παραφόρῳ ποδί,   1050
παίδων τε δισσῶν σώμαθ᾽, οὓς ἔκτειν᾽ ἐγὼ
σὺν ταῖς ἀρίσταις Τρῳάσιν· δίκην δέ μοι
δέδωκε· χωρεῖ δ᾽, ὡς ὁρᾷς, ὅδ᾽ ἐκ δόμων.
ἀλλ᾽ ἐκποδὼν ἄπειμι κἀποστήσομαι
θυμῷ ῥέοντι Θρῃκὶ δυσμαχωτάτῳ.   1055

ΠΟΛΥΜ. ὤμοι ἐγώ, πᾷ βῶ,
πᾷ στῶ, πᾷ κέλσω;
τετράποδος βάσιν θηρὸς ὀρεστέρου
τιθέμενος ἐπὶ χεῖρα κατ᾽ ἴχνος ποίαν
ἢ ταύταν ἢ τάνδ᾽   1060
ἐξαλλάξω, τὰς
ἀνδροφόνους μάρψαι
χρῄζων Ἰλιάδας, αἵ με διώλεσαν;
τάλαιναι κόραι τάλαιναι Φρυγῶν,
ὦ κατάρατοι,   1065
ποῖ καί με φυγᾷ πτώσσουσι μυχῶν;
εἴθε μοι ὀμμάτων αἱματόεν βλέφαρον
ἀκέσσαιο τυφλὸν ἀκέσσαι᾽, Ἅλιε,
φέγγος ἀπαλλάξας.
ἆ ἆ.
σίγα· κρυπτὰν βάσιν αἰσθάνομαι   1070
τάνδε γυναικῶν. πᾷ πόδ᾽ ἐπᾴξας
σαρκῶν ὀστέων τ᾽ ἐμπλησθῶ,
θοίναν ἀγρίων τιθέμενος θηρῶν,
ἀρνύμενος λώβαν
λύμας ἀντίποιν᾽ ἐμᾶς; ὦ τάλας.   1075
ποῖ πᾷ φέρομαι τέκν᾽ ἔρημα λιπὼν
βάκχαις Ἅιδου διαμοιρᾶσαι,
σφακτὰν κυσί τε φονίαν δαῖτ᾽ ἀνήμερον
οὐρείαν τ᾽ ἐκβολάν;

πᾷ στῶ, πᾷ βῶ, πᾷ κάμψω,   1080
ναῦς ὅπως ποντίοις πείσμασι, λινόκροκον
φᾶρος στέλλων, ἐπὶ τάνδε συθεὶς
τέκνων ἐμῶν φύλαξ
ὀλέθριον κοίταν;

ΧΟ. ὦ τλῆμον, ὥς σοι δύσφορ᾽ εἴργασται κακά·   1085
δράσαντι δ᾽ αἰσχρὰ δεινὰ τἀπιτίμια.   1086

ΠΟΛΥΜ. αἰαῖ, ἰὼ Θρῄκης   1088
λογχοφόρον ἔνοπλον εὔιππον Ἄ-
ρει κάτοχον γένος.   1090
ἰὼ Ἀχαιοί, ἰὼ Ἀτρεῖδαι.
βοὰν βοὰν ἀϋτῶ, βοάν·
ὦ ἴτε, μόλετε πρὸς θεῶν.
κλύει τις, ἢ οὐδεὶς ἀρκέσει; τί μέλλετε;
γυναῖκες ὤλεσάν με,   1095
γυναῖκες αἰχμαλώτιδες.
δεινὰ δεινὰ πεπόνθαμεν·
ὤμοι ἐμᾶς λώβας.
ποῖ τράπωμαι, ποῖ πορευθῶ;
ἀμπτάμενος οὐράνιον   1100
ὑψιπέτης ἐς μέλαθρον, Ὠρίων
ἢ Σείριος ἔνθα πυρὸς φλογέας, ἀφίησιν ὄσσων αὐγάς, ἢ τὸν ἐς Ἀίδα
μελανοχρῶτα πορθμὸν ᾄξω τάλας;   1105

ΧΟ. ξυγγνώσθ᾽, ὅταν τις κρεῖσσον᾽ ἢ φέρειν κακὰ
πάθῃ, ταλαίνης ἐξαπαλλάξαι ζόης.

ΑΓ. κραυγῆς ἀκούσας ἦλθον· οὐ γὰρ ἥσυχος
πέτρας ὀρείας παῖς λέλακ᾽ ἀνὰ στρατὸν   1110
Ἠχὼ διδοῦσα θόρυβον. εἰ δὲ μὴ Φρυγῶν
πύργους πεσόντας ᾖσμεν Ἑλλήνων δορί,
φόβον παρέσχεν οὐ μέσως ὅδε κτύπος.

ΠΟΛΥΜ. ὦ φίλτατ᾽, ᾐσθόμην γάρ, Ἀγάμεμνον, σέθεν
φωνῆς ἀκούσας, εἰσορᾷς ἃ πάσχομεν; 1115

ΑΓ. ἔα.
Πολυμῆστορ ὦ δύστηνε, τίς σ᾽ ἀπώλεσεν;
τίς ὄμμ᾽ ἔθηκε τυφλὸν αἱμάξας κόρας,
παῖδάς τε τούσδ᾽ ἔκτεινεν; ἢ μέγαν χόλον
σοὶ καὶ τέκνοισιν εἶχεν ὅστις ἦν ἄρα.

ΠΟΛΥΜ. Ἑκάβη με σὺν γυναιξὶν αἰχμαλωτίσιν 1120
ἀπώλεσ᾽, οὐκ ἀπώλεσ᾽, ἀλλὰ μειζόνως.

ΑΓ. τί φής; σὺ τοὖργον εἴργασαι τόδ᾽, ὡς λέγει;
σὺ τόλμαν, Ἑκάβη, τήνδ᾽ ἔτλης ἀμήχανον;

ΠΟΛΥΜ. ὤμοι, τί λέξεις; ἦ γὰρ ἐγγύς ἐστί που;
σήμηνον, εἰπὲ ποῦ ᾽σθ᾽, ἵν᾽ ἁρπάσας χεροῖν 1125
διασπάσωμαι καὶ καθαιμάξω χρόα.

ΑΓ. οὗτος, τί πάσχεις;

ΠΟΛΥΜ. πρὸς θεῶν σε λίσσομαι,
μέθες μ᾽ ἐφεῖναι τῇδε μαργῶσαν χέρα.

ΑΓ. ἴσχ᾽· ἐκβαλὼν δὲ καρδίας τὸ βάρβαρον
λέγ᾽, ὡς ἀκούσας σοῦ τε τῆσδέ τ᾽ ἐν μέρει 1130
κρίνω δικαίως ἀνθ᾽ ὅτου πάσχεις τάδε.

ΠΟΛΥΜ. λέγοιμ᾽ ἄν. ἦν τις Πριαμιδῶν νεώτατος,
Πολύδωρος, Ἑκάβης παῖς, ὃν ἐκ Τροίας ἐμοὶ
πατὴρ δίδωσι Πρίαμος ἐν δόμοις τρέφειν,
ὕποπτος ὢν δὴ Τρωικῆς ἁλώσεως. 1135
τοῦτον κατέκτειν᾽· ἀνθ᾽ ὅτου δ᾽ ἔκτεινά νιν,
ἄκουσον, ὡς εὖ καὶ σοφῇ προμηθίᾳ.
ἔδεισα μὴ σοὶ πολέμιος λειφθεὶς ὁ παῖς
Τροίαν ἀθροίσῃ καὶ ξυνοικίσῃ πάλιν,
γνόντες δ᾽ Ἀχαιοὶ ζῶντα Πριαμιδῶν τινα 1140
Φρυγῶν ἐς αἶαν αὖθις ἄρειαν στόλον
κἄπειτα Θρῄκης πεδία τρίβοιεν τάδε

λεηλατοῦντες, γείτοσιν δ' εἴη κακὸν
Τρώων, ἐν ᾧπερ νῦν, ἄναξ, ἐκάμνομεν.
Ἑκάβη δὲ παιδὸς γνοῦσα θανάσιμον μόρον   1145
λόγῳ με τοιῷδ' ἤγαγ', ὡς κεκρυμμένας
θήκας φράσουσα Πριαμιδῶν ἐν Ἰλίῳ
χρυσοῦ· μόνον δὲ σὺν τέκνοισί μ' εἰσάγει
δόμους, ἵν' ἄλλος μή τις εἰδείη τάδε.
ἵζω δὲ κλίνης ἐν μέσῳ κάμψας γόνυ·   1150
πολλαὶ δὲ χειρὸς αἱ μὲν ἐξ ἀριστερᾶς,
αἱ δ' ἔνθεν, ὡς δὴ παρὰ φίλῳ, Τρώων κόραι
θάκους ἔχουσαι, κερκίδ' Ἠδωνῆς χερὸς
ᾔνουν, ὑπ' αὐγὰς τούσδε λεύσσουσαι πέπλους·
ἄλλαι δὲ κάμακα Θρηκίαν θεώμεναι   1155
γυμνόν μ' ἔθηκαν διπτύχου στολίσματος.
ὅσαι δὲ τοκάδες ἦσαν, ἐκπαγλούμεναι
τέκν' ἐν χεροῖν ἔπαλλον, ὡς πρόσω πατρὸς
γένοιντο, διαδοχαῖς ἀμείβουσαι χεροῖν.
κᾆτ' ἐκ γαληνῶν, πῶς δοκεῖς; προσφθεγμάτων   1160
εὐθὺς λαβοῦσαι φάσγαν' ἐκ πέπλων ποθὲν
κεντοῦσι παῖδας, αἱ δὲ πολεμίων δίκην
ξυναρπάσασαι τὰς ἐμὰς εἶχον χέρας
καὶ κῶλα· παισὶ δ' ἀρκέσαι χρῄζων ἐμοῖς,
εἰ μὲν πρόσωπον ἐξανισταίην ἐμόν,   1165
κόμης κατεῖχον, εἰ δὲ κινοίην χέρας,
πλήθει γυναικῶν οὐδὲν ἤνυον τάλας.
τὸ λοίσθιον δέ, πῆμα πήματος πλέον,
ἐξειργάσαντο δείν'· ἐμῶν γὰρ ὀμμάτων,
πόρπας λαβοῦσαι, τὰς ταλαιπώρους κόρας   1170
κεντοῦσιν αἱμάσσουσιν· εἶτ' ἀνὰ στέγας
φυγάδες ἔβησαν· ἐκ δὲ πηδήσας ἐγὼ
θὴρ ὣς διώκω τὰς μιαιφόνους κύνας,

ἅπαντ' ἐρευνῶν τοῖχον ὡς κυνηγέτης
βάλλων ἀράσσων. τοιάδε σπεύδων χάριν 1175
πέπονθα τὴν σὴν πολέμιόν τε σὸν κτανών,
'Αγάμεμνον. ὡς δὲ μὴ μακροὺς τείνω λόγους,
εἴ τις γυναῖκας τῶν πρὶν εἴρηκεν κακῶς,
ἢ νῦν λέγων ἔστιν τις ἢ μέλλει λέγειν,
ἅπαντα ταῦτα συντεμὼν ἐγὼ φράσω· 1180
γένος γὰρ οὔτε πόντος οὔτε γῆ τρέφει
τοιόνδ'· ὁ δ' ἀεὶ ξυντυχὼν ἐπίσταται.

ΧΟ. μηδὲν θρασύνου, μηδὲ τοῖς σαυτοῦ κακοῖς
τὸ θῆλυ συνθεὶς ὧδε πᾶν μέμψῃ γένος·
πολλαὶ γὰρ ἐσμέν· αἱ μέν εἰσ' ἐπίφθονοι, 1185
αἱ δ' εἰς ἀριθμὸν οὐ κακῶν πεφύκαμεν.

ΕΚ. 'Αγάμεμνον, ἀνθρώποισιν οὐκ ἐχρῆν ποτὲ
τῶν πραγμάτων τὴν γλῶσσαν ἰσχύειν πλέον.
ἀλλ', εἴτε χρήστ' ἔδρασε, χρήστ' ἔδει λέγειν,
εἴτ' αὖ πονηρά, τοὺς λόγους εἶναι σαθροὺς 1190
καὶ μὴ δύνασθαι τἄδικ' εὖ λέγειν ποτέ.
σοφοὶ μὲν οὖν εἰσ' οἱ τάδ' ἠκριβωκότες,
ἀλλ' οὐ δύνανται διὰ τέλους εἶναι σοφοί,
κακῶς δ' ἀπώλοντ'· οὔτις ἐξήλυξέ πω.
καί μοι τὸ μὲν σὸν ὧδε φροιμίοις ἔχει· 1195
πρὸς τόνδε δ' εἶμι καὶ λόγοις ἀμείψομαι,
ὃς φῂς 'Αχαιῶν πόνον ἀπαλλάσσων διπλοῦν
'Αγαμέμνονός θ' ἕκατι παῖδ' ἐμὸν κτανεῖν.
ἀλλ', ὦ κάκιστε, πρῶτον οὐ ποτ' ἂν φίλον
τὸ βάρβαρον γένοιτ' ἂν Ἕλλησιν γένος 1200
οὐδ' ἂν δύναιτο. τίνα δὲ καὶ σπεύδων χάριν
πρόθυμος ἦσθα; πότερα κηδεύσων τινὰ
ἢ συγγενὴς ὤν, ἢ τίν' αἰτίαν ἔχων;
ἢ σῆς ἔμελλον γῆς τεμεῖν βλαστήματα

πλεύσαντες αὖθις ; τίνα δοκεῖς πείσειν τάδε;
ὁ χρυσός, εἰ βούλοιο τἀληθῆ λέγειν,   1206
ἔκτεινε τὸν ἐμὸν παῖδα καὶ κέρδη τὰ σά.
ἐπεὶ δίδαξον τοῦτο· πῶς, ὅτ' ηὐτύχει
Τροία, πέριξ δὲ πύργος εἶχ' ἔτι πτόλιν,
ἔζη τε Πρίαμος Ἕκτορός τ' ἤνθει δόρυ,   1210
τί δ' οὐ τότ', εἴπερ τῷδ' ἐβουλήθης χάριν
θέσθαι, τρέφων τὸν παῖδα κἂν δόμοις ἔχων
ἔκτεινας ἢ ζῶντ' ἦλθες Ἀργείοις ἄγων;
ἀλλ' ἡνίχ' ἡμεῖς οὐκέτ' ἐσμὲν ἐν φάει,
καπνῷ δ' ἐσήμην' ἄστυ πολεμίων ὕπο,   1215
ξένον κατέκτας σὴν μολόντ' ἐφ' ἑστίαν.
πρὸς τοῖσδέ νυν ἄκουσον, ὡς φανῇς κακός.
χρῆν σ', εἴπερ ἦσθα τοῖς Ἀχαιοῖσιν φίλος,
τὸν χρυσὸν ὃν φὴς οὐ σὸν ἀλλὰ τοῦδ' ἔχειν
δοῦναι φέροντα πενομένοις τε καὶ χρόνον   1220
πολὺν πατρῴας γῆς ἀπεξενωμένοις·
σὺ δ' οὐδὲ νῦν πω σῆς ἀπαλλάξαι χερὸς
τολμᾷς, ἔχων δὲ καρτερεῖς ἔτ' ἐν δόμοις.
καὶ μὴν τρέφων μὲν ὥς σε παῖδα χρῆν τρέφειν
σώσας τε τὸν ἐμόν, εἶχες ἂν καλὸν κλέος·   1225
ἐν τοῖς κακοῖς γὰρ ἀγαθοὶ σαφέστατοι
φίλοι· τὰ χρηστὰ δ' αὔθ' ἕκαστ' ἔχει φίλους.
εἰ δ' ἐσπάνιζες χρημάτων, ὃ δ' ηὐτύχει,
θησαυρὸς ἄν σοι παῖς ὑπῆρχ' οὑμὸς μέγας·
νῦν δ' οὔτ' ἐκεῖνον ἄνδρ' ἔχεις σαυτῷ φίλον, 1230
χρυσοῦ τ' ὄνησις οἴχεται παῖδές τε σοί,
αὐτός τε πράσσεις ὧδε. σοὶ δ' ἐγὼ λέγω,
Ἀγάμεμνον, εἰ τῷδ' ἀρκέσεις, κακὸς φανεῖ·
οὔτ' εὐσεβῆ γὰρ οὔτε πιστὸν οἷς ἐχρῆν,
οὐχ ὅσιον, οὐ δίκαιον εὖ δράσεις ξένον·   1235

αὐτὸν δὲ χαίρειν τοῖς κακοῖς σε φήσομεν
τοιοῦτον ὄντα· δεσπότας δ' οὐ λοιδορῶ.

ΧΟ. φεῦ φεῦ· βροτοῖσιν ὡς τὰ χρηστὰ πράγματα
χρηστῶν ἀφορμὰς ἐνδίδωσ' ἀεὶ λόγων.

ΑΓ. ἀχθεινὰ μέν μοι τἀλλότρια κρίνειν κακά, 1240
ὅμως δ' ἀνάγκη· καὶ γὰρ αἰσχύνην φέρει,
πρᾶγμ' ἐς χέρας λαβόντ' ἀπώσασθαι τόδε.
ἐμοὶ δ', ἵν' εἰδῇς, οὔτ' ἐμὴν δοκεῖς χάριν
οὔτ' οὖν Ἀχαιῶν ἄνδρ' ἀποκτεῖναι ξένον,
ἀλλ' ὡς ἔχῃς τὸν χρυσὸν ἐν δόμοισι σοῖς. 1245
λέγεις δὲ σαυτῷ πρόσφορ' ἐν κακοῖσιν ὤν.
τάχ' οὖν παρ' ὑμῖν ῥᾴδιον ξενοκτονεῖν·
ἡμῖν δέ γ' αἰσχρὸν τοῖσιν Ἕλλησιν τόδε.
πῶς οὖν σε κρίνας μὴ ἀδικεῖν φύγω ψόγον;
οὐκ ἂν δυναίμην· ἀλλ' ἐπεὶ τὰ μὴ καλὰ 1250
πράσσειν ἐτόλμας, τλῆθι καὶ τὰ μὴ φίλα.

ΠΟΛΥΜ. οἴμοι, γυναικός, ὡς ἔοιχ', ἡσσώμενος
δούλης ὑφέξω τοῖς κακίοσιν δίκην.

ΕΚ. οὔκουν δικαίως, εἴπερ εἰργάσω κακά; 1254

ΠΟΛΥΜ. οἴμοι τέκνων τῶνδ' ὀμμάτων τ' ἐμῶν, τάλας.

ΕΚ. ἀλγεῖς; τί δὴ 'μέ; παιδὸς οὐκ ἀλγεῖν δοκεῖς;

ΠΟΛΥΜ. χαίρεις ὑβρίζουσ' εἰς ἔμ', ὦ πανοῦργε σύ;

ΕΚ. οὐ γάρ με χαίρειν χρή σε τιμωρουμένην;

ΠΟΛΥΜ. ἀλλ' οὐ τάχ', ἡνίκ' ἄν σε ποντία νοτὶς

ΕΚ. μῶν ναυστολήσῃ γῆς ὅρους Ἑλληνίδος; 1260

ΠΟΛΥΜ. κρύψῃ μὲν οὖν πεσοῦσαν ἐκ καρχησίων.

ΕΚ. πρὸς τοῦ βιαίων τυγχάνουσαν ἁλμάτων;

ΠΟΛΥΜ. αὐτὴ πρὸς ἱστὸν ναὸς ἀμβήσει ποδί.

ΕΚ. ὑποπτέροις νώτοισιν ἢ ποίῳ τρόπῳ;

ΠΟΛΥΜ. κύων γενήσει πύρσ' ἔχουσα δέργματα. 1265

ΕΚ. πῶς δ' οἶσθα μορφῆς τῆς ἐμῆς μετάστασιν;

ΠΟΛΥΜ. ὁ Θρηξὶ μάντις εἶπε Διόνυσος τάδε.

ΕΚ. σοὶ δ᾽ οὐκ ἔχρησεν οὐδὲν ὧν ἔχεις κακῶν;

ΠΟΛΥΜ. οὐ γάρ ποτ᾽ ἂν σύ μ᾽ εἶλες ὧδε σὺν δόλῳ.

ΕΚ. θανοῦσα δ᾽ ἢ ζῶσ᾽ ἐνθάδ᾽ ἐκπλήσω βίον; 1270

ΠΟΛΥΜ. θανοῦσα· τύμβῳ δ᾽ ὄνομα σῷ κεκλήσεται

ΕΚ. μορφῆς ἐπῳδόν, ἢ τί, τῆς ἐμῆς ἐρεῖς;

ΠΟΛΥΜ. κυνὸς ταλαίνης σῆμα, ναυτίλοις τέκμαρ.

ΕΚ. οὐδὲν μέλει μοι σοῦ γέ μοι δόντος δίκην.

ΠΟΛΥΜ. καὶ σήν γ᾽ ἀνάγκη παῖδα Κασάνδραν θανεῖν.

ΕΚ. ἀπέπτυσ᾽· αὐτῷ ταῦτά σοι δίδωμ᾽ ἔχειν. 1276

ΠΟΛΥΜ. κτενεῖ νιν ἡ τοῦδ᾽ ἄλοχος, οἰκουρὸς πικρά.

ΕΚ. μήπω μανείη Τυνδαρὶς τοσόνδε παῖς.

ΠΟΛΥΜ. καὐτόν γε τοῦτον, πέλεκυν ἐξάρασ᾽ ἄνω.

ΑΓ. οὗτος σύ, μαίνει καὶ κακῶν ἐρᾷς τυχεῖν; 1280

ΠΟΛΥΜ. κτεῖν᾽, ὡς ἐν Ἄργει φόνια λουτρά σ᾽ ἀναμένει.

ΑΓ. οὐχ ἕλξετ᾽ αὐτόν, δμῶες, ἐκποδὼν βίᾳ;

ΠΟΛΥΜ. ἀλγεῖς ἀκούων; ΑΓ. οὐκ ἐφέξετε στόμα;

ΠΟΛΥΜ. ἐγκλῇετ᾽· εἴρηται γάρ.

ΑΓ. οὐχ ὅσον τάχος
νήσων ἐρήμων αὐτὸν ἐκβαλεῖτέ ποι, 1285
ἐπείπερ οὕτω καὶ λίαν θρασυστομεῖ;
Ἑκάβη, σὺ δ᾽, ὦ τάλαινα, διπτύχους νεκροὺς
στείχουσα θάπτε· δεσποτῶν δ᾽ ὑμᾶς χρεὼν
σκηναῖς πελάζειν, Τρῳάδες· καὶ γὰρ πνοὰς
πρὸς οἶκον ἤδη τάσδε πομπίμους ὁρῶ. 1290
εὖ δ᾽ ἐς πάτραν πλεύσαιμεν, εὖ δὲ τὰν δόμοις
ἔχοντ᾽ ἴδοιμεν τῶνδ᾽ ἀφειμένοι πόνων.

ΧΟ. ἴτε πρὸς λιμένας σκηνάς τε, φίλαι,
τῶν δεσποσύνων πειρασόμεναι
μόχθων· στερρὰ γὰρ ἀνάγκη. 1295

NOTES.

1. σκότου πύλας for the more usual Ἀιδου πύλας. Hom. Il. ix. 312, Aesch. Ag. 1291, Eur. Hipp. 56.

2. Ἀιδης...ᾤκισται, 'where Hades' abode has been fixed.' Ἀιδης here is the god (as always in Homer: cf. Leaf on Il. i. 3), not his realm. The use of the word οἰκίζω implies that he is regarded as a settler in a new (and undesirable, χωρὶς θεῶν) land.

3. Κισσέως. So Virgil Aen. vii. 320 calls her 'Cisseis,' though Homer Il. xvi. 718 says she was daughter of Dymas.

6. ὑπεξέπεμψε, 'sent me *secretly* (ὑπ-) out' of the country.

8. The Thracian Chersonese (so called to distinguish it from other χερσόνησοι, 'peninsulas,' e. g. the Tauric, mod. Crimea) was early colonised by the Greeks. Herodotus vi. 34 sq. tells how the family of the 'tyrant of the Chersonese' first came there in the days of Peisistratus; probably several other Athenian families had valuable estates there too.

9. σπείρει. Corn and wine were the chief products of Thrace: probably the accounts of the severity of the climate were exaggerated. Corn was especially exported from the Chersonese, and was. of good quality, Plin. xviii. 12. Homer Il. xx. 485 calls Thrace ἐριβῶλαξ.

φίλιππον. The Thracians were at all times famous for their horses (Il. xiv. 227): a white breed is specially mentioned, λευκότεροι χιόνος, θείειν δ' ἀνέμοισιν ὁμοῖοι, Il. x. 437.

δορί implies unconstitutional rule by force.

13. ὅ=δι' ὅ. So ταῦτα, Andr. 212 ταῦτά τοί σ' ἔχθει πόσις: Ar. Nub. 320 ταῦτ' ἄρ' ἀκούσασ' αὐτῶν τὸ φθέγμ' ἡ ψυχή μου πεπότηται: cf. Soph. Phil. 142 τό μοι ἔννεπε, 'tell me therefore.' Hom. Il. iii. 176.

14. ὅπλα defensive, ἔγχος offensive.

16. ὀρθ' ἐκειθ' ὁρίσματα. This probably refers to the boundary stones (Il. xxi. 405 τόν ῥ' ἄνδρες πρότεροι θέσαν ἔμμεναι οὖρον ἀρούρης) which would be thrown down on the conquest of the country.

20. 'beneath his nurturing like some young plant I grew in stature —bootlessly.' For the plur. τροφαῖς, cf. Aesch. Ag. 1158 ἀμφὶ σὰς ἀϊόνας τάλαιν' ἠνυτόμαν τροφαῖς. So infr. 82 φυλακαῖσιν. For the metaphor, cf. Od. xiv. 175 τὸν ἐπεὶ θρέψαν θεοὶ ἔρνεϊ ἴσον, of Telemachus.

23. αὐτὸς, sc. πατήρ, supplied from πατρῴα in the previous line.

θεοδμήτῳ. Poseidon and Apollo had worked as builders for Laomedon, King of Troy, who, when the task was finished, βιήσατο μισθὸν ἅπαντα | ...ἀπειλήσας δ' ἀπέπεμπέν, Il. xxi. 451.

24. ἐκ, 'at the hand of': the action is viewed as *proceeding from* the author: this use of ἐκ for the more usual ὑπό, though common in Herodotus, is rare in Attic. Soph. O. T. 854 διεῖπε χρῆναι παιδὸς ἐξ ἐμοῦ θανεῖν, Ant. 63.

The slaughter of Priam by Pyrrhus is not mentioned by Homer, but cf. Eur. Tro. 16 πρὸς δὲ κρηπίδων (base of the altar) βάθροις | πέπτωκε Πρίαμος Ζηνὸς 'Ερκείου θανών: Virg. Aen. ii. 547 'altaria ad ipsa trementem | traxit, etc.' This same Pyrrhus was to sacrifice another victim at the altar, Polyxena, last (save Cassandra) of Priam's daughters: infr. 566 sq. σφάζειν is properly used of cutting the throat of victims.

26. The emphatic position of ξένος πατρῷος marks the atrocity of the criminal, who added to murder breach of hospitality.

27. ἔχῃ more vivid than the regular ἔχοι. Thompson's Gr. Synt. p. 255.

28. Before ἐπ' ἀκταῖς supply ἄλλοτε, as in Soph. Tr. 11 φοιτῶν ἐναργὴς ταῦρος, ἄλλοτ' αἰόλος | δράκων κ.τ.λ. Others read ἐπ' ἀκτῆς and take κεῖμαι to mean 'I am now lying.'

29. 'tossed in the waves' frequent ebb and flow': the ebb and flow of the waves reminds the poet of the δίαυλος, where the track lay up one side of the course and down again to the starting-place.

30. νῦν δ' ὑπὲρ κ.τ.λ. 'My wraith is present in a dream to my mother.' Cf. Od. iv. 803 of the vision of a friend appearing to Penelope, στῆ δ' ἄρ' ὑπὲρ κεφαλῆς καί μιν πρὸς μῦθον ἔειπεν.

31. ᾁσσω. This is perhaps the only exception to the rule that in Tragedy ᾁσσω, not ἀΐσσω, is found in trimeter verse. Homer on the contrary always uses the trisyllabic form.

32. τριταῖον φέγγος: a similar redundance (δευτεραῖος τριταῖος etc. meaning on the second, third etc. *day*) is found Hipp. 275 τριταίαν ἡμέραν. Thuc. v. 75 προτεραίᾳ ἡμέρᾳ.

αἰωρούμενος, 'hovering': cf. Soph. El. 1390 ὄνειρον αἰωρούμενον. αἰώρημα was the stage machine used for representing figures above the usual level.

35. **ναῦς ἔχοντες,** '*though* provided with ships, *yet* sit idle...*for* the son of Peleus, etc.'

37. **τύμβος** is properly the mound or barrow, on the summit of which was placed the στήλη, a pillar commemorating the deceased, often adorned with a sculptured likeness, amid surroundings suggested by his vocation: representations of banquets and parting scenes are frequently found also. In Hom. Il. xi. 371 Paris takes aim at Diomedes

στήλῃ κεκλιμένος ἀνδροκμήτῳ ἐπὶ τύμβῳ | Ἴλου Δαρδανίδαο.

39. **εὐθύνοντας,** sc. στρατιώτας, understood from στράτευμα above.

40. **ἀδελφὴν** is direct object to αἰτεῖ, and λαβεῖν an explanatory infinitive.

One post-Homeric version of Achilles' death was that, enamoured of Polyxena, he came to a rendezvous assigned by her, and was there slain by Paris. This would account for his demand for her sacrifice. Cf. Seneca, Tro. 204 *desponsa nostris cineribus Polyxena*.

41. Cf. I. T. 243 δίπτυχοι νεάνιαι, | θεᾷ φίλον πρόσφαγμα καὶ θυτήριον | Ἀρτέμιδι. **φίλον,** 'desired.'

44. **τῷδ'...ἐν ἤματι,** 'this coming day': as it is now supposed to be night or early morning.

47. The souls of the unburied could not enter the Elysian fields: hence the importance attached by the Greeks to the due burial even of enemies: cf. Elpenor's prayer to Odysseus (Od. xi. 72) μή μ' ἄκλαυτον ἄθαπτον ἰὼν ὄπιθεν καταλείπειν | νοσφισθείς, μή τοί τι θεῶν μήνιμα (cause of divine anger) γένωμαι.

51. **ὅσονπερ τυχεῖν.** 'The neut. plur. accus. of pronouns and adjectives can stand after τυγχάνειν and κυρεῖν, not as an accus. directly governed by the verb, but rather as a species of cognate or adverbial accusative.' Jebb on Soph. O. T. 1298. This passage shows that the usage is not confined to *plural* accusatives. Cf. Aesch. Cho. 711 τυγχάνειν τὰ πρόσφορα, Eur. Ph. 1666 οὐ γὰρ ἂν τύχοις τάδε.

53. **πέρᾳ πόδα.** Verbs signifying motion take an accusative of the instrument or limb used, is Porson's remark on Eur. Or. 1427: thus he explains the common phrase βαίνειν πόδα, found in e.g. Eur. El. 94, 1173, Heracl. 805, Phoen. 1412. Prof. Jebb regards βαίνειν in these passages as transitive.

55. 'who after a royal home hast come to see the day of slavery': **ἐκ,** 'after,' denoting change, as Soph. O. T. 454 τυφλὸς ἐκ δεδορκότος: Xen. Cyr. 3. 1. 17 ἐξ ἄφρονος σώφρων γεγένηται.

56. **δούλειον ἦμαρ.** This Homeric use of ἦμαρ to denote a condition occurs also Andr. 99. I know of no other instance in tragedy.

57. 'making equipoise of present woe with past prosperity.' σήκωμα is a weight in the balance: cf. Eur. Heracl. 690 σμικρὸν τὸ σὸν σήκωμα προστίθης φίλοις.

59. Hecuba, in a frenzy of alarm at the visions of her sleep, appears supported by her fellow captives. πρὸ δόμων: the conventional background on the Greek stage from the middle of the fifth century was a palace or temple front. In 17 out of the 25 extant plays of Soph. and Eur. this is required (Haigh, Attic Theatre, p. 168): in the Hecuba however an encampment is the background, a fact which the poet seems to have forgotten, when he uses the words πρὸ δόμων.

60. Cf. Andr. 64 ὦ φιλτάτη σύνδουλε, σύνδουλος γὰρ εἶ | τῇ πρόσθ' ἀνάσσῃ τῇδε, νῦν δὲ δυστυχεῖ.

62. Anapaestic systems as a rule avoid successions of short syllables; a proceleusmatic (◡◡◡◡) is accordingly very rare, and a proceleusmatic followed, as here, by an anapaest, quite extraordinary: it is intended to express frenzied excitement.

63. γεραιᾶς: cf. Hipp. 170. The quantity of -αι- in such cases is due to the change of *i* to *y* in pronunciation.

64. προσλαζύμεναι: λάζομαι is Epic: λάζυμαι Attic, except in the imperat., when λάζου is used: cf. Elmsley on Med. 1185.

65. 'and I, resting my weight upon thine arm, staff-like, albeit curved, setting forward will quicken the slow-paced goings of my feet.' σκίπων χερὸς is the staff, consisting in thy hand (epexegetic genit.), which differs from real staves, which are straight, by being curved (σκολιός). See Blomfield's Glossary on Aesch. Ag. 81, who well illustrates the poetic usage of softening down a violent metaphor by the addition of a contradictory epithet, marking clearly and at once the distinction between the reality and the similitude: a simple instance is in Aesch. Theb. 64 κῦμα χερσαῖον στρατοῦ, 'a wave (but a *land* wave) consisting in the army.' προτιθεῖσα, setting one foot before the other.

68. στεροπὰ Διός is taken by most editors as=the sun, which seems inconsistent with ἔννυχος in the next line. Possibly the shooting beams of the rising sun are meant.

70. Her agitation is expressed by the asyndeton, δείμασι φάσμασιν. δείματα νυκτίπλαγκτα (Aesch. Cho. 524) are terrifying visions, which drive men from their beds.

71. μελανοπτερύγων ὀνείρων, cf. infr. 705 φάσμα μελανόπτερον.

72. ἀποπέμπομαι, 'I strive to avert' by invocation and prayer: so infr. 97.

76. ἐδάην, found in Trag. only in lyrical passages.

80. **ἄγκυρ'**, a slight anachronism, as in the times in which the action of this play is placed, not anchors, but heavy perforated stones (εὐναί), were used.

Porson quotes a fragment of Soph. ἀλλ' εἰσὶ μητρὶ παῖδες ἄγκυραι βίου.

82. **ξείνου πατρίου**, cf. supr. 26 ξένος πατρῷος : Cobet distinguishes πατρῷον = τὸ τοῦ πατρός, πάτριον = τὸ τῶν προγόνων.

φυλακαῖσιν : perhaps the plur. conveys the notion of ' continued protection': see τροφαῖς, supr. 20.

85. **ἄλαστος**, epic word, ' unabating.' Cf. Il. xxiv. 549 μηδ' ἄλαστον ὀδύρεο.

86. **φρίσσει ταρβεῖ** : for the asyndeton, cf. supr. 70.

87. Helenus and Cassandra were two of Priam's children, who had the gift of prophecy. From Homer we learn little of Helenus, but other writers tell us that he became reconciled to the Greeks, and settled in Epirus, where he received Aeneas (Virg. Aen. iii. 346 sq.). Cassandra is famous for her beauty only in Homer (ἰκέλη χρυσέῃ Ἀφροδίτῃ), who knows nothing of the prophetic powers, which the later Epic writers assigned to her.

θεῖος, ' inspired.' ἐσίδω, deliberative ; Thompson Gr. Synt. § 132.

90. ' for in my dream I saw a dappled hind, and a wolf rending her throat with bloody fangs: and the hind had been torn ruthlessly from my knees.' Notice the change of tense, σφαζομέναν (the word suggests sacrifice, cf. supr. 24 n.) of continuous, σπασθεῖσαν of momentary action.

αἵμων, only here and Aesch. Supp. 847. χαλᾷ, ' jaw': so Hesychius, though the usual meaning of χηλή is ' hoof' or ' talons.'

92. **τόδε**, ' this too,' viz. the following.

93. Cf. supr. 37, 40.

96. **ἀπὸ...πέμψατε**, ' avert': supr. 72.

98. **ἐλιάσθην** seems to mean ' have come hither out of my way ': λιάζομαι is entirely an epic word = ' to go aside.' It was doubtless suggested to the poet by ἄλαστος, supr. 85, and is a good instance of the tendency in the poets, in Euripides especially, to repeat a rare word, often in an entirely different meaning and connection, very soon after they have first employed it.

102. ' spear-won at the lance's point,' a redundant expression, easy to parallel, e.g. Bacch. 571 εὐδαιμονίας ὀλβοδόταν (Pflugk).

105. ' laden with a burden of heavy tidings.'

108. **δόξαι**, the regular term for expressing the resolutions of the

Athenian assembly: infr. 124 ῥήτορες would be equally familiar to Athenian ears.

109. θέσθαι=ποιήσασθαι, by Ionic usage, allowed in Tragedy.

110. The arms described in Il. xviii. were given to Ulysses. χρυσέοις: that in the heroic age gold was very plentiful, is proved not only by the frequent references to it in Homer (where the epithet χρύσεος is often merely picturesque, or means 'ornamented with gold,') but by the evidence of the tombs at Mycenae and elsewhere, which yielded a profusion of solid gold cups and ornaments of all kinds. India, Arabia, Lydia and the Caucasus provided the metal in the early period: the famous gold mines of Thrace were not fully worked till Philip of Macedon developed them.

112. In this passage and in I. T. 1134 πρότονοι are explained to be the ropes '*quibus vela vel contrahuntur vel expanduntur*' (Hermann): elsewhere they are the two forestays of the mast, fastened from the masthead to the bows, the backstay being called ἐπίτονος. I see no reason to depart from the traditional meaning here; we must remember that Greek ships were square-rigged, and a favourable or following breeze would belly the sails out till they pressed upon the forestays, running forward from the mast. In the passage from the I. T. the reading is doubtful.

116. 'clashing waves of great strife met.'

ξυνέπαισε, intr. Cf. Soph. O. C. 1503 χάλαζ' ἐπιρράξασα, 'bursting on' one: Herod. i. 80 ὁ ποταμὸς συρρήγνυσι: Ar. Plut. 805 ἐς τὴν οἰκίαν ἐπεισπέπαικεν: Eur. Hipp. 1198 ἔρημον χῶρον εἰσεβάλλομεν: Soph. O. T. 1252 εἰσέπαισεν Οἰδίπους.

117. lit. 'opinion spread dividedly,' a Homeric phrase: cf. δίχα θυμὸν ἔχοντες: Herod. vi. 109 ἐγίνοντο δίχα αἱ γνῶμαι.

118. With τοῖς μὲν διδόναι supply δοκοῦν from οὐχὶ δοκοῦν in the next line. δοκοῦν is accus. abs., cf. Hadley Gr. Gr. § 973.

121. ἀνέχων, 'remaining constant to': cf. Soph. Aj. 212 σε στέρξας ἀνέχει Αἴας.

Βάκχης is Cassandra: cf. supr. 88.

123. τὼ Θησείδα. Acamas and Demophon, the Scholiast tells us. Homer does not mention these two sons of Theseus and Phaedra. Virgil (Aen. ii. 262) includes Acamas in the list of the warriors concealed in the wooden horse. ὄζω, cf. Homeric ὄζος Ἄρηος, and supr. 20.

124. δισσῶν, i.e. one speech each; it does not mean 'taking opposite sides,' for γν. μιᾷ συνεχωρείτην: the word was probably introduced merely for the verbal antithesis with μιᾷ.

In Athens by ῥήτορες were meant habitual speakers in the ἐκκλησία: references to these professional politicians of the democracy are very frequent and often uncomplimentary. Eur. himself says (fr. 600) νόμον ...ἄνω τε καὶ κάτω | ῥήτωρ ταράσσων πολλάκις λυμαίνεται. It is not without significance that these two early ῥήτορες were ὅζω Ἀθηνῶν.

126. στεφανοῦν, 'honour with libations,' for the more usual στέφειν, Soph. Ant. 431 χοαῖσι τρισπόνδοισι τὸν νέκυν στέφει.

127. χλωρῷ, 'fresh.'

128. The military services of Achilles establish a claim on the Greeks not to be postponed to the mere connection of their general Agamemnon with a Trojan captive.

130. 'on either side the eager heat of contentious speech was equal.'

κατατειν. means 'strained to the full': cf. the intr. use of the participle κατατείνας = 'strenuously,' Plat. Rep. 358 D διὸ κατατείνας ἐρῶ, τὸν ἄδικον βίον ἐπαινῶν: id. ib. 367 B.

131. 'shifty prater, smooth-tongued flatterer of the mob.' κόπις, a prater; κοπίς, a knife.

135. δούλων σφ. εἵνεκ' = 'to save a slave girl's life.' ἀπωθεῖν, 'to slight.'

139. οἰχομένοις, 'departed,' i.e. dead.

141. ὅσον οὐκ ἤδη, 'almost immediately.' ὅσον οὐκ is only used in this sense ('almost') when speaking of time: μόνον οὐκ is used in other connections. Thuc. i. 36 τὸν μέλλοντα καὶ ὅσον οὐ παρόντα πόλεμον: iv. 125 νομίσαντες πολλαπλασίου ἐπιέναι, ὅσον δὲ οὔπω παρεῖναι.

143. ὁρμήσων κ.τ.λ., 'and to tear her from thy aged arms.' ὁρμάω is generally used of 'urging towards' not 'taking from.'

145. There is a metrical objection to this line, the succession of four short syllables caused by the anapaest ἱκέτις following the dactyl -μεμνονος: cf. supr. 62 n.

146. κήρυσσε, 'summon.' Il. ii. 51 κηρύσσειν ἀγορήνδε Ἀχαιούς.

150. ἐπιδεῖν, 'live to see.' Cf. Thompson on Plat. Gorg. 473 C.

τύμβου προπετῆ, 'quick hasting to her grave.' This seems better than ' falling before the tomb' of Achilles.

152. 'while the darkly-gleaming tide | welleth, welleth from the neck, which the golden mockeries deck' is Mr Way's translation.

μελαναυγὴς is ἅπαξ λεγόμενον.

'*mas erat apud veteres virginibus plurimum auri gestare*' remarks Porson, quoting Il. ii. 872 of the Carian leader ὃς καὶ χρυσὸν ἔχων πόλεμόνδ' ἴεν, ἠΰτε κούρη.

154. ἀπύσω. ἠπύειν is found in Tragedy only in lyric passages, and always in this, the Doric, form.

156. Observe the heavy spondaic rhythm of these mournful lines.
γήρως. Causal genit. 'wretched by reason of,' Thompson Gr. Synt. p. 94.

161. πρέσβυς, Priam.

162. ποίαν, sc. ὁδόν: for this ellipse cf. the expression τὴν ἄλλως, Plat. Theaet. 172 E οἱ ἀγῶνες οὐδέποτε τὴν ἄλλως ἀλλ' ἀεὶ τὴν περὶ αὐτοῦ, 'the trial is never for an indifferent stake, but always immediately concerns the speaker' (Campbell). Dem. (Ol. 3) 34. 11 (Reiske) καὶ ταῦτ' οὐ τὴν ἄλλως (*frustra*) προῄρημαι λέγειν.

163. ἥσω, sc. ἐμαυτόν: the text however is not certain.

167. ἀπωλέσατ' ὠλέσατ', by a common Greek idiom only the simple verb is repeated: cf. Bacch. 1065 κατῆγεν ἦγεν ἦγεν: Hipp. 1374 προσαπόλλυτέ μ' ὄλλυτε τὸν δυσδαίμονα. ' Ye have undone me with your news' (κάκ' ἐνεγκοῦσαι).

170. ἄγησαι...ἄγησαι. The repeated words and phrases in this lament of Hecuba heighten the pathetic effect. 'O weary, weary feet, lead me bowed with years, lead me' etc.

173. These lines are parodied in Ar. Nub. 1165 ὦ τέκνον, ὦ παῖ, ἔξελθ' οἴκων, | ἄιε σοῦ πατρός. As the Nubes was produced in B.C. 423, the date of the Hecuba must be placed earlier than that year.

177. 'what fresh horror hast thou announced, drawing me forth in such amaze from the palace, scared even as a bird?'

179. ἐξέπταξας, 'scared me from' the house: this causal use of πτήσσω is perhaps without parallel; for Hom. Il. xiv. 40 is condemned, partly on the ground of this very use: and Theogn. 1015 (quoted by L. and S.) is plainly intr.

181. δυσφημεῖν τινά is to speak in an ill-omened way of a person. Here οἴμοι conveys the omen. In Heracl. 600, Iolaus bids Makaria, who is about to be sacrificed, χαῖρε· δυσφημεῖν γὰρ ἄζομαι θεὰν | ᾗ σὸν κατῆρκται σῶμα: Soph. El. 1182.
φροίμια, i.e. οἴμοι: cf. Hipp. 566 τὸ μέντοι φροίμιον (referring to ἐξειργάσμεθα in the previous line) κακὸν τόδε. Phoen. 1336.

182. σᾶς ψυχᾶς, for genit. cf. 156 n.

183. δαρόν: this, the Doric form, is alone found in Trag.: so too κυναγός, ὀπαδός etc. (Pors. on Or. 26): cf. Rutherford, New Phrynichus, p. 496.

184. δειμαίνω τί ποτ' ἀναστένεις = δειμαίνω, ἀποροῦσα ὅ τι ἀναστένεις. For τί = ὅ τι, cf. Soph. Aj. 794 ὥστε μ' ὠδίνειν (= δεῖσασαν ἀπορεῖν) τί φῄς.

188. σφάξαι σε συντείνει, 'is bent upon thy sacrifice.'

192. ἀμέγαρτα κακῶν, cf. Hipp. 849 φίλα γυναικῶν: infr. 716 κατάρατ' ἀνδρῶν.

195. 'that a decree concerning thy life has been made by vote of the Greeks' is a somewhat vague statement to come *after* the plain words of 188—190: some editors transpose the lines.

199. αὖ, in addition to thy previous woes.

202. 'thou hast me now no more, no more, thy child, to share in wretchedness the bondage of thy wretched age.'

205. σκύμνον οὐριθρέπταν, cf. Or. 1493 βάκχαι σκύμνον ἐν χεροῖν ὀρείαν ξυνήρπασαν.

206. δειλαία δειλαίαν, 'woe is me! woe is thee!'

207. χειρὸς ἀναρπαστὰν, cf. supr. 90.

210. her marriage will be with the shades: cf. her lament infr. 416.

211. σοῦ, sc. τὸν βίον.

213. 'my life, all misery and insult, I weep not after, but the better lot, to die, has fallen to me.'

214. μετακλαίομαι, 'pursue with lamentation'; the force of μετα- seen in μετέρχομαι: others take μετα- here of succession, 'lament in turn,' and compare μεταστένω, Med. 996.

216. καὶ μὴν, introducing the new person: Hipp. 899 καὶ μὴν ὅδ' αὐτὸς παῖς σὸς εἰς καιρὸν πάρα | Ἱππόλυτος: Soph. Ant. 526, 1180: O. C. 549: Eur. Andr. 515 καὶ μὴν δέδορκα τόνδε Πηλέα πέλας | σπουδῇ τιθέντα δεῦρο γηραιὸν πόδα.

219. ψῆφον κρανθεῖσαν, cf. Aesch. Supp. 942 τοιάδε δημόπρακτος ἐκ πόλεως μία | ψῆφος κέκρανται: Eur. Andr. 1273.

220. ἔδοξ' Ἀχαιοῖς κ.τ.λ. This is framed on the analogy of an Athenian ψήφισμα: notice its blunt, businesslike wording.

221. ὀρθὸν χῶμ', cf. 37 n.

223. ἐπιστάτης ἐπέστη: such repetition was not disagreeable to Greek ears: it is akin to expressions like δραμεῖν δρόμον etc.

224. τοῦδε—pointing towards Achilles' tomb.

225. οἶσθ' οὖν ὃ δρᾶσον; 'dost thou know, what thou must do?' The Greek imperative can be used in subordinate clauses: cf. Thompson Gr. Synt. p. 137, Hadley Gr. Gr. § 875: and by all means Jebb's note on Soph. O. T. 543.

μήτ' ἀποσπασθῇς βίᾳ, 'do not make force necessary to take her from thee.' Verbs of depriving take a double accusative (cf. Thompson Gr. Synt. p. 72), e.g. Soph. O. C. 866 ὅς μ', ὦ κάκιστε, ψιλὸν ὄμμ' ἀποσπάσας κ.τ.λ.: in the passive construction one accus. becomes the subject: so here, active, μὴ ἀποσπάσῃς με τὴν θυγατέρα: passive, μὴ ἀποσπασθῆς τὴν θυγατέρα.

227. 'recognize what strength you have,' i.e. how little.

228. τοι introduces a remark of a proverbial nature, cf. Soph. Aj. 1350 τόν τοι τύραννον εὐσεβεῖν οὐ ῥᾴδιον.

231. κἄγωγ', I too, as well as my husband and children.

ἄρ' οὐκ ἔθνησκον οὗ με χρῆν θανεῖν, 'I did not, as now I know (ἄρα), die, where I should have died,' i.e. in Troy: cf. for sense of ἄρα, Hipp. 359.

232. ὅπως ὁρῶ κακῶν κ.τ.λ.: this is the ἀγὼν μέγας of 229.

234—237. The literal translation seems to be, 'if it is permitted to a slave to put to a freeman such questions as are not offensive nor calculated to wound his feelings, then it is fitting for an answer to have been given by you, and for me, who put the questions, to listen.' Hecuba asks in a somewhat roundabout fashion, 'if I ask you, meaning no offence, certain questions, will you reply to them?' It is possible that εἰ, l. 234, means 'whether': in that case the sense would be, 'it is for you to say, for me to acquiesce in your decision, whether I a slave may ask you certain questions.'

235. καρδίας δηκτήρια: 'the genitive is used with adjectives of transitive action, where the corresponding verbs would have the accusative.' Hadley Gr. Gr. § 754 a: so ὀψιμαθὴς ἀδικίας, 'late in learning injustice.'

237. τοὺς ἐρωτῶντας: when persons speak of themselves in the plural instead of the singular (using *we* for *I*), even though a woman be speaking, the masculine plural is used. Cf. Soph. El. 399 πεσούμεθ', εἰ χρή, πατρὶ τιμωρούμενοι (Electra is speaking).

238. χρόνου, emphatic: 'mere *time* I do not grudge': for the genit. cf. H. F. 333 οὐ φθονῶ πέπλων.

239. Cf. Hom. Od. iv. 244 sq. αὐτόν μιν πληγῇσιν ἀεικελίῃσι δαμάσσας, | σπεῖρα κάκ' (rags) ἀμφ' ὤμοισι βαλών, οἰκῆι ἐοικὼς, | ἀνδρῶν δυσμενέων κατέδυ πόλιν εὐρυάγυιαν. Eur. (?) Rhes. 710 sq. ἔβα καὶ πάρος | κατὰ πόλιν, ὕπαφρον ὄμμ' ἔχων, | ῥακοδύτῳ στολᾷ πυκασθείς. Odysseus disguised as a beggar made his way as a spy into Troy, κατὰ δὲ φρόνιν (information) ἤγαγε πολλήν.

242. ἄκρας καρδίας, the mere surface of the heart, cf. Aesch. Ag. 805 νῦν δ' οὐκ ἀπ' ἄκρας φρενός κ.τ.λ. 'it lies deep-printed in my heart.'

243. Cf. Od. iv. 250 ἐγὼ (Helen) δέ μιν οἴη ἀνέγνων τοῖον ἐόντα. Eur. makes her share the secret with Hecuba.

246. ἐνθανεῖν, 'become numb with holding.'

247. δοῦλος ὤν ἐμός τότε, as I now am yours.

254. 'yours is a thankless generation, who yearn with striving for the honours of the demagogue.'

255. 'nor be ye friends of mine, who etc.' The poet here is looking at contemporary politics, and lamenting the growing influence of that product of democracy, the trained speaker (ῥήτωρ), whose only aim is self-advancement, and who does not hesitate to desert the friend, to whose help he perhaps owes everything, if he may thereby improve his position with his patrons and audience, the mob. Odysseus, deserting in her need Hecuba, who had preserved his life, serves as his text. If we wish to grasp Eur.'s position with regard to this class of his contemporaries, the following passages are noteworthy: Or. 893 sqq., Hipp. 488 sqq., Bacch. 269 sqq., Supp. 421 sqq.

258. But even adopting for the moment this standard, what clever subtlety can you devise for condemning this child to death? what specious pretext can you adduce? Not the necessity of human sacrifice certainly on an altar intended for oxen. Does Achilles' blood call for the blood of those who brought about his death? Then Helen, not the guiltless Polyxena, should be the victim. She too is fairest of the captives, if beauty be an object. So much for the mere justice of the case. But think further, how great a claim I have on your personal gratitude. Once you were my suppliant: now I am yours: shall it go for nothing, that I saved your life? This child is all I have left to me in the wide world: spare her: it becomes the possessors of power to set due limits to its exercise, to reflect that it is fleeting: one day brought me low, and may you. This is the day of your might: if you do but ask a boon of the Greeks, you will obtain it: so prevailing is the petition of the powerful.

260. τὸ χρῆν, a shortened form either of the infin. χρῆναι (cf. ζῆν, διψῆν), or of the partic. χρεών. In Eur. H. F. 828 τὸ χρῆν νιν ἐξέσωζεν, we meet the same difficulty. Nauck would in both passages read τὸ χρή. Philologically χρῆν may be a regular infinitive: χρή-εν = χρῆν, as λέγε-εν = λέγειν.

263. εἰς τήνδ' is emphatic, 'is Achilles acting justly in aiming (metaphor from a bow) death at Polyxena?'

264. ἥδε γ', she at any rate, whatever others may have done.

265. τάφῳ προσφάγματα: cf. supr. 41. χρῆν = ἐχρῆν, imperf. It would appear that χρῆν = χρὴ ἦν, and that ἐ- is due to the origin of the word being forgotten, and its consequent treatment as an ordinary

imperfect: its accentuation ἐχρῆν (ἔχρην would be natural, if it were an augmented tense) favours this view.

268.   οὐχ ἡμῶν τόδε, lit. 'this requirement is not found with us,' i.e. Polyxena speaking through her advocate Hecuba.

270.   οὐδὲν ἧσσον = 'far more,' an instance of litotes.   This figure of speech was a favourite one with the Greeks, who were in the habit of emphasizing a case by intentionally understating it.

271.   ἁμιλλᾶσθαι is to contend with a person: the kind of contest may be added as a cognate accusative, e.g. Plat. Legg. 833 A ἁμιλλᾶσθαι στάδιον : Eur. Hel. 546 σὲ, τὴν ὄρεγμα δεινὸν ἡμιλλημένην | τύμβου 'πὶ κρηπῖδα, 'who hast contended with me in a desperate effort to reach the tomb,' i.e. to reach it before I could reach you : Hel. 164 ποῖον ἁμιλλαθῶ γόον; lit. 'in what competition of lamentation am I to engage' in order to express myself adequately : so here, 'his claims based on strict justice (cf. ἐνδίκως, 263) I contend with in this argument,' i.e. I bring this argument against them.   So Hipp. 971 τί ταῦτα σοῖς ἁμιλλῶμαι λόγοις ; τῷ δικαίῳ, 'strict justice,' is opposed to ἃ ἀντιδοῦναι δεῖ σε, 'the personal claim I have on you.'

274.   προσπίτνων, 'in your supplication.'

275.   ἀνθ-, 'in my turn.'

276.   ἀπαιτῶ, 'demand *as my due.*'   Cf. L. and S. s.v. ἀποδίδωμι I. 1: so in Latin, *reddo.*

277.   ἀποσπάσῃς...κτάνητε: the first is the work of Odysseus alone: the latter of the Greeks generally, who had voted for the sacrifice.

281.   Porson quotes from a fragment of Eur. ἀλλ' ἥδε μ' ἐξέσωσεν· ἥδε μοι τροφὸς | μήτηρ ἀδελφὴ δμωῒς ἄγκυρα στέγη: cf. too Soph. Aj. 518 τίς δῆτ' ἐμοὶ γένοιτ' ἂν ἀντὶ σοῦ πατρίς ; | τίς πλοῦτος; Ov. Her. iii. 52 *tu dominus, tu vir, tu mihi frater eras:* and the touching appeal of Andromache, Il. vi. 429 "Εκτορ, ἀτὰρ σύ μοί ἐσσι πατὴρ καὶ πότνια μήτηρ | ἠδὲ κασίγνητος, σὺ δέ μοι θαλερὸς παρακοίτης.

284.   κἀγὼ γὰρ ἦ, sc. εὐτυχής.

285.   On double accus. cf. 225 n.

288.   παρηγ.   παρηγορεῖν is Ion. and Trag. : παραμυθεῖσθαι Attic. 'Counsel them soothingly, and say it is held shameful etc.'

φθόνος, sc. ἐστί = it is an invidious thing to do.

291.   ἐν ὑμῖν, in Greece: cf. Dem. c. Mid. § 46 κἂν εἰς δοῦλον ὑβρίζῃ τις, ὁμοίως ἔδωκεν ὁ νομοθέτης ὑπὲρ τούτου γραφήν· οὐ γὰρ ὅστις ὁ πάσχων ᾤετο δεῖν σκοπεῖν, ἀλλὰ τὸ πρᾶγμα ὁποῖόν τι τὸ γιγνόμενον.

293.   κἂν κακῶς λέγῃς, 'even if you speak in a bad cause' or 'a cause which most of your hearers think bad' (Paley) : it may be how-

ever that κακῶς means 'haltingly.' So Tro. 914. These lines are translated by Ennius, *haec tu etsi pervorse dices, facile Achivos flexeris;* | *nam opulenti quom loquontur pariter atque ignobiles,* | *eadem dicta eademque oratio aequa non aeque valet.*

295. τῶν δοκούντων, sc. εἶναί τι, 'men of position.' Plat. Gorg. 472 A, Euthyd. 303 C τῶν σεμνῶν καὶ δοκούντων τι εἶναι: cf. Pind. Nem. vii. 30 ἀλλὰ κοινὸν γὰρ ἔρχεται | κῦμ' Ἀίδα, πέσε δ' ἀδόκητον ἐν καὶ δοκέοντα. Cf. ὁ ἔχων, 'rich.'

296. οὕτω στερρός, ἥτις κ.τ.λ., cf. Hel. 501 ἀνὴρ γὰρ οὐδεὶς ὧδε βάρβαρος φρένας | ὃς ὄνομ' ἀκούσας τοὐμὸν οὐ δώσει βοράν.

297. μακρῶν, prob. 'loud,' like Hom. μακρὸν ἀυτεῖν: lit. 'so as to be heard afar.'

298. ἐκβάλοι δάκρυ, a favourite phrase with Eur., who uses it very frequently, e.g. I. A. 451, 477, Ion 924, Hel. 957, 1563, H. F. 1356. It occurs in Hom. Od. 19. 362. Neither Soph. nor Aesch. I believe employs it.

299. τῷ θυμουμένῳ, 'through anger.' For the neut. partic. used in an abstract sense, where the infin. would be usual, cf. Soph. Phil. 675 τὸ γὰρ | νοσοῦν ποθεῖ σε συμπαραστάτην λαβεῖν. Thuc. i. 36 τὸ δεδιός, vii. 68 τὸ θυμούμενον τῆς γνώμης, i. 142 τὸ μὴ μελετῶν (failure to practise). This use is specially frequent in Thuc. Antiphon too (118, 16) has τὸ θυμούμενον τῆς γνώμης.

300. ποιοῦ, 'consider.'

301. τὸ σὸν σῶμα, 'you personally.'

305. σὴν παῖδα δοῦναι σφάγιον, in apposition to ἅ, supr. 303. ἅ εἶπον means 'the suggestion I made.'

306. Hecuba, in the corresponding part of her speech, had brought a charge of ingratitude against Odysseus and selfish politicians generally (254 ἀχάριστον ὑμῶν σπέρμα κ.τ.λ.). Here Odysseus retorts: the real ingratitude, an ingratitude which is a source of weakness in a state, is the failure to duly recompense deserving citizens: 'if we fail to grant Achilles his request, we shall be no better than you barbarians (inf. 327), and Greece, if she resembles you in this respect, will also resemble you in her decay (330).'

308. φέρηται. φέρεσθαι is used of carrying off a prize. Il. xxiii. 663 αὐτὰρ ὁ νικηθεὶς δέπας οἴσεται ἀμφικύπελλον, ix. 127 and very frequently. Herod. i. 31 δοκέων πάγχυ δευτερεῖα οἴσεσθαι 'win second place.' Soph. O. T. 500 μάντις πλέον ἢ 'γὼ φέρεται.

309. ἡμῖν ἄξιος τιμῆς, 'worthy of honour at our hands': cf. Alc. 433 ἀξία δέ μοι | τιμῆς: Ar. Ach. 633 φησὶν δ' εἶναι πολλῶν ἀγαθῶν ἄξιος

ὑμῖν ὁ ποιητής. Akin is the use of the dat. with δέχομαι: cf. Hom. Il.
i. 186 δέξατό οἱ σκῆπτρον πατρώϊον: infr. 535 δέξαι χοάς μοι (so Porson)
τάσδε κηλητηρίους: Aesch. Cho. 762 Ὀρέστην ἐξεδεξάμην πατρί.

310. 'who died for Hellas nobly as man may' (Way).   Notice
the emphatic position of ἀνήρ.

311. βλέποντι, 'alive,' cf. 295 n.

φίλῳ χρώμεσθ', 'treat as a friend.'

317—320. 'in life I can be content with little, but I would have my
tomb honoured after death.'

319. ἀξιούμενον, absol. 'honoured.' Cf. Thuc. v. 16. 3 βουλόμενος,
ἐν ᾧ ἀπαθὴς ἦν καὶ ἠξιοῦτο, διασώσασθαι τὴν εὐτυχίαν: Aesch. Ag. 903
τοιοῦσδέ τοί νιν ἀξιῶ προσφθέγμασιν: Eur. Or. 1210 ὑμεναίοισιν ἀξιουμένη.
ἀξ. is predicate. ὁρᾶσθαι, 'be seen to be.'

·320. τὸν ἐμὸν, emphatic. 'I should wish my tomb to be honoured,
and therefore I am anxious to honour the tomb of another.' Cf. the
Sophoclean Odysseus in Aj. 1365 urging the burial of Ajax, his enemy,
καὶ γὰρ αὐτὸς ἐνθάδ' ἵξομαι.

διὰ μακροῦ, 'lasting.' The usual meaning would be 'after a long
interval.' It is possible so to take it here: χάρις was not his in life,
but came after death, διὰ μακροῦ, i.e. delayed.

323. γραῖαι, supr. 274. The use of ἠδὲ, 'and,' is rare in tragedy,
but it occurs ten times in Aesch., twice in Soph., and twice in Eur.
(here and H. F. 30). σέθεν is out of place. πρεσβῦται, masc.

327. ἀμαθία signifies 'the absence of training or discipline, and the
condition which this absence produces.' Verrall on Med. 223. Thus
it is naturally to be expected in βάρβαροι, the point of the present
passage.

For ὀφλεῖν, 'incur the reproach of,' cf. Soph. Ant. 1028 αὐθαδία τοι
σκαιότητ' ὀφλισκάνει. ὀφλισκάνειν means to bring on oneself some
disadvantage, e.g. βλάβην, or the reputation for some bad quality
(expressed by the name of the quality simply), e.g. μωρίαν, ἀνομίαν,
δειλίαν, κακίαν.

328. οἱ βάρβαροι, nom. for voc., Hadley Gr. Gr. § 707.

330. ὡς ἄν=so that, in that case. Both ὡς and ὡς ἄν in final
clauses are extremely rare in Attic prose. For the sense, cf. supr. 306 n.

332. τὸ δοῦλον, 'slavery,' cf. Ion 556 ἐκπεφεύγαμεν τὸ δοῦλον.

333. τολμᾷ, 'endures,' cf. supr. 326. χρὴ of what is right)(δεῖ of
what is expedient.

335. μάτην ῥιφθέντες, cf. Med. 1404 μάτην ἔπος ἔρριπται.

337. 'as from nightingale's throat, pour forth each various strain of

supplication.' In the Greek, Polyxena is compared to the nightingale's throat, not the nightingale: cf. κόμαι χαρίτεσσιν ὁμοῖαι, Il. xvii. 51. For the sad and varied song of the nightingale, cf. the beautiful lines in Od. xix. 518 ὡς δ᾽ ὅτε...χλωρηὶς ἀηδὼν | καλὸν ἀείδησιν ἔαρος νέον ἱσταμένοιο | δενδρέων ἐν πετάλοισι καθεζομένη πυκινοῖσιν, | ἥ τε θαμὰ τρωπῶσα χέει πολυηχέα φωνήν, | παῖδ᾽ ὀλοφυρομένη.

340. πρόφασιν, 'plea.' The Scholiast explains it = ἀφορμὴν τοῦ πείθειν, 'a starting-place for persuasion.'

345. τὸν ἐμὸν is hard to translate literally: rendered freely the sense is 'I invoke not Zeus, the suppliant's help, so thou art safe from him.'

348. φιλόψυχος, cf. supr. 315.

349. δεῖ, cf. supr. 333 n.

350. 'this was the first element in my life.'

351. ἐλπίδων καλῶν ὕπο, 'with fair hope': for ὑπὸ, of accompanying circumstances, cf. Hipp. 1299 ὡς ὑπ᾽ εὐκλείας θάνῃ, 'with honour': H. F. 289 ὥστ᾽ οὐκ ἀνεκτὸν δειλίας θανεῖν ὕπο, 'with cowardice': Ar. Ach. 1001 πίνειν ὑπὸ σάλπιγγος.

352. 'causing no small contention for my hand, to whose hearth and home I am to come.' ζῆλος is honourable rivalry. γάμων, objective genit., Thompson Gr. Synt. § 98.

353. ἔχουσα, 'causing': ἔχειν sometimes almost = παρέχειν. The shade of meaning is not difficult to catch, as to be in possession of a thing implies the ability to offer or present it to the attention of another: cf. Thuc. ii. 41 μόνη (Athens) οὔτε τῷ πολεμίῳ ἐπελθόντι ἀγανάκτησιν ἔχει ὑφ᾽ οἵων κακοπαθεῖ, 'contains no grounds for indignation at the thought of being conquered by so unworthy a foe': iv. 1 ὁρῶντες προσβολὴν ἔχον τὸ χωρίον τῆς Σικελίας, 'affording an approach.'

ἀφίξομαι, the future here and infr. 360 ὠνήσεται is due to the vivid mental realising of the situation by the speaker.

355. μετά, with dat. 'among': poet. and somewhat rare, cf. Eur. fr. 362 (Erechtheus). 26 ἀλλ᾽ ἐμοίγ᾽ ἔστω τέκνα | ἃ καὶ μάχοιτο καὶ μετ᾽ ἀνδράσιν πρέποι: Il. xxiv. 258 Ἕκτορα ὃς θεὸς ἔσκε μετ᾽ ἀνδράσιν.

356. 'peer of the gods in all beside, save only in my mortality.' Before πλὴν understand πάντα.

358. ἐρᾶν τίθησιν, 'makes me to desire,' cf. Med. 718 παίδων γονὰς | σπεῖραί σε θήσω.

οὐκ εἰωθὸς ὄν. For the double partic. Porson compares Ar. Ran. 721 οὔτε γὰρ τούτοισιν οὖσιν οὐ κεκιβδηλευμένοις.

359. ὠμῶν φρένας, 'cruel-hearted.' δεσποτῶν...ὅστις, 'when the

antecedent is plural, the relative is sometimes singular, referring to an individual of the number. Plat. Rep. 566 D ἀσπάζεται πάντας, ᾧ ἂν περιτυγχάνῃ.' Hadley Gr. Gr. § 629 b.

361. Cf. the very similar passage, Tro. 490 (Hecuba speaks) δούλη γυνὴ γραῦς Ἑλλάδ' εἰσαφίξομαι. | ἃ δ' ἐστὶ γήρᾳ τῷδ' ἀσυμφορώτατα, | τούτοις με προσθήσουσιν, ἢ θυρῶν λάτριν | κλῇδας φυλάσσειν, τὴν τεκοῦσαν Ἕκτορα, | ἢ σιτοποιεῖν, κ.τ.λ.

365. As 357—364 answers 349, 350, so 365, 6 answers 351—353. Notice the contempt implied by ποθεν.

366. χρανεῖ, 'will pollute.' As slaves were incapable of legitimate marriage, Polyxena regards connection with one as mere defilement.

367. Polyxena dismisses with horror the prospect of such an union, and announces her intention of becoming the bride of Hades ("Αιδη προστιθεῖσ' ἐμὸν δέμας).

ἐλευθέρων, she regards herself as still free, in comparison with the slavery she has just depicted: cf. Aesch. Ag. 328 οὐκέτ', ἐξ ἐλευθέρου | δέρης ἀποιμώζουσι φιλτάτων μόρον. ἀφίημ' is used of voluntary action.

372. μῆτερ, σὺ δ'. This order of words is regular. 'When we suddenly turn our conversation from one person to another, the order is first the name, then the pronoun, and third the particle δέ,' is Porson's note on Or. 614. Cf. Soph. El. 150 Νιόβα, σὲ δ' ἔγωγε νέμω θεόν : infr. 1287, and very frequently.

373. μὴ must be understood before λέγουσα: cf. Soph. Phil. 771 ἐφίεμαι | (μήτε) ἑκόντα μήτ' ἄκοντα μήτε τῳ τέχνῃ | κείνοις μεθεῖναι ταῦτα : Ant. 267: Ar. Av. 695. συμβούλου, 'join with me in wishing for death' not only for me, but for yourself; cf. infr. 391.

374. μὴ κατ' ἀξίαν, for μὴ, cf. Hadley Gr. Gr. 1027.

377. μᾶλλον εὐτυχέστερος, cf. Hipp. 485 μᾶλλον ἀλγίων : Aesch. Supp. 673: Soph. Ant. 1210.

379. 'a marvellous stamp and of credit among men is it to come of a good stock, and the glory of high birth becometh more and more glorious for those whose life is worthy of their lineage.'

χαρακτὴρ and ἐπίσημος, metaphor from coining: cf. Med. 519.

The meaning of δεινὸς is well shown by the opening words of the chorus in Soph. Antig. 331 πολλὰ τὰ δεινὰ κοὐδὲν ἀνθρώπου δεινότερον πέλει, 'wonders are many, and none is more wonderful than man,' Jebb.

380. κἀπὶ μεῖζον ἔρχεται, cf. Soph. Phil. 259 ἡ δ' ἐμὴ νόσος | ἀεὶ τέθηλε κἀπὶ μεῖζον ἔρχεται.

382. 'well hast thou spoken, daughter, well: but in that word lies bitter grieving.'

384. ψόγον, of neglecting the dead hero.

387. κεντεῖτε, 'stab,' cf. infr. 1162.

388. Homer gives no account of Achilles' death, though the dying Hector (Il. xxii. 359) prophesies of that day ὅτε κέν σε Πάρις καὶ Φοῖβος Ἀπόλλων | ἐσθλὸν ἐόντ' ὀλέσωσιν ἐνὶ Σκαιῇσι πύλῃσιν. The later accounts of the manner of his death vary greatly.

389. ὦ γεραιά, emphatic: almost = τὴν γεραιάν.

391. ἀλλά: 'after a conditional clause expressed or implied, ἀλλά is often to be rendered 'at least': Soph. fr. 855 εἰ σῶμα δοῦλον, ἀλλ' ὁ νοῦς ἐλεύθερος: El. 411 συγγένεσθέ γ' ἀλλὰ νῦν, 'help me (if not before) now at least.' Hadley Gr. Gr. 1046. 2 a. Here the implied condition is 'if you will not accept me as a substitute for my daughter.'

395. μηδὲ τόνδ' ὠφείλομεν: although in this expression οὐ should logically be the negative employed, the phrase as a whole is felt to express a wish, and hence μὴ is used: cf. Soph. Phil. 969 μήποτ' ὤφελον λιπεῖν | τὴν Σκῦρον: Hadley Gr. Gr. § 871 a.

τόνδ', sc. θάνατον, that of Polyxena.

397. Odysseus resents the use of the word ἀνάγκη by a slave, and its application to his own action. For the partic. κεκτημένος after a verb of knowing, cf. Thompson Gr. Synt. § 167: for the nomin. § 165. 2.

398. 'I will cling fast to her, I the ivy, she the oak.' For the double comparison cf. Tro. 147 μάτηρ δ' ὥς τις πτανοῖς κλαγγὰν | ὄρνισιν ὅπως ἐξάρξω 'γώ. ὁποῖα = 'like': cf. Soph. O. T. 915 οὐδ', ὁποῖ' ἀνὴρ | ἔννους, τὰ καινὰ τοῖς πάλαι τεκμαίρεται.

400. ὡς, i.e. ἴσθι ὡς: cf. Med. 609 ὡς οὐ κρινοῦμαι τῶνδέ σοι τὰ πλείονα: the construction 'expresses a point resolved and certain.' Andr. 587.

401. ἀλλ' οὐδ' ἐγὼ μὴν κ.τ.λ., 'nay, but I will not etc.' Cf. Soph. O. C. 28 ἀλλ' ἐστὶ μὴν οἰκητός, 'nay, inhabited it surely is.' ἀλλὰ μὴν is the recognized phrase to introduce the second horn of a dilemma.

403. τοκεῦσιν: the plural is used for the singular to give a more general meaning to the expression: in English we should say 'be indulgent to *a parent*.' In the next line too κρατοῦσι refers to Odysseus alone.

406. γέροντα χρῶτα: for γέρων as adj. cf. Soph. O. C. 1259 γέρων πίνος: Theocr. vii. 17 γέρων πέπλος: H. F. 26 γέρων λόγος: ἄρτος νεανίας is found in Ar. Lys. 1207. So in Latin *anus charta*, Cat. lxviii. 46.

407. ἀσχημονῆσαι, 'be put to open shame': a prose word, not found in Aesch. or Soph. For ἐκ = ὑπό, cf. supr. 24 n.

408. μὴ σύ γε *blandientis est*, says Valckenaer on Phoen. 535 'do not, I beg you.' Cf. Bacch. 951: Ion 1334: Ar. Lys. 189.

410. 'and let me lay my cheek on thine.' προσβαλεῖν after δός, which also governs χέρα.

411, 412. These two lines occur also in Alc. 208, 209.

416. lit. 'without the husband, without the marriage-song, which I ought to have obtained.' ὧν has for antecedent the nouns (understood) contained in the adjectives ἄνυμφος ἀνυμέναιος. For the genit. after adjectives compounded with a-privative, cf. Hadley Gr. Gr. § 753 c. Cf. Thuc. ii. 65. 5 ἀδωρότατος χρημάτων (of Pericles): Soph. O. C. 49 μή μ' ἀτιμάσῃς, ὧν σε προστρέπω φράσαι.

417. 'wretched art thou, my child, but all-wretched I.' ἀθλία is far the stronger word.

419. ποῖ τελευτήσω βίον; lit. 'whither shall I take my life and end it?' Cf. Soph. O. C. 476 τὸ δ' ἔνθεν ποῖ τελευτῆσαί με χρή; 227 ἃ δ' ὑπέσχεο ποῖ καταθήσεις; 'to what fulfilment wilt thou bring thy promise?' Thuc. iii. 104. 5 ἐτελεύτα ἐς τάδε τὰ ἔπη, 'he proceeded to these lines, and then stopped.' In Prose τελευτᾶν is intrans. This line is in answer to the preceding one, in which Polyxena lamented her impending separation from her mother. Hecuba replies with a wish, expressed in question form, that she too might find death.

421. Euripides seems here to assign to Hecuba the credit which should belong to Priam only. In Il. xxiv. 495 Priam laments πεντήκοντά μοι ἦσαν, ὅτ' ἤλυθον υἷες Ἀχαιῶν· | ἐννεακαίδεκα μέν μοι ἰῆς ἐκ νηδύος (one wife, Hecuba) ἦσαν, | τοὺς δ' ἄλλους μοι ἔτικτον ἐνὶ μεγάροισι γυναῖκες. Theocr. xv. 139 οὔθ' Ἕκτωρ Ἑκάβας ὁ γεραίτατος εἴκατι παίδων. Probably however Hecuba regards them all as having formed one family, of which she was the head. ἄμμοροι τέκνων, cf. Med. 1395 στείχω, δισσῶν γ' ἄμορος τέκνων.

424. στέρνα. Homer never uses this word of a woman's breasts, though it is commonly found in that sense in Trag. στέρνον and στῆθος (which latter word Homer uses of men and women) are wider terms than μαστός, which denotes a single breast (generally of a woman). Correctly rendered by Mr Way, 'O bosom, breasts that sweetly nurtured me.'

426. Cassandra was her last surviving sister. ἐμοί, ethic dat.: cf. Phoen. 618 μῆτερ, ἀλλά μοί σὺ χαῖρε.

427. 'others *fare well*—not for thy mother this.' Way.

428. Cf. 328 n. κάσις, a poet. word, not used by Homer, except in the compound form κασίγνητος.

431. 'dead am I of sorrow, before dead indeed.'

432. She desires Odysseus to cover her head, that no one may see the traces of her tears.

433. **ἐκτέτηκα**, 'I am melted': καρδίαν, accus. of respect. ἐκτήκω trans.

435. As Odysseus prepares to muffle and lead her away, she calls upon the sun, whose light she is so soon to lose.

436. 'except for such time as I am going between this spot and the place of sacrifice at Achilles' pyre.' ξίφους καὶ πυρᾶς Ἀχιλλέως together form one idea, 'sacrifice at Achilles' pyre.' μεταξὺ ξίφους κ.τ.λ. : for this use of μεταξύ, where one only of the two points, between which extension is indicated, is expressed, cf. Aesch. Cho. 63 τὰ δ' ἐν μεταιχμίῳ (distance between) σκότου (supply καὶ φάους) : Soph. O. C. 290 τὰ δὲ | μεταξὺ τούτου (between the present time *and an expected event*) μηδαμῶς γίγνου κακός: Ar. Av. 187 ἐν μέσῳ ἀήρ ἐστι γῆς (καὶ οὐρανοῦ).

438. **προλείπω**, intr. 'I swoon.' Cf. Thuc. vii. 75. 3 (of the retreat of the Athenians from Syracuse) εἴ τῳ δὲ προλίποι ἡ ῥώμη καὶ τὸ σῶμα, οὐκ ἄνευ ὀλίγων ἐπιθειασμῶν καὶ οἰμωγῆς ὑπολειπόμενοι κ.τ.λ. These three broken lines are the mother's last utterances in the agony of separation from her child, culminating in the ἀπωλόμην, φίλαι which she cries, as she turns from the disappearing figure of Polyxena to seek the sympathy of her fellow-slaves. Then, in frenzied and impotent desire for vengeance, she curses the 'Spartan woman,' who is the source of all her sorrows. Nothing surely could be more artistic, more consistent with the vengeful Oriental character, which Euripides draws so clearly in the latter part of the play, than this last touch : and yet ' *damnavit Hartungius, choro tribuit Hermannus.*'

441. **ὧς**, 'thus,' i.e. led off, like Polyxena, to death. The use of ὧς for οὕτως is rare in Attic Greek except in certain phrases (καὶ ὧς, οὐδ' ὧς), but it occurs in Aesch. Ag. 930 εἰ πάντα δ' ὧς πράσσοιμ' ἄν, εὐθαρσὴς ἐγώ. Thuc. iii. 37 (speech of Cleon) ὧς οὖν χρὴ καὶ ἡμᾶς ποιοῦντας κ.τ.λ.

443. **Ἑλένην...εἶλε.** For the pun, cf. Aesch. Ag. 689 τίς ποτ' ὠνόμαζεν ὧδ' ἐς τὸ πᾶν ἐτητύμως...Ἑλέναν; ἐπεὶ πρεπόντως ἑλέναυς, ἕλανδρος, ἑλέπτολις, εἰ τῶν ἁβροτίμων προκαλυμμάτων ἔπλευσε κ.τ.λ. Eur. Tro. 890 Hecuba says αἰνῶ σε, Μενέλα', εἰ κτενεῖς δάμαρτα σήν. | ὁρῶν δὲ τήνδε φεῦγε, μή σ' ἕλῃ πόθῳ. | αἱρεῖ γὰρ ἀνδρῶν ὄμματ', ἐξαιρεῖ πόλεις | πίμπρησι δ' οἴκους. The close parallel afforded by the lines in the Troades to this passage is noticeable. Plato was addicted to punning: cf. Symp. 198 c Γοργίου κεφαλὴν δεινοῦ λέγειν: Apol. 25 c

ἀλλὰ γάρ, ὦ Μέλητε, σαφῶς ἀποφαίνεις τὴν σαυτοῦ ἀμέλειαν. At the conclusion of these lines Hecuba falls insensible.

444. The metre of this chorus is glyconic; the rhythm is founded on the trochee (– ◡), but admits of very free construction.

The stage is now clear, save for the prostrate form of Hecuba, and the chorus mark the end of the first act by singing the first *stasimon*: at its conclusion the sacrifice is supposed to have been completed, and Talthybius arrives to give a description of the scene. They speculate in what Grecian land fate has fixed the place of their slavery, whether on the northern mainland, or one of the islands of the Aegean, or in Pallas' city of Athens: then with a brief lament the ode concludes. The parallel chorus, Tro. 197—234, should be carefully read with this one: there, as here, Talthybius appears at the finish of the ode, and announces to Hecuba among other things the sacrifice of Polyxena: εὐδαιμόνιζε παῖδα σήν· ἔχει καλῶς. It must be borne in mind that the Hecuba is the earlier play by eight or ten years.

ποντιάς, this form of the femin. of πόντιος is found here and twice in Pindar.

446. θοὰς ἀκάτους: the adjective is not picturesque merely, for ἄκατοι or ἀκάτια were small fast-sailing boats, popular with pirates (cf. Thuc. iv. 67): holding, Strabo tells us, from 25 to 30 men : large merchant vessels sometimes carried an ἄκατος on board. They were at any rate small boats, and not particularly adapted, one would think, for the conveyance of a number of females. (They were not πελαγοδρομοῦσαι, Etym. M. s.v.)

οἶδμα λίμνας, 'swelling waste of waters.' The same expression occurs in a line of Sophocles (fr. 423), introduced by Aristophanes into the Aves (1337).

448. δουλόσυνος is ἅπαξ λεγόμενον. Cf. δεσπόσυνος supr. 99.

449. κτηθεῖσ', cf. supr. 360: this passive aorist is rare, and does not occur elsewhere in Trag., though Thuc. (i. 123) uses it.

450. Δωρίδος αἴας. Eur. no doubt refers to the Dorian settlements in the Peloponnese, and is thereby guilty of an anachronism, as Dorians are only once mentioned in the Homeric poems (Od. xix. 177) and then as a tribe in Crete. Achaeans at that early time dwelt in what was destined to become the heritage of the then obscure tribe, whose home was north of the Corinthian gulf. (Doris proper had no sea-board.)

451. Φθιάδος. Achaia Phthiotis, the home of Achilles and the original nursery of the Hellenes : by Ἑλλάς Homer always understands this district: cf. Il. ii. 683, 4 : ix. 395.

454. **Ἀπιδανόν.** It is probable that Eur. means the Enipeus, which, rising in Mt Othrys, flows northward through Achaia Phthiotis and the plain of Thessaly, and falls into the Peneus shortly after receiving the waters of the Apidanus, a tributary which runs parallel with it through most of Thessaly. The two streams are frequently confused. Cf. Bacch. 572 Λυδίαν (the river Lydias) τε τὸν τᾶς εὐδαι-μονίας | βροτοῖς ὀλβοδόταν, πατέρα τε, | τὸν ἔκλυον εὔιππον χώραν ὕδασι | καλλίστοισι λιπαίνειν. The plain of Thessaly was the richest pasture-land in Greece, and supported the flocks and herds, which formed the wealth of a powerful aristocracy, who, but for mutual jealousy, might have been a great influence in Greece: cf. Theocr. xvi. 36 πολλοὶ δὲ Σκοπάδαισιν ἐλαυνόμενοι ποτὶ σακοὺς | μόσχοι σὺν κεραῆσιν ἐμυκήσαντο βόεσσι. The Scopadae of Krannon, like the Aleuadae of Larissa, were a powerful family of this haughty and luxurious aristocracy.

455. **νάσων...ἔνθα** (458), 'to that one of the islands, where' etc.

456. **τάλαιναν**, the accusatives follow πορεύσεις, l. 447.

The island of Delos, to which reference is made in these lines, was one of the holy places of Greece: for here Leto, pursued by the jealousy of Hera, found a resting-place, where she might give birth to Apollo and Artemis. The island, which, once floating, was fixed by Zeus for the reception of Leto, was little more than a rock, rising in Mt Cynthus to a height of 500 feet, and not more than 5 miles in circumference. It became the centre of the worship of Apollo, and there every fifth year from early times were celebrated the Delia, a festival at which the Ionians of the islands and the neighbouring coasts assembled to do honour to their θεὸς πατρῷος. After falling into desuetude, the Delia were restored by the Athenians in 426 B.C., and the island purified. (Thuc. v. 1 tells us that the completion of the purification consisted in the deportation of the inhabitants: this took place in 422 B.C.) At the time of the production of the Hecuba (425 B.C. probably), this revival would be fresh in men's memories, and suggested to Eur. no doubt the mention of the island in this place.

458. Tradition said that Leto, when giving birth to Apollo, sup-ported herself by grasping a palm tree, which henceforth became sacred to her offspring. Cf. Hymn. ad Ap. 118: Theogn. 929 Φοῖβε ἄναξ, ὅτε μέν σε θεὰ τέκε πότνια Λητώ, | φοίνικος ῥαδινῆς χερσὶν ἐφαψαμένη, κ.τ.λ. The Delians maintained in Cicero's time that the original palm tree was still to be seen. (Cic. de legg. i. 1. 2.) Cf. Homer Od. vi. 162 where Odysseus likens Nausicaa to the young palm tree growing in Apollo's shrine in Delos. The palm tree was not found in Greece.

460. **Λατοῖ φίλᾳ**, probably dative after ἀνέσχε, 'for the service of dear Leto': then **ἄγαλμα ὠδῖνος Δίας** is in apposition to πτόρθους, 'the pride of her Zeus-born son.' For ὠδίς (properly 'birth-pangs') = child, cf. Aesch. Ag. 1418 ἔθυσεν αὑτοῦ παῖδα, φιλτάτην ἐμοὶ | ὠδῖνα. A very parallel passage to this is I. T. 1097—1105, where Λατοῦς ὠδῖνα φίλαν occurs in connection with the palm, the olive and the bay: both reading and interpretation are doubtful, and the parallelism seems to prove little more than that mere verbal echoes from former plays often led Eur. to the repetition of a phrase in a different sense: cf. infr. 482 n.

463. The common tradition made Artemis twin-sister of Apollo. Many statues of Artemis have been discovered at Delos : nearly all are of the archaic type, completely draped, with the hair confined at the front by the ἄμπυξ (a metal headband, usually assigned to goddesses): the later type, while keeping the ἄμπυξ, usually discarded the long draperies, and added the quiver and arrows, realising the conception of Artemis the Huntress.

464. **τε** is wrongly placed : it should follow χρυσέαν.

466. The chief ornament of the Great Panathenaic festival, which was celebrated in August, every four years, was the saffron-coloured πέπλος, newly embroidered by maidens with a representation of the battle of the giants (cf. I. T. 224), which was carried sail-wise on a ship, supported on wheels, in a magnificent procession from the outer Ceramicus to the temple of Athene Polias. (Probably the ship was not introduced prominently till the 4th century.)

467. **καλλιδίφρου**: on the seated type of Athene statues, cf. Miss Harrison's Mythology and Monuments of Ancient Athens, p. 495.

469. **ζεύξομαι πώλους** means of course ' I shall represent in my embroidery yoked steeds.'

473. **ἀμφιπύρῳ**, cf. Hipp. 559 βροντᾷ ἀμφιπύρῳ. The thunderbolt is often represented in works of art with tongues of flame *above and below*; this would rightly be the meaning of ἀμφίπυρος, ἀμφι- meaning ' on both sides,' περι- ' on all sides."

474. **κοιμίζει**, 'casteth into the sleep of death': cf. Hipp. 1387 εἴθε με κοιμίσειε τὸν δυσδαίμον' | Ἅιδου μέλαινα νύκτερὸς τ' ἀνάγκα. Soph. Aj. 832.

478. **δορίκτητος Ἀργείων**, 'spear-won prize of the Greeks': the genit. is due to the idea of possession : still the absence of a preposition is harsh.

482. Eur. uses the word θεράπνα six times : I. A. 1499 Μυκηναῖαι

τ' ἐμαὶ θεράπναι: Bacch. 1043 θεράπνας τῆσδε Θηβαίας χθονός: H. F. 370
Πηλιάδες θεράπναι: Tro. 1070 τὰν καταλαμπομέναν ζαθέαν θεράπναν (of a
place): Tro. 211 μὴ γὰρ δὴ (ἔλθοιμεν) δίναν γ' Εὐρώτα, τὰν ἐχθίσταν
θεράπναν Ἑλένας, ἔνθ' ἀντάσω Μενέλᾳ δούλα. Thus in each case it is to
be translated 'dwelling,' 'homestead.' Θεράπνη or Θεράπναι was also a
not uncommon place-name: the best known Θεράπνη was in the valley
of the Eurotas in Sparta, and is made the subject of a play on words in
the passage from the Troades (211, quoted above). The ode in which
it occurs is almost identical with the present chorus of the Hecuba: and
that the word is purposely chosen there is certain from the fact that the
Spartan Therapne stood on Mt Menelaius, which derived its name from
a temple of Menelaus, where he and Helen were buried. Eur. must
have had this ode from the Hecuba in his mind, when he wrote the
chorus in the Troades: it is curious too that Εὐρώπας θεράπναν here is
echoed by Εὐρώτα...θεράπναν there, cf. 460 n.

483. **ἀλλάξασ'**, lit. 'having taken in exchange a dwelling in Europe.'
Ἀίδα θαλάμους is in apposition to θεράπναν.

484. **δή ποτε**, 'erstwhile': cf. Supp. 1130 σποδοῦ τε πλῆθος ὀλίγον
ἀντὶ σωμάτων | εὐδοκίμων δή ποτ' ἐν Μυκήναις.

486. Cf. 443 n. Editors are at pains to explain that Hecuba is on
her back, because the attendants so placed her, that she might recover
from her swoon. They might also explain why the attendants failed at
the same time to loosen her clothing: it is certainly unsuitable for a
fainting person to be συγκεκλημένη ('tightly muffled') πέπλοις.

488. 'What shall I say, O Zeus? Whether that thou regardest
men, or that idly to no purpose hast thou (with thy fellow-gods) gotten
thee this so false repute, seeming to be a race of gods indeed?' I do not
see sufficient reason for expelling line 490; the poet's mind passes
quickly from the mention of one god to the thought of all, so that not σε
but ὑμᾶς is subject to κεκτῆσθαι. The piling up of kindred words to
produce a mass-effect (ἄλλως—μάτην—ψευδῆ) is characteristically Greek.
δοκοῦντας is emphatic: 'seeming and seeming only': a bitter echo of
δόξαν (489), 'false reputation.'

491. **ἐπισκοπεῖν, ἐπίσκοπος** are used specially of tutelary gods.
Solon 2. 3 (in Hiller's Anth. Lyr.) τοίη γὰρ μεγάθυμος ἐπίσκοπος ὀβριμο-
πάτρη | Παλλὰς Ἀθηναίη χεῖρας ὕπερθεν ἔχει. Pind. Ol. xiv. 4 Χάριτες
Ὀρχομενοῦ, παλαιγόνων Μινυᾶν ἐπίσκοποι. Eur. I. T. 1414: Aesch.
Eum. 517 ἔσθ' ὅπου τὸ δεινὸν εὖ | καὶ φρενῶν ἐπίσκοπον | δεῖ μένειν καθή-
μενον.

493. **μέγ' ὀλβίου**, cf. Aesch. Prom. 647 ὦ μέγ' εὔδαιμον: the adver-

bial use with adjectives is Homeric. It is however found in Herod. and Xen. also: cf. Rutherford, New Phryn. p. 28.

494. ἀνέστηκεν, passive of ἀνίστημι, 'make people remove'; e.g. Thuc. ii. 27 ἀνέστησαν δὲ καὶ Αἰγινήτας ἐξ Αἰγίνης Ἀθηναῖοι. So Thuc. i. 12 ἐπεὶ καὶ μετὰ τὰ Τρωϊκὰ ἡ Ἑλλὰς ἔτι μετανίστατό τε καὶ κατῳκίζετο, ὥστε μὴ ἡσυχάσασα αὐξηθῆναι...μόλις τε ἐν πολλῷ χρόνῳ ἡσυχάσασα ἡ Ἑλλὰς βεβαίως καὶ οὐκέτι ἀνισταμένη ἀποικίας ἐξέπεμψεν. Applied to a country it means 'depopulated.' So too ἀνάστατος, which is found in Poetry, though the verb is confined to Prose (except in this passage). ἀνάστατον δορί is found in Soph. Tr. 240.

498. αἰσχρᾷ, 'vile.' περιπεσεῖν, common in all Greek = 'encounter' (evil).

499. μετάρσιον, proleptic, 'from the ground.'

501. τίς οὗτος κ.τ.λ. 'who art thou there, who' etc. Cf. Il. x. 82 τίς δ᾿ οὗτος κατὰ νῆας ἀνὰ στρατὸν ἔρχεαι οἶος | νύκτα δι᾿ ὀρφναίην;

503. Talthybius in the Il. is Agamemnon's herald, i. 320: he was worshipped in Sparta after his death, and the hereditary heralds at Sparta were called Talthybiadae: cf. Herod. vii. 134. Δαναϊδῶν is used with special reference to his connection with the Argive prince Agamemnon.

504. πέμψαντος μέτα, 'having sent me for you': cf. Soph. Phil. 343 ἦλθόν με νηῒ ποικιλοστόλῳ μέτα: cf. infr. 509 μεταστείχων σε: 512.

505. Observe Hecuba's welcome to the messenger, as she thinks, of death.

506. δοκοῦν, acc. absol., cf. supr. 118 n.: lit. 'it being a resolution of the Greeks.' δόξαν would mean 'it having been resolved by': the present calls attention to the abiding nature of the decree. Cf. Thuc. iii. 38. 2 καὶ δῆλον ὅτι ἢ τῷ λέγειν πιστεύσας τὸ πάνυ δοκοῦν ἀνταποφῆναι ὡς οὐκ ἔγνωσται ἀγωνίσαιτ᾽ ἂν κ.τ.λ.

507. ἐγκονῶμεν. Homer uses only the partic. pres. of this verb, in an adverbial sense = 'speedily': in other writers it is only found in imperative sentences.

511. οἴμοι, τί λέξεις; a Euripidean formula on the receipt of bad news: the use of the future implies that the speaker cannot at once realise what he hears: cf. infr. 712, 1124: Hipp. 353: Ion 1113: Med. 1310.

512. κακά, the sad news of her daughter's death.

514. τοὐπὶ σέ, quod ad te attinet.

515. πῶς καί νιν ἐξεπράξατ᾽; 'how, tell me, did ye take her life?'

This seems to be the force of καὶ *interrogativis postpositum*: cf. infr. 1066: Alc. 834: Hipp. 92, 1171: Soph. Aj. 1290.

ἐκπράσσειν, lit. 'to finish': cf. διεργάζεσθαι, διαχρῆσθαι, Lat. *conficere*.
'How did ye slay her?—how?—with reverence meet,
Or with brute outrage, as men slay a foe?' Way.

518. 'once more, lady, thou wouldst have me renew the sad solace of tears.' Cf. Soph. O. C. 363 δὶς γὰρ οὐχὶ βούλομαι | πονοῦσά τ᾽ ἀλγεῖν καὶ λέγουσ᾽ αὖθις πάλιν.

519. **λέγων**, 'at the recital.'

520. Supply ἔτεγξα.

523. **χερὸς**, for the genit. cf. Thompson Gr. Synt. § 97 B.

526. 'whose hands should curb the strugglings of thy lamb.' Way. For μόσχος=child, cf. I. A. 1623: Andr. 712.

527. **πλῆρες**, supr. 522: for similar carelessness, cf. χεροῖν 526, χεροῖν 527, χειρὶ 528: τίθεται 655, τιθεμένα 656: μάθῃ 601, μαθὼν 602, μάτην 603: πρευμενὴς 538, πρύμνας 539, πρευμενοῦς 540 (the latter may be intentional). This preliminary libation would be wine, or a mixture of meal, honey and oil (πέλανος): cf. Aesch. Cho. 92, the χοαί sent by Clytaemnestra to appease the shade of Agamemnon.

531. Cf. I. A. 1563 στὰς δ᾽ ἐν μέσῳ Ταλθύβιος, ᾧ τόδ᾽ ἦν μέλον, | εὐφημίαν ἀνεῖπε καὶ σιγὴν στρατῷ. The account of the sacrifice of Iphigeneia should be compared with this passage.

532. **σῖγα**, the adverb: cf. Ar. Ach. 238 σῖγα πᾶς (ἔστω). Eur. Phoen. 1224 κελεύσας σῖγα κηρῦξαι στρατῷ.

535. **κηλητηρίους**, cf. Alc. 359 ὥστ᾽ ἢ κόρην Δήμητρος ἢ κείνης πόσιν | ὕμνοισι κηλήσαντά σ᾽ ἐξ Ἅιδου λαβεῖν.

536. **νεκρῶν ἀγωγούς**, 'that bring up the departed.' Compare the account of the sacrifice offered by Odysseus in Od. xi. 35 on his descent to the lower world, ῥέε δ᾽ αἷμα κελαινεφές· αἱ δ᾽ ἀγέροντο | ψυχαὶ ὑπ᾽ ἐξ Ἐρέβευς νεκύων κατατεθνηώτων. For the genit. cf. Tro. 1130 πολλῶν ἐμοὶ δακρύων ἀγωγός.

539. **πρύμνας—πρευμενής**: the paronomasia may be intentional: cf. supr. 443 n. Cf. too infr. 650 τὸν εὔροον Εὐρώταν.

χαλινωτήρια are the ropes that 'bridle' the ship's course.

541. **δὸς ἡμῖν...τυχόντας**, a common irregularity: τυχοῦσι would be expected: cf. Aesch. Cho. 140 αὐτῇ τέ μοι δὸς σωφρονεστέραν πολὺ | μητρὸς γενέσθαι χεῖρά τ᾽ εὐσεβεστέραν.

νόστου, 'home-coming': one of the later Epic poems was the Νόστοι, or the narrative of the returns of the heroes from Troy.

543. **ἀμφίχρυσον**, 'inlaid with gold on both sides': cf. supr. 474 n.

κώπης, cf. supr. 523 n.   Such swords have been found at Mycenae.

546.   ἐφράσθη, 'observed.' This middle use of the pass. aorist is found in Homer (Od. xix. 485 etc.) and Herod. (i. 84 sub fin., vii. 46). Both Soph. and Aesch. use the perf. pass. as middle.

ἐσήμηνεν λόγον, cf. supr. 217 σημανῶν ἔπος.

550.   cf. supr. 367.

551.   'I have a queenly pride that brooks not the name of slave among the dead.' 'She will hold in Hades the same position, servile or free, that she held at the moment of her death.' Paley.

552.   δούλη κεκλῆσθαι, cf. supr. 480 κέκλημαι δούλα.

553.   ἐπερρόθησαν, 'shouted approval': cf. Phoen. 1238 πάντες δ' ἐπερρόθησαν Ἀργεῖοι τάδε | Κάδμου τε λαός, ὡς δίκαι' ἡγούμενοι. Or. 901.

558.   It is simpler to take ἐξ ἄκρας ἐπωμίδος as referring to the top of the shoulder, than to one of the many fashions of wearing the chiton, which prevailed among Greek women : cf. Becker's Charicles, p. 425 (Eng. tr.).

560.   ὡς ἀγάλματος κάλλιστα. It is significant as showing the perfection reached in the plastic arts, that ἄγαλμα is frequently used to denote extraordinary or divine beauty: cf. Hipp. 631 γέγηθε κόσμον προστιθεὶς ἀγάλματι | καλὸν κακίστῳ. Plat. Charm. 154 C πάντες ὥσπερ ἄγαλμα ἐθεῶντο αὐτόν. Phaedr. 251 A θύοι ἂν ὡς ἀγάλματι καὶ θεῷ τοῖς παιδικοῖς. Eur. fr. 284. 10 λαμπροὶ δ' ἐν ἥβῃ καὶ πόλεως ἀγάλματα | φοιτῶσ'.

ἔδειξε, 'displayed': the first meaning of δείκνυμι; cf. Tro. 801 ὄχθοις ἱεροῖς, ἵν' ἐλαίας | πρῶτον ἔδειξε κλάδον γλαυκᾶς Ἀθάνα.

562.   τλημονέστατον, 'heroic.'

566.   οἴκτῳ κόρης, 'in pity for the maiden' : cf. 519 σῆς παιδὸς οἴκτῳ: the genitive is objective, cf. Thompson Gr. Synt. § 98.

οὐ θέλων τε καὶ θέλων : cf. El. 1230 (Electra addressing the corpse of Clytaemnestra) ἰδού, φίλαν τε κοὐ φίλαν φάρεά σέ γ' ἀμφιβάλλομεν: Phoen. 357 μῆτερ, φρονῶν εὖ κοὐ φρονῶν ἀφικόμην | ἐχθροὺς ἐς ἄνδρας.

568.   κρουνὸς is a 'well-head': 'and the welling blood leapt forth': cf. Rhesus 790 θερμὸς δὲ κρουνὸς δεσπότου παρὰ σφαγαῖς | βάλλει με δυσθνητοῦντος αἵματος νέου, where the force of κρουνός, the strong gush of blood, is heightened by the use of βάλλει and νέου: for ἐχώρουν, cf. Med. 1174 ἀνωλόλυξε, πρὶν γ' ὁρᾷ διὰ στόμα | χωροῦντα λευκὸν ἀφρόν.

569.   This verse is quoted by Pliny Ep. iv. 11. 9, in his account of the judicial murder by Domitian of the Vestal, Cornelia. Paley quotes an imitation from Ovid Fasti ii. 833 *tum quoque iam moriens ne non*

procumbat honeste | respicit: haec etiam cura cadentis erat. With this passage should certainly be compared Ovid's version of it, Met. xiii. 449—480.

570. For the double accus. after κρύπτειν, cf. Thompson Gr. Synt. § 88.

572. 'Each Argive 'gan his task—no man the same.' Way.

573. ἐκ χερῶν, supply ἱέντες.

574. φύλλοις ἔβαλλον: her courage was rewarded with the same honours as were bestowed on victors in the games: cf. Pind. Pyth. ix. 131 ἔνθ' Ἀλεξίδαμος, ἐπεὶ φύγε λαιψηρὸν δρόμον, | παρθένον κεδνὰν χερὶ χειρὸς ἑλὼν | ἆγεν ἱππευτᾶν Νομάδων δι' ὅμιλον. πολλὰ μὲν κεῖνοι δίκον (cast) | φύλλ' ἔπι καὶ στεφάνους.

576. Cf. Alc. 704 εἰ δ' ἡμᾶς κακῶς | ἐρεῖς, ἀκούσει πολλὰ κοὐ ψευδῆ κακά. Ar. Thesm. 385 βαρέως φέρω...ὁρῶσ' ἡμᾶς ὑπὸ | Εὐριπίδου τοῦ τῆς λαχανοπωλητρίας | καὶ πολλὰ καὶ παντοῖ' ἀκουούσας κακά. Soph. Phil. 608 ὁ πάντ' ἀκούων αἰσχρὰ καὶ λωβήτ' ἔπη | δόλιος Ὀδυσσεύς. More frequently ἀκούω and κλύω are used either with adverbs (κακῶς ἀκ. 'to have an ill repute') or the nomin. of adjectives: they serve as the passive of λέγειν = to call a person such and such a thing: so *audire*, e.g. Hor. Ep. i. 16. 17 *tu recte vivis, si curas esse quod audis.* (Cf. Milton Areop. p. 24 (ed. Hales) 21 'Next what more nationall corruption, for which England hears ill abroad, than houshold gluttony?' Ben Jonson in his dedication of the Fox to those 'most equal sisters, the two famous universities' says 'hence is it, that I now render myself grateful, and am studious to justify the bounty of your act: to which, though your mere authority were satisfying, yet it being an age wherein poetry and the professors of it hear so ill on all sides, there will be a reason be looked for in the subject.')

578. For the custom of casting garments and offerings of all kinds on funeral pyres, cf. Lucian de Luctu 14 πόσοι γὰρ καὶ ἵππους καὶ παλλακίδας, οἱ δὲ καὶ οἰνοχόους ἐπικατέσφαξαν καὶ ἐσθῆτα καὶ τὸν ἄλλον κόσμον συγκατέφλεξαν ἢ συγκατώρυξαν;

579. τῇ περίσσ' εὐκαρδίῳ, cf. supr. 493 n.

583. ἐπέζεσε, cf. I. T. 987 δεινή τις ὀργὴ δαιμόνων ἐπέζεσε. 'Herein (τόδε) by fate some heaven-sent bane hath burst seething upon the children of Priam and my country.'

585. Hecuba half-personifies her various troubles: they all crowd round her, claiming her attention and aid, nor does she know to which she should turn first: if she embrace the cause of one, another (τόδε) straightway will not suffer his claims to be postponed, while if she listen

to the second, there is always a third, inheritor of woe from woe, to summon her away in turn by his cries for help (παρακαλεῖ).

588. διάδοχος κακῶν κακοῖς. The poet is not strictly logical: first he regards the different Woes as urging their separate claims, to the exclusion of others, on Hecuba; then he proceeds to speak of one of them as receiving in his turn a burden of misery from another. Hecuba would herself more properly be styled διάδοχος κακῶν κακοῖς: we should then read διάδοχον: for the phrase, cf. Supp. 71 ἀγὼν ὅδ' ἄλλος ἔρχεται γόων γόοις διάδοχος. The usual construction of διάδοχος is genit. of thing received and dat. of the person received from: cf. the dat. after δέχομαι, e.g. Il. ii. 186 δέξατό οἱ ('from him') σκῆπτρον, and many instances quoted by Porson on supr. 535 (where he reads δέξαι χοάς μοι).

591. 'excess of grieving the tidings of thy noble bearing hath taken from me.' This line serves as an apology for the following philosophical reflections, which might seem out of place at a time of such distress. Similar apologies are found in Hipp. 252: Med. 119.

592. δεινόν, cf. supr. 379 n.: the context there is very similar to this. **γῆ,** 'soil.' 'Strange,' says Hecuba, 'that poor land may under some conditions bring forth good fruit, and good land evil fruit: but a good man's works are always good, and an evil man's evil. What is the reason? Is it heredity, or early nurture?' Euripides' answer to the claims of the former is negative: El. 369 ἤδη γὰρ εἶδον παῖδα γενναίου πατρὸς | τὸ μηδὲν (worthless) ὄντα, χρηστὰ δ' ἐκ κακῶν τέκνα. In Supp. 911 he inclines to give the credit to early education; τὸ γὰρ τραφῆναι μὴ κακῶς αἰδῶ φέρει· | αἰσχύνεται δὲ τἀγάθ' ἀσκήσας ἀνὴρ | κακὸς γενέσθαι πᾶς τις· ἡ δ' εὐανδρία | διδακτός, εἴπερ καὶ βρέφος διδάσκεται | λέγειν ἀκούειν θ' ὧν μάθησιν οὐκ ἔχει. Eur. does not go as far as his contemporary Socrates, and assert that no one is vicious, except through ignorance, and that any one knowing good will ensue it (cf. Hipp. 380 τὰ χρήστ' ἐπιστάμεσθα καὶ γιγνώσκομεν, | οὐκ ἐκπονοῦμεν δέ), but still attaches great weight to the knowledge of good as a means to the identification of evil, infr. 601 τοῦτο (ἐσθλὸν) δ' ἤν τις εὖ μάθῃ | οἶδεν τό γ' αἰσχρόν, κανόνι τοῦ καλοῦ μαθών. It is true that Euripides' expressions are not always quite consistent, but we must remember that to dogmatize was not his failing, and, like Socrates, he propounds many a question, and argues on many a theme, yet leaves the question unanswered and the theme a sketch.

597. οὐδέ. For this use of οὐ after εἰ (592) consult Shilleto's note on Thuc. i. 121. 7. His rule is, that in a bi-membered sentence, like the present, when in the second clause the indicative is used, the

negative is οὐ: from this rule however there are many exceptions.

599. τροφαί, for the plural cf. supr. 82 n.

600. ἔχει, cf. supr. 353 n. Lit. 'involves a teaching of virtue.'
δίδαξις seems ἀπ. λεγ.

603. ἐτόξευσεν, cf. Aesch. Supp. 446 καὶ γλῶσσα τοξεύσασα μὴ τὰ
καίρια. Eur. Supp. 456 καὶ ταῦτα μὲν δὴ πρὸς τάδ' ἐξηκόντισα. μὲν δὴ
dismisses the philosophical reflections.

605. θιγγάνειν, sc. τῆς παιδός: μοι, ethic dative: cf. infr. 728.

606. τοι, 'thou knowest': cf. supr. 228 n.

607. ναυτική τ' ἀναρχία, cf. I. A. 913 ἀφῖγμαι δ', ὥσπερ εἰσορᾶς,
γυνὴ | ναυτικὸν στράτευμ' ἄναρχον κἀπὶ τοῖς κακοῖς θρασύ, | χρήσιμον δ'
ὅταν θέλωσιν. Eur. probably had in view the frequent disorders of
Piraeus. It was and remains a commonplace that water-side population
is hard to manage.

608. κρείσσων πυρός, cf. Andr. 271 ἃ δ' ἔστ' ἐχίδνης καὶ πυρὸς
περαιτέρω, | οὐδεὶς γυναικὸς φάρμακ' ἐξεύρηκέ πω | κακῆς. κακὸς, 'poor
creature.'

610. ποντίας ἁλός, partitive genitive after βάψασ' ἔνεγκε, which =
'draw and bring.'

612. It may well be that Hecuba refers here to the union in death
of Achilles and Polyxena: in this shadowy wedlock she could not be
regarded as strictly wife or strictly maid: and the ceremonial bath,
which took place before marriage (at Athens the water for the bath was
fetched from Callirrhoe, Thuc. ii. 15), assumes the form of the last
washing of the corpse before burial.

613. προθῶμαι, 'lay out': cf. Alc. 664 (παῖδας, οἳ) περιστελοῦσι καὶ
προθήσονται νεκρόν. Ph. 1319.

614. ὡς δ' ἔχω...κόσμον τ' ἀγείρασ', i.e. with my own resources, so
far as they go, and with whatever contributions my fellow-captives may
be able to make. τί γὰρ πάθω; the exact meaning in this passage is
somewhat difficult to determine: 'what else can I do?' i.e. except ὡς
ἔχω, seems to me to represent the sense. The strict meaning of the
phrase is 'what is to happen to me?' 'What is to happen to me, if I do
not do so?' Valckenaer says the formula is *eorum, quos invitos natura
vel fatum vel quaecunque tandem cogit vix superanda necessitas* (ad
Phoen. 902). It is found in Homer Il. xi. 404 where Odysseus in a
dilemma says ὤ μοι ἐγώ, τί πάθω; Paley remarks that the subj. is not
deliberative, but has the future sense common in epic usage: cf. Monro
Hom. Gr. § 274: Tro. 792: Supp. 257.

616. **τῶνδε**, deictic: cf. supr. 59 n.

618. **κλέμμα τῶν αὐτῆς δόμων.** Notice the bitter irony of this phrase: 'aught she hath pilfered from her home.'

619. **ὦ σχήματ' οἴκων,** 'O vision of home, once happy home.' Or it may be that σχῆμα implies something striking and impressive to the eye.

620. **ὦ πλεῖστ' ἔχων κ.τ.λ.** To take ὦ πλ. ἔχων κάλλιστά τε together, punctuating at τε, and translating 'thou who hadst very many and very beautiful things,' seems unsatisfactory: Porson's κάλλιστά τ' εὐτεκνώτατε, where κάλλιστα is adverbial (cf. supr. 579 n.), leaves ὦ πλεῖστ' ἔχων particularly bare and feeble: I see no difficulty in understanding from εὐτεκνώτατε in this line and τέκνων in the next τέκνα as object of ἔχων: reference to the number and beauty of Priam's children is frequent and here apposite: cf. supr. 280, 421 n. Further the pathos of the reference to herself in the next line is heightened if we supply πλείστων καλλίστων τε with τέκνων.

622. **εἰς τὸ μηδὲν ἥκομεν,** 'have come to nought': cf. Herod. i. 32. 1 ἡ ἡμετέρη εὐδαιμονίη ἀπέρριπται ἐς τὸ μηδέν. Soph. El. 1000 δαίμων δὲ τοῖς μὲν εὐτυχὴς καθ' ἡμέραν, | ἡμῖν δ' ἀπορρεῖ κἀπὶ μηδὲν ἔρχεται.

φρονήματος τοῦ πρὶν στ., 'shorn of our former pride.'

623. **στερέντες:** this aorist is found only in Poetry.

δῆτα, used in a scornful sense: it is more frequently found in interrogative sentences. **εἶτα** also is *indignantis.*

626. **τά,** on the article used as a demonstrative, cf. Thompson Gr. Synt. § 36: Soph. O. C. 742 πᾶς σε Καδμείων λεὼς | καλεῖ δικαίως, ἐκ δὲ τῶν μάλιστ' ἐγώ, where Jebb points out that usually, when the article is used in this way, it stands first in the sentence.

ἄλλως, 'mere,' cf. supr. 489: Tro. 476 οὐκ ἀριθμὸν ἄλλως ἀλλ' ὑπερτάτους Φρυγῶν. Fr. 362 (Erechtheus). 27 ἀλλ' ἐμοίγ' ἔστω τέκνα | ἃ καὶ μάχοιτο καὶ μετ' ἀνδράσιν πρέποι, | μὴ σχήματ' ἄλλως ἐν πόλει πεφυκότα.

628. Cf. Ennius in Cic. de fin. ii. 13 *nimium boni est, cui nil mali est.*

629. This short choral interlude, performed while Hecuba is absent, collecting the ornaments mentioned in 615, is mainly glyconic (cf. supr. 444 n.): it marks a break in the action, as the news of Polydorus' death, which arrives at its conclusion, supplies a fresh theme for the remainder of the play. The chorus trace the origin of their calamities in the fatal judgment of Paris. The ode in Androm. 274—308 on the same subject should be compared.

χρῆν, imperfect: cf. supr. 260 n. The force of the tense is, 'that was the moment when my present misfortunes became inevitable.'

631. Cf. Med. 3 (εἴθ' ὤφελε) μηδ' ἐν νάπαισι Πηλίου πεσεῖν ποτε | τμηθεῖσα πεύκη, μηδ' ἐρετμῶσαι χέρας | ἀνδρῶν ἀριστέων κ.τ.λ. Hel. 229 φεῦ φεῦ, τίς ἢ Φρυγῶν | ἢ τίς Ἑλλανίας ἀπὸ χθονὸς | ἔτεμε τὰν δακρυόεσσαν Ἰλίῳ | πεύκαν; ἔνθεν ὀλόμενον | σκάφος συναρμόσας | ὁ Πριαμίδης ἔπλευσε βαρβάρῳ πλάτᾳ | τὰν ἐμὰν ἐφ' ἑστίαν.

634. **τὰν**=ἄν.

638. **πόνων ἀνάγκαι κρείσσονες**, 'constraint of slavery more torturing than mere suffering.' ἀνάγκαι, cf. supr. 82 n.

640. 'On all from the folly of one (Paris) hath come a curse, a curse of destruction on the land of Simoïs, and ruin from stranger-hands.'

644. Lit. 'the strife, which a herdsman on Ida set himself to determine (κρίνει) between the three goddesses, hath been determined finally (aorist, ἐκρίθη), hath resulted, in ruin and bloodshed.' In ἐκρίθη we see the sense of the word as used by Hippocrates to denote the 'crisis' of a disease.

645. **ἂν παῖδας κρίνει**, for the double accus., one accus. being cognate, cf. Plat. Apol. 19 B Μέλητός με ἐγράψατο τὴν γραφὴν ταύτην. Hadley Gr. Gr. § 725.

646. **ἀνὴρ βούτας**, cf. Andr. 280 σταθμοὺς ἔπι βούτα: for βούτης as adj., cf. Hipp. 537 βούταν φόνον: Tro. 490 γραῦς γυνή: Aesch. Cho. 805 γέρων φόνος: Lat. *anus charta*. See 406 n. The βούτης was of course Paris, ὁ τὰς θεὰς κρίνας (I. A. 71). There seems to be a tinge of contempt in the use of the word ἀνὴρ here and infr. 682.

650. **τις**, 'many a one': cf. supr. 270 n.

ἀμφὶ, 'by the banks of.' εὔροον Εὐρώταν, cf. supr. 539 n.

655. **τίθεται χέρα**, meiosis: cf. supr. 270 n. Mr Way translates, 'and her cheeks with woe-furrows are gory | and her fingers are red.'

656. **τιθεμένα**. This use of τιθέναι=ποιεῖν is Ionic, but found sometimes in Attic poets: cf. Cobet V. L. p. 302. δίαιμον, 'bloody': only here and in Hippocrates.

658. The **ἀρχαία λάτρις**, despatched by Hecuba (l. 609) for water, returns bringing with her the corpse of Polydorus, which she has discovered as foretold, supr. 47 sq. It is covered with a cloth, which is thrown back at l. 679. **παναθλία**. To an ear so sensitive to suggestions of sound as Euripides', there would be a sad play on the word παναθλία (connected of course with ἄθλος, 'contest') and νικῶσα 659, στέφανον 660, κηρύγματα ('proclamation of victor') 662.

659. **θῆλυν**, this form of the feminine is found frequently in Poetry from Homer onwards.

661. **τάλαινα σῆς κ. β.**, lit. 'wretched by reason of thy ill-omened cry': cf. for the genit. Thompson Gr. Synt. § 101, n. 1.

662. **εὕδει**, 'is still': cf. Il. v. 524 ὄφρ' εὕδησι μένος Βορέαο. Solon 2. 19 (Hiller) πόλεμον εὕδοντ' ἐπεγείρει. So σιγᾶν, Theocr. ii. 38 (of the jealous Simaetha) ἠνίδε σιγᾷ μὲν πόντος, σιγῶντι δ' ἀῆται· | ἁ δ' ἐμὰ οὐ σιγᾷ στέρνων ἔντοσθεν ἀνία.

663. **τόδ' ἄλγος**, 'this weight of woe,' pointing to Polydorus' body.

665. **καὶ μὴν** introduces the fresh arrival, supr. 216 n. **περῶσα ὑπὲρ δόμων**, 'passing out of the house': 'through and beyond,' i.e. 'out of,' seems the sense of ὑπέρ here.

668. **οὐκέτ' εἶ βλέπουσα φῶς**, 'though alive, art dead': i.e. dead in the sense of having lost all which gives life a value.

670. Hecuba imagines that she refers to the death of Polyxena. The repetition of similar sounds in εἶπας εἰδόσιν δ' ὠνείδισας is characteristic of Euripides, cf. supr. 527 n.

εἰδόσιν, cf. supr. 237 n. 'No news this: 'tis but taunting me who knew.' Way.

673. **σπουδὴν ἔχειν** generally = σπουδάζειν, 'to be in earnest': here it must either = 'receive attention,' or (cf. supr. 353 n.) 'involve, cause exertion.'

674. This couplet is spoken half-aside, but Hecuba hears enough to learn that the body is that of some fresh victim.

675. **ἅπτεται**, 'grasps.'

676. **βακχεῖον**, 'inspired': for Cassandra, cf. supr. 87 n.

678. 'She liveth whose name thou shriekest aloud, but the dead man at thy feet thou mournest not.' λάσκειν of agitated or rapid speech: an entirely poet. word, used chiefly of animals or things by Homer.

679. **γυμνωθὲν**, at this word the attendant draws aside the covering and displays to the horror-stricken mother the features of her son.

682. **Θρῇξ ἀνήρ**, so supr. 646 ἀνὴρ βούτας.

684. **ὦ τέκνον τέκνον κ.τ.λ.** This κόμμος or lament, sung by one of the characters of the play and the chorus alternately (θρῆνος κοινὸς χοροῦ καὶ ἀπὸ σκηνῆς, Arist. Poet. 12. 3), is partly iambic and partly dochmiac. The dochmiac rhythm is used by the Tragedians to express wild excitement; strictly its construction is a bacchius (‿ – –) followed by an iambus (‿ –), but very great license is permitted: it seems probable that the nature of the metre suggested to the poet the use of the word βακχεῖον, l. 686; νόμος βακχεῖος would then mean a wild strain in the frenzied manner of the votaries of Bacchus : it is observable

also that the vintage songs frequently were dirges, having for their subject the premature death of a youth (e.g. αἴλινος, sung by a boy to the vintagers, Il. xviii. 570 τοῖσιν δ᾽ ἐν μέσσοισι πάις φόρμιγγι λιγείῃ | ἱμερόεν κιθάριζε, λίνον δ᾽ ὑπὸ καλὸν ἄειδεν | λεπταλέῃ φωνῇ), thus typi- fying the departing summer: Hecuba's lament over her dead son, cut off before manhood, might appropriately be compared to one of these ancient and well-known dirges, nor is it inconceivable that ὦ τέκνον τέκνον may actually have been the opening of some such funeral- song.

685. **κατάρχομαι,** ' I begin': usually of making a due commence- ment of a sacrifice: cf. Od. iii. 444 γέρων δ᾽ ἱππηλάτα Νέστωρ | χέρνιβά τ᾽ οὐλοχύτας (meal) τε κατήρχετο, πολλὰ δ᾽ Ἀθήνῃ | εὔχετ᾽: Eur. I. T. 40 κατάρχομαι μὲν (perform preliminary rites), σφάγια δ᾽ (actual sacrifice) ἄλλοισιν μέλει. The genit. is regularly found with it, but cf. Or. 960 κατάρχομαι στεναγμόν, and Homer quoted above.

686. **ἐξ ἀλάστορος** should be connected with κακῶν, 'ills sent by some avenging power': cf. Soph. Tr. 1235 τίς ταῦτ᾽ ἄν, ὅστις μὴ 'ξ ἀλαστόρων νοσοῖ, | ἕλοιτο; Eurip. very frequently uses the word ἀλάστωρ, and always in the sense of a malignant power, exacting vengeance to the uttermost for a man's trespasses either on himself or his family: cf. infr. 949.

687. **ἀρτιμαθής** (ἀπ. λεγ.), 'grasping but now my woes,' cf. Alc. 940 λυπρὸν διάξω βίοτον· ἄρτι μανθάνω: for the genit. κακῶν cf. Thompson Gr. Synt. § 112. She had had *forebodings* of ill for Polydorus, supr. 73 sq.

688. 'Ah then, thou dost recognize the working of thy son's curse?' ἔγνως is aor. of instantaneous action. I am inclined to think that this is the better rendering: the son is of course Paris, with whose original transgression, as the source of all subsequent calamity, the chorus have just dealt, supr. 629 sq., and the mention of κακὰ ἐξ ἀλά- στορος, supr. 686, seems also to favour this version: further, the mean- ing of ἄτη as an active working curse is, by this rendering, preserved. It may be of course that the question is prompted by Hecuba's use of the word ἀρτιμαθής. 'Didst thou then know of thy son's (Polydorus') death?' γὰρ = γ᾽ ἄρ᾽, 'ah then.'

692. **ἐπισχήσει** probably means 'prevent me' from grieving. 'No tearless day, no day without a sigh, shall ever come to rid me of my grieving.'

696. **κεῖσαι,** 'art thou lying dead?'

698. **νιν,** for the accus. with κυρεῖν, cf. Aesch. Theb. 699 βίον εὖ

κυρήσας. πέσημα, 'a fallen victim': cf. Andr. 652 οὗ πεσήματα | πλεῖσθ' Ἑλλάδος πέπτωκε δοριπετῆ νεκρῶν. πτῶμα is usual in this sense.

700. **ἐν ψαμάθῳ λευρᾷ** should be taken with ἔκβλητον (ἡ πέσημα φ. δ. is parenthetic); a body cast up by the sea would be found on the *smooth* sand, the part of the shore covered at high water.

701. **πελάγιος** is used of the open sea: hence πελ. κλύδων ἐξήνεγκε implies that the body has drifted in from some distance.

702. **ἔμαθον**, 'I interpreted aright': for the dream cf. supr. 70 sq.

704. **οὔ με παρέβα φ. μελ.**, these words are parenthetical, as ἅν in the next line refers back to ὄψιν. παρέβα, 'did not escape me': Hecuba is thinking of the gloomy interpretation she gave of the dream, supr. 79 sq. μελανόπτερον is an echo of the μελανοπτερύγων of that passage (l. 71).

706. **ἀμφί σ' οὐκέτ' ὄντα**, 'concerning thee, who even then wast dead.'

709. **γάρ** (as above 688) in interrogative sentences often expresses surprise. Hadley Gr. Gr. § 1050, 4 b. 'Does thy knowledge of dream-lore enable thee to tell?'

710. **ἱππότας**, cf. supr. 9 n. A poet. word, for which ἱππεύς is found in Prose.

711. **ἵνα**, 'with whom,' lit. 'where.'

712. **τί λέξεις**; cf. supr. 511 n.

714. The sanctity of the ties of hospitality, one of the most pleasing traits of the heroic age, continued to be regarded in Greece long after the dangers of travel and absence of public accommodation, which in early civilizations led to the extraordinary value attached to the institution of hospitality, had been remedied to a large extent by the construction of good roads and the establishment of inns: compare the conduct of Miltiades (Herod. vi. 35) towards the Dolonchian envoys, whom once when sitting at his front door, he saw ἐσθῆτα ἔχοντας οὐκ ἐγχωρίην in the streets of Athens: προσεβώσατο, καί σφι προσελθοῦσι ἐπηγγείλατο καταγωγὴν καὶ ξείνια. To this behaviour he owed his kingdom in the Chersonese. Thucydides too (ii. 13) tells us of the ξενία existing between Pericles and Archidamos the Spartan, which led Pericles to fear that Archidamos would, while ravaging the property of other Athenians, spare that of his friend, and to his public declaration ὅτι Ἀρχίδαμος μέν οἱ ξένος εἴη, οὐ μέντοι ἐπὶ κακῷ γε τῆς πόλεως γένοιτο, and that if his property should be excepted from the general devastation, ἀφίησιν αὐτὰ δημόσια εἶναι. Crito too offered Socrates a safe retreat in Thessaly, εἰσὶν ἐμοὶ ἐκεῖ ξένοι, οἵ σε περὶ πολλοῦ ποιήσονται καὶ

ἀσφάλειάν σοι παρέξονται. To violate hospitality was regarded as a heinous offence against both gods and men (οὐχ ὅσια οὐδ' ἀνεκτά, 715), and was visited by the wrath of Zeus the protector of strangers and suppliants: cf. supr. 345 n.

715. ποῦ δίκα ξένων; 'where is the retributive justice, which an injured guest may invoke?' ξένων is possessive genitive: the position of the words immediately following οὐδ' ἀνεκτά makes this the more probable sense. It would be possible to translate 'where (i.e. in the doings of Polymestor) do we find the rightful custom of hosts?' (It should be remembered that δίκη is right as based upon custom.)

716. κατάρατ' ἀνδρῶν, cf. supr. 192 n. The sight of wounds on the body of her son rouses a fresh paroxysm of wrath and grief. To the Greeks, who reverenced above other races the beauty of the human form, the infliction of disfiguring wounds was especially painful. Cf. Hipp. 1376 for διεμοιράσω, 'didst rend.'

722. ἔθηκεν, cf. supr. 656 n.; 'whoever among deities it be, that presseth so grievously upon thee.' The indef. relat. (ὅστις) is not used when the antecedent is definite: when the antecedent seems to be of this nature, an indefinite idea is really connected with it. Hadley Gr. Gr. § 699 a.

724. ἀλλ'...γάρ, 'with γάρ a remark is sometimes inserted parenthetically, which introduces the principal sentence *following*, and serves to explain what is said in it.' Madv. Gr. Synt. § 196 b. Frequently however it is best to explain ἀλλὰ γάρ as = ἀλλά γ' ἄρα, 'but then': cf. Plat. Apol. 20 c ἐγὼ γοῦν καὶ αὐτὸς ἐκαλλυνόμην τε καὶ ἡβρυνόμην ἂν εἰ ἠπιστάμην ταῦτα· ἀλλ' οὐ γὰρ ἐπίσταμαι, 'but then I don't know.' Prot. 336 A.

δέμας Ἀγαμέμνονος, cf. I. A. 417 μήτηρ δ' ὁμαρτεῖ, σῆς Κλυται-μνήστρας δέμας: Or. 107 τί δ' οὐχὶ θυγατρὸς Ἑρμιόνης πέμπεις δέμας; I. T. 1439 δεῦρ' ἦλθ' Ὀρέστης...ἀδελφῆς Ἄργος εἰσπέμψων δέμας. The Homeric distinction, δέμας of the living, σῶμα of the dead body, does not hold in Attic Greek: cf. infr. 735.

727. ἐφ' οἷσπερ κ.τ.λ. = ἐπὶ τούτοις, ἃ κ.τ.λ. 'under those condi-tions, which Talthybius reported to me, namely that no one of the Greeks' etc.: cf. supr. 605 sq.

731. τἀκεῖθεν = τὰ ἐκεῖ: cf. Soph. O. C. 505 τοὐκεῖθεν ἄλσους, 'the farther side of the grove.' Aesch. Theb. 40 σαφῆ τἀκεῖθεν φέρω: the idea of the facts, or rather the account of them, being brought from the place of occurrence to the place of recital, probably accounts for this use.

732. 'If to aught of this we may apply the word *well* done.'

734. **οὐ—'Αργεῖον** go closely together: 'his garb tells me he is no Greek.'

736. Hecuba does not address Agamemnon directly till l. 752: meanwhile, her back turned to the king, she debates with herself, whether she shall appeal to Agamemnon for assistance in her scheme of vengeance, finally deciding to throw herself on his clemency. δύστηνε, she addresses herself: then as though she had said δύστηνε σύ, she continues ἐμαυτὴν λέγω λέγουσα σέ (where in English we should say, 'by the word 'thou' I mean myself').

737. **προσπέσω**, delib. subj.; Hadley Gr. Gr. § 866. 3: for the accus. after προσπέσω, cf. Aesch. Theb. 95 πότερα δῆτ' ἐγὼ προσπέσω βρέτη τίμια δαιμόνων; Many verbs, which in a simple form are intrans., when compounded acquire a transitive meaning, and therewith a transitive construction: cf. Soph. Aj. 82 φρονοῦντα γάρ νιν οὐκ ἂν ἐξέστην ὄκνῳ, where ἐκστῆναι has acquired the transit. force of 'shun.' Herod. v. 103 ἐπεὶ ἐξῆλθον τὴν Περσίδα χώρην: cf. Thompson Gr. Synt. § 90. 2.

739. **προσώπῳ νῶτον ἐγκ. σὸν**, 'turning thy back upon my face.'

742. **ἄλγος ἄν προσθείμεθ' ἄν**, ἄν is frequently repeated twice or even three times with the same verb either to make the conditional force felt throughout a long sentence, or to emphasize particular words affected by the contingency: cf. Goodwin, Syntax of Greek Moods and Tenses § 223.

744. 'to search out the path of thy designs': for ὁδόν in a metaphorical sense, cf. Hipp. 290 γνώμης ὁδόν: Aesch. Eum. 989 γλώσσης ὁδόν.

745. **ἆρ' ἐκλογίζομαι κ.τ.λ.** lit. 'am I, I wonder, reckoning up this man's state of mind too much on the side of hostility?' i.e. 'am I crediting Agamemnon with greater hostility towards me than he really feels?' μᾶλλον, 'over-much.'

748. **ἐς ταὐτὸν ἥκεις**, sc. ἐμοί: i.e. you and I agree entirely: cf. Or. 1278 Α. καλῶς τά γ' ἐνθένδ'. ἀλλὰ τἀπὶ σοῦ σκόπει. Β. εἰς ταὐτὸν ἥκεις· καὶ γὰρ οὐδὲ τῇδ' ὄχλος.

749. **τιμωρεῖν** is to help those to right who suffer wrong, or from another point of view, to punish the guilty in the interests of the injured: hence the dative is used of the person whose wrong is redressed (*dativus commodi*): the accusative of the person punished (direct accus., sometimes the crime committed is regarded as the offender and is in the accus.): the genitive of the wrong done (genit. of cause). The middle means 'to avenge oneself upon,' and so to 'punish' generally.

752. Hecuba suddenly turns round and before Agamemnon can prevent her (as Odysseus, supr. 342, proposed to prevent Polyxena), becomes his suppliant by touching his knees, his chin, and his right hand.

753. δεξιᾶς τ' εὐδαίμονος, 'that right hand of thine, that ever prospers.' Hecuba contrasts his position with her own.

754. μαστεύουσα. Both μαστεύω and ματεύω are found in Attic poets: Homer uses ματεύω only: cf. infr. 779, 815, and supr. 98 n.

755. θέσθαι, cf. supr. 656 n. Notice the force of the middle, 'to get thy days set free.'

ῥάδιον γάρ ἐστί σοι, i.e. 'it is an easy boon from me to thee': this is preferable to regarding μῶν ἐλ. αἰῶνα θ. as equivalent to 'to put an end to thy life, and so free thyself,' in which case these words would = 'it is open to thee so to do.'

757 corresponds closely to 755. The emphasis lies on τιμωρου-μένη, 'if only I may punish those who have worked me ill, right gladly will I be a slave for all my days.'

760. οὗ, 'on which': cf. H. F. 934 ἀφρὸν κατέσταξ' εὐτρίχου γενειάδος: the genit. is used with κατά in the sense of 'down upon.'

762. ζώνης ὕπο, cf. Aesch. Cho. 992 τέκνων ἤνεγχ' ὑπὸ ζώνης βάρος. Eum. 608.

765. ἦ γάρ in surprised or eager questions: cf. Soph. Phil. 248 ἦ γὰρ μετέσχες καὶ σὺ τοῦδε τοῦ πόνου; is Neoptolemus' rejoinder to Philoctetes' mention of the expedition against Troy: cf. infr. 1047, 1124.

766. ἀνόνητα, cf. Hipp. 1144 ὦ τάλαινα μᾶτερ, ἔτεκες ἀνόνατα.

768. ὀρρωδῶ is a favourite word with Herodotus (in its Ionic form ἀρρωδῶ) and is frequent in Attic prose: Eurip. uses it three times (ὀρρωδία also several times), but it does not occur in Soph. or Aesch. In two out of the three passages, Eur. constructs it (most unusually) with the infin., here and fr. 128: Ammonius the Alexandrine grammarian says, quoting Euripides, ὀρρωδεῖν εἴρηται ἐπὶ τοῦ εὐλαβεῖσθαι: so here we may translate, 'taking precautions that he should not die': εὐλαβεῖσθαι is similarly used with the infin.: cf. Soph. O. T. 616 εὐλαβουμένῳ πεσεῖν.

771. For the inclusion of Πολυμήστωρ in the relative clause, cf. Hipp. 101 τήνδ' ἢ πύλαισι σαῖς ἐφέστηκεν Κύπρις.

772. πικροτάτου is proleptic, 'the cause of his undoing.' Cf. supr. 12.

774. Θρήξ νιν ὤλεσε ξένος. Notice the emphatic position of ξένος.

H. E.   6

The reputation enjoyed in Greece by the Thracians was not good. They were proverbial for their cruelty, in proof of which may be adduced the slaughter of the Mycalessians, described by Thucydides (vii. 29), who adds that, when successful, τὸ γένος τὸ τῶν Θρᾳκῶν φονικώτατόν ἐστιν, and the murder of prisoners by Seuthes, narrated in the Anabasis (vii. 4). Their cruelty was accentuated by their faithlessness, as in the latter case, while some of the maritime tribes, notably in Salmydessus (ἐχθρόξενος ναύταισι, μητρυιὰ νεῶν, Aesch. Prom. 727), were professional wreckers. Horace is witness to their quarrelsome and intemperate habits in his day—*natis in usum laetitiae scyphis pugnare Thracum est*—and human sacrifices are stated by Herod. (ix. 119) to have been not unheard of. They were the Switzers of their time, ready to sell their swords to any hirer and in any cause : ready too to betray a falling master : a natural recruiting ground for Athenian policemen (τοξόται) and Roman gladiators, for bravos and assassins ; like the Highland clansmen, terrible in their onset, but, like them too, soon discouraged ; most terrible, when victory placed plunder before their eyes. We cannot feel surprise, that members of the peace party at Athens had little affection for allies such as these, and that the herald of the great Sitalces meets with scant courtesy at the hands of Dicaeopolis (Ar. Ach. 134). Thracian ξένοι and their doings had probably been often on men's lips in Athens, since the time of Sitalces' alliance in 431 : and no doubt the allusions in this play to the faithlessness, cruelty and avarice of the barbarian despot of an earlier age did not fall on unheeding ears.

775. ἦ που asks a hesitating question, or rather perhaps puts a statement in a hesitating, enquiring form. Elmsley (Med. 1275) denies the directly interrogative force of this collocation of particles, which, though common in Eurip., occurs perhaps only once in Soph., and rarely in Aesch.

χρυσόν. On the greed of the Thracians, especially their kings, cf. Thuc. ii. 97. 4 οὐ γὰρ ἦν πρᾶξαι οὐδὲν μὴ διδόντα δῶρα.

776. τοιαῦτα, 'even so': cf. El. 645 A. ξυνῆχ'· ὕποπτος οὖσα γιγνώσκει πόλει· | B. τοιαῦτα· μισεῖται γὰρ ἀνόσιος γυνή. So ταῦτα, Ar. Pax 275.

782. ὧδε διατεμὼν χρόα, cf. supr. 716 n.

783. σχετλία...τῶν πόνων : for the genit. cf. Thompson Gr. Synt. § 101, n. 1.

784. 'there remains nought of misery untried,' lit. 'there is nought of misery remaining over.'

786 sqq. Hear my story, and be thou judge betwixt him and me : if thou hold him guiltless, I say no more : if guilty, then do thou be my helper and avenger on this wicked man, who hath broken the laws of gods and men : who, after eating at our table, hath slain the son entrusted to his keeping, nay, hath refused him burial and cast him to the waves. I am but a slave, and weak : but gods are strong, and stronger still is that Law, which, centering in you as the gods' vicegerent, will be outraged, if the breakers of troth and despisers of holy things escape. Think then on this and reverence my supplication : pity me : contemplate my woes, once queen and mother, now a slave, childless friendless cityless and old. · (Ah stay, turn not from me : woe is me—bootlessly do we mortals toil at other arts, yet leave neglected the sovereign art of all, Persuasion.) Why henceforth, with my fate before his eyes, should a man hope for prosperity? My children dead, myself a slave, my home ashes. But stay, one other ground there is, on which (vainly maybe) I claim thy help. Bethink thee of her, who sleeps beside thee, my child, Cassandra : is there to be no return of pity for her love? That dead man thou seest claims kin with thee, and claiming kin, he claims revenge. Oh would there were voices in my arms hands feet ; then would they cling about thee, crying out for pity. Master, hear me ; stretch out thy hand to me : old and useless as I am, still be my helper. It behoves the good man to succour justice and destroy the wicked.

786. 'none so unfortunate indeed, save only Misfortune's self.' Parallel expressions are Plaut. Capt. 529 *neque iam Salus servare, si volt, me potest.* Ter. Ad. 761 : Cic. Tusc. iv. 31 *Fortunam ipsam anteibo fortunis meis.*

790. τιμωρὸς ἀνδρός. The genitive is used with adjectives of transitive action, where the corresponding verbs would have the accusative. It is better to regard τιμωρὸς as an adjective than as a noun : in the latter case, the genitive is used of the person assisted, not the person punished. Cf. supr. 235 n.

791. τοὺς γῆς νέρθεν, sc. θεούς : the χθόνιοι θεοί as distinguished from τοὺς ἄνω, the οὐράνιοι or ὕπατοι θεοί. It must be borne in mind that ὅσιος means either what is in accordance with divine law, holy, as opposed to δίκαιος, sanctioned by human law (so here, Polymestor is ἀνόσιος as transgressing divine law), or what is merely permitted, not forbidden by the divine law, and so secular (L. *profanus*) : cf. Dem. Timocr. 9 Τιμοκράτης οὑτοσὶ τοσοῦτον ὑπερεῖδεν ἅπαντα τὰ πράγματα, ὥστε τίθησι τουτονὶ τὸν νόμον, δι' οὗ τῶν ἱερῶν μὲν χρημάτων τοὺς θεούς, τῶν ὁσίων δὲ τὴν πόλιν ἀποστερεῖ.

84   HECUBA.

794. 'Often have we sat at the same table: our hospitality he has
shared more frequently than any other of our friends: yet though he has
experienced such kindness at our hands, he has slain and robbed of
burial our son.' Such is my interpretation of this vexed passage: ξενίας
I take as genitive following τυχών l. 793 (it may either be from the
substantive ξενία, 'hospitality,' or from the adj. ξένιος, when it would
agree with τραπέζης: for ξεν. τραπ. cf. Od. xiv. 158 ἴστω νῦν Ζεὺς πρῶτα
θεῶν ξενίη τε τράπεζα); ἀριθμῷ I connect adverbially with πρῶτα:
τυχών then in line 795 is resumptive and forcible: λαβὼν προμηθίαν
I take as correlative to ἔχω προμηθίαν, 'have consideration for' (cf.
Alc. 1054 ἐγὼ δὲ σοῦ προμηθίαν ἔχω), and render 'having received
consideration at our hands.'

796. A condensed expression: 'assuming there might be some
excuse for his desire to kill the boy, he might at any rate have given
him burial: but he did not.'

797. ἀφῆκε πόντιον, 'cast him to the waves.'

798. 'I am a weak slave, it may be (ἴσως): yes, but gods are
strong.' For δοῦλοι cf. supr. 237 n.

799. χὠ κείνων κρατῶν νόμος, cf. Pind. fr. 151 νόμος ὁ πάντων
βασιλεὺς θνατῶν τε καὶ ἀθανάτων ἄγει. Euripides, like his friend and
teacher Anaxagoras, recognized one mighty intelligence as supreme
governor of the universe, though by what name he is to be called the poet
professes doubt: Ζεύς, αἰθήρ, νοῦς, ἀνάγκη, νόμος in turn are used to
express the ruling principle, which to his devout albeit questioning mind
was God: cf. Tro. 884 (Hecuba speaks) ὦ γῆς ὄχημα κἀπὶ γῆς ἔχων
ἕδραν, | ὅστις ποτ' εἶ σύ, δυστόπαστος εἰδέναι, | Ζεύς, εἴτ' ἀνάγκη φύσεος
εἴτε νοῦς βροτῶν, | προσευξάμην σε· πάντα γὰρ δι' ἀψόφου | βαίνων κελεύ-
θου κατὰ δίκην τὰ θνήτ' ἄγεις. (To which Menelaus replies τί δ' ἔστιν;
εὐχὰς ὡς ἐκαίνισας ('revolutionized') θεῶν.) Whether he really recognized the gods of the mythology as subordinate agencies, or regarded
them as convenient embodiments only, calculated to impress the popular
imagination, is hard to decide. At any rate, like Plato, he discarded
all discreditable stories of the gods as ἀοιδῶν δύστηνοι λόγοι: indeed in
the Bellerophon he says (fr. 294. 7) εἰ θεοί τι δρῶσιν αἰσχρόν, οὐκ εἰσὶν
θεοί.

νόμῳ γὰρ τοὺς θεοὺς ἡγούμεθα, 'it is by reason of the existence
of law, that we believe in the existence of gods,' i.e. by observation of
the law and order of the universe, we infer the existence of a great
directing power.

ἡγεῖσθαι θεοὺς (like νομίζειν θεοὺς, cf. Plat. Apol. 24 B Σωκράτη φησὶν ἀδικεῖν, θεούς, οὓς ἡ πόλις νομίζει, οὐ νομίζοντα): cf. El. 583 χρὴ μηκέθ' ἡγεῖσθαι θεοὺς | εἰ τἄδικ' ἔσται τῆς δίκης ὑπέρτερα. Plat. Apol. 27 D, and often: the meaning is to 'believe in the existence of gods.'

802. ὅς, sc. νόμος: ἀνελθὼν is used as passive of ἀναφέρειν, 'to refer.' In the Homeric times kings were regarded as vicegerents of the gods, who prompted the θέμιστες or judgments, which they delivered. If justice is to be corrupted at its source, Hecuba argues, then farewell to all fair dealing among men.

804. φέρειν, 'plunder': cf. Bacch. 759: Thuc. i. 7 ἔφερον γὰρ ἀλλήλους τε καὶ τῶν ἄλλων ὅσοι ὄντες οὐ θαλάσσιοι κάτω ᾤκουν. φέρειν καὶ ἄγειν is the common phrase.

807. ἀποσταθείς, 'having placed yourself a short distance off,' seems to be the meaning; the metaphor is from an artist falling back a few paces from his model, in order to take in the general effect. Euripides had been an art-student in his youth.

810. γραῦς, old, and therefore with no hope of more children.

812. ὑπεξάγεις πόδα, 'withdrawest thy foot,' is equivalent to 'leavest,' and thus acquiring a transitive sense takes after it the accusative με: cf. supr. 737 n. For ποῖ, cf. supr. 419 n. We must suppose that Agamemnon turns away at this point, either to conceal his emotion at Hecuba's piteous appeal, or to escape from her persistent entreaties.

814. The defect, which Euripides represents Hecuba as deploring, the lack of systematic training in persuasiveness, was, at the time of the production of this play, in a fair way to be remedied. Only a year or two before (427) there had appeared at Athens, as envoy from his native city, Leontini in Sicily, the celebrated rhetorician Gorgias: quick-witted and dramatic, the Sicilian Greeks had amid the change and stir of falling despotisms and rising democracies discovered the value of the art of speaking, whether for offence or defence, to persuade a jury or to dazzle an assembly, and professors of this art, Corax, Tisias and the rest, were not slow to appear. From Sicily both the art and its professors found their way into Greece proper, where a ready welcome was extended to them, and though the old-fashioned folk disliked and feared these forgers of new weapons, they, with the teachers of the modern philosophic theories of Anaxagoras and his school, practically took in hand the higher education of Greek youth. Shallow as were often the methods and unworthy the ends proposed by these new teachers, on the whole the verdict of history is in their favour. Attacked on the one side by old Toryism in the caricatures of Aristophanes, on the other by philo-

sophic radicalism in the misrepresentations of Plato, assailed by the former as dangerous innovators, devoid of reverence for institutions which had justified their existence in times of national peril, by the latter as shallow empirics with no real knowledge of the abuses they proposed to remedy, and by both as venal and corrupt seekers after private gain, it was not till Grote demonstrated their true position as a necessary link in the intellectual evolution of the race, as the needed solvent of old prejudices and outworn traditions in religion and politics, that the Sophists were recognized as a truly progressive body, working indeed singly, and without organization, but bound together by a common purpose, and invincible by reason of their fitness for the epoch of change and re-combination, in which they lived, and of which they were a product.

816. **πειθὼ τὴν τύραννον**, imitated by Pacuvius, *O flexanima atque omnium regina rerum oratio* (quoted by Cicero de orat. ii. 187 and referred to by Quintil. i. 12. 18).

817. **ἐs τέλος** is to be taken with μανθάνειν, 'thoroughly.'

818. **μισθοὺς διδόντες.** The Sophists were attacked on the ground that they took fees for the instruction they gave: cf. Xen. Mem. i. 6. 13.

ἵν' ἦν: for the past tense of the indicative, expressing a purpose which could only be attained in an imagined case, contrary to reality, cf. Hadley Gr. Gr. § 884.

820. She resumes her direct appeal to Agamemnon.

τί οὖν, Porson (Phoen. 892) denied that this hiatus is admissible in tragedy: but cf. Aesch. Theb. 704 τί οὖν ἔτ' ἂν σαίνοιμεν ὀλέθριον μόρον; Soph. Phil. 100 : Aesch. Eum. 902 : so εὖ ἴσθι, Soph. O. T. 959.

ἐλπίσαι, the forms of the 1 aor. opt. in -σαις, -σαι are much rarer than those ending in -σειας, -σειε.

821. **οἱ μὲν γὰρ ὄντες παῖδες**, the children who were left survivors after the fall of Troy, Polyxena and Polydorus: an easily intelligible paradox, 'even my surviving children are now dead.'

822. **ἐπ' αἰσχροῖς**, 'for a menial fate.'

823. **τόνδ'**, deictic.

824. **καὶ μὴν** introduces the new thought: τοῦ λόγου depends on τόδε, 'this part of my argument.' κενὸν, 'unavailing.'

825. **εἰρήσεται**, Hom. Poet. and Herod.; ῥηθήσομαι, Attic Prose.

826. **κοιμίζειν** is always used in a metaphorical sense = 'to still': Soph. Aj. 674 δεινῶν τ' ἄημα πνευμάτων ἐκοίμισε | στένοντα πόντον· Phoen. 184 Νέμεσι, σύ τοι μεγαλαγορίαν ὑπεράνορα κοιμίζεις: especially

of the sleep of death, supr. 474: Hipp. 1387. So here we must connect it closely with ἡ φοιβάς, 'my child's frenzied spirit sinks to sleep by thy side.'

828. 'In what way will you show your gratitude for those nights of love you call (δῆτ') so dear?' ποῦ δείξεις is an odd phrase: it may= 'in what esteem (ποῦ) will you show that you hold?' εὐφρόνας, an intentionally chosen word, perhaps influencing the meaning of δείξεις, 'how will you show those dear nights of love were nights of love indeed?' i.e. as leading to εὖ φρονεῖν now.

830. κείνης δ' ἐγώ, i.e. τίνα χάριν (gratitude for) κείνης ἐγὼ ἕξω;

835. δράσεις, sc. καλῶς.

836. After the doubtful delicacy of ll. 825—830 this beautiful passage comes as a relief.

εἰ, for the usual εἴθε or εἰ γάρ, in the expression of a wish is rare: cf. Soph. O. T. 863 εἴ μοι ξυνείη φέροντι μοῖρα τὰν εὔσεπτον ἁγνείαν λόγων.

838. Δαιδάλου τέχναισιν, schol. περὶ τῶν Δαιδάλου ἔργων ὅτι ἐκινεῖτο καὶ προῖει φωνήν, αὐτός τε Εὐριπίδης ἐν Εὐρυσθεῖ λέγει· οὐκ ἔστιν, ὦ γεραιέ, μὴ δείσῃς τάδε· | τὰ Δαιδάλεια πάντα κινεῖσθαι δοκεῖ | βλέπειν τ' ἀγάλμαθ'· ὧδ' ἀνὴρ κεῖνος σοφός. To Daedalus were attributed many of the old wooden statues of the gods, which were regarded with peculiar veneration. The improvements in statuary assigned to him are that he opened the ὄμματα μεμυκότα—the closed eyes, and divided the σκέλη συμβεβηκότα—closed legs, of the still more archaic ξόανα. His statues were called διαβεβηκότα.

839. ὁμαρτῇ=ὁμοῦ (Hesych.) occurs also Hipp. 1195, Heracl. 138.

840. κλαίοντ' ἐπισκήπτοντα κ.τ.λ., cf. Aeschin. 76. ὁ κλαίοντας ἱκετεύοντας ἐπισκήπτοντας μηδενὶ τρόπῳ τὸν ἀλιτήριον στεφανοῦν.

841. ὦ δέσποτ'. The pathos of this appeal to her 'master' from the fallen queen is great.

843. εἰ καί, 'although': καὶ εἰ, 'even if.'

ἀλλ' ὅμως, cf. Bacch. 1027 ὥς σε στενάζω, δοῦλος ὢν μέν, ἀλλ' ὅμως. Ar. Ach. 402 ΔΙ. ἐκκάλεσον αὐτόν. ΚΗ. ἀλλ' ἀδύνατον. ΔΙ. ἀλλ' ὅμως, where Aristophanes is ridiculing Eur.'s fondness for ἀλλ' ὅμως at the end of a line.

846. 'Strange indeed is it, how everything, probable and im-probable, comes to pass for men: and how Necessity's laws determine, making friends of bitterest foes and bringing former friends to enmity.' Nothing short of ἀνάγκης νόμος could have reconciled Hecuba to the author of the ruin of her family and her country. See crit. n.

ἅπαντα, Lat. *nihil non*, 'everything, likely or unlikely.'

848. **τιθέντες**, cf. supr. 656 n.

851. **δι' οἴκτου ἔχω** = 'pity.' On this and many similar phrases (δι' ὀργῆς ἔχειν, δι' αἰτίας ἔχειν, δι' ἔχθρας γίγνεσθαι and the like), cf. Thompson Gr. Synt. p. 308.

852. **θεῶν θ' εἵνεκ'**, as a breach of hospitality was an offence against heaven.

853. **δικαίου**, 'justice between man and man': cf. supr. 791 n.

854. Two constructions are here confused : εἴ πως φανείη γ', ὥστε σοί τ' ἔχειν καλῶς, στρατῷ τε ἐμὲ μὴ δόξαι and εἴ πως φανείη θ', ὥστε σοι ἔχειν καλῶς, στρατῷ τε μὴ δόξαιμι. In other words the δόξαιμι clause should be parallel with the ἔχειν καλῶς clause, and depend on ὥστε, but instead of δόξαι, which would be expected, the writer, by an attraction to the εἴ πως φανείη clause, has written δόξαιμι.

φανείη, sc. δίκη.

860. **χωρὶς τοῦτο κοὐ κοινὸν στρατῷ**, 'that is a purely personal feeling, and not shared by the army.'

862. **ταχὺν προσαρκέσαι**, 'swift to help you,' if it depends on myself alone.

863. **εἰ διαβληθήσομαι**, 'if I am to fall into disfavour with': cf. Thuc. iv. 22. 3 μὴ ἐς τοὺς ξυμμάχους διαβληθῶσιν εἰπόντες καὶ οὐ τυχόντες, 'lose favour with the allies by speaking without success': Heracl. 420 ταῦτ' οὖν ὅρα σὺ καὶ συνεξεύρισχ' ὅπως | αὐτοί τε σωθήσεσθε καὶ πέδον τόδε, | κἀγὼ πολίταις μὴ διαβληθήσομαι.

866. **πόλεος**. Jebb (on Ant. 412) gives the instances of this form found in trimeters (one in Soph., two in Aesch., and three, besides the present case, which he omits, in Eur.): also ὄφεος, and in Comedy φύσεος, ὕβρεος. They are due to metrical convenience.

867. **εἴργουσι χρῆσθαι μή**, 'prevent him from using.' The μὴ is out of place: the order should be εἴργ. μὴ χρ.: for the so-called redundant negative, cf. Hadley Gr. Gr. § 1029: Heracl. 963 εἴργει δὲ δὴ τίς τόνδε μὴ θανεῖν νόμος;

868. Notice Hecuba's contemptuous reference to the στρατὸς as ὄχλος, 'mob.'

869. **ἐγώ**, 'I, your slave': emphasis is added both by its place in the line and its juxtaposition to σε.

870. 'Be my accomplice in plan, but not in action.'

872. **ἢ 'πικουρία**, infr. 878: cf. supr. 527 n.

873. **πάσχοντος οἷα πείσεται**. *Hujusmodi formulis utuntur Graeci, quando de rebus injucundis breviter effari volunt.* Blomfield gloss. ad Aesch. Ag. 66), who gives many instances: Soph. O. T. 1376

βλαστοῦσ' ὅπως ἔβλαστε: O. C. 273 ἱκόμην ἵν' ἱκόμην: Med. 1011
ἤγγειλας οἷ' ἤγγειλας: El. 289 ἔκυρσεν ὡς ἔκυρσεν.

874. **μὴ δοκῶν ἐμὴν χάριν,** 'without seeming to be doing so for my
sake': 'μὴ is often used instead of οὐ with participles or other words,
through an influence of the verbs on which they depend, when these
verbs either have μή, or would have it, if negative.' Hadley Gr. Gr.
§ 1027.

ἐμὴν χάριν, cf. Soph. Tr. 485 κείνου τε καὶ σὴν ἐξ ἴσου κοινὴν
χάριν.

875. **θήσω καλῶς,** a formula of reassurance: cf. Hipp. 521, and
very freq. When the middle voice is used (εὖ, καλῶς, θήσομαι), reference
is made to a person's private interests: see examples in Elmsley's note
on Medea 896.

880. **στέγαι αἴδε,** pointing to the encampment in the background:
cf. supr. 59 n.

882. **φονέα,** only here and El. 599, 763.

883. **ἀρσένων κράτος,** 'mastery over men': cf. Tro. 949 ὃς τῶν μὲν
ἄλλων δαιμόνων ἔχει κράτος, | κείνης δὲ δοῦλός ἐστι.

884. **σὺν δόλῳ τε,** 'and when aided by stratagem.'

885. **μέμφομαι,** 'have a poor opinion of.' Cf. fr. 199 τὸ δ' ἀσθενές
μου καὶ τὸ θῆλυ σώματος | κακῶς ἐμέμφθης. So καταμέμφομαι = 'distrust.'

886. The fifty daughters of Danaos married and slew on the
wedding night the fifty sons of Aegyptos, Danaos' brother, with the
solitary exception of Hypermnestra, who spared Lynceus.

887. The Lemnian women, having slain all their husbands, chose
Hypsipyle, the daughter of their late king, Thoas, as their queen; and
were living without male companionship, when the Argonauts on their
wanderings visited the Λαμνιᾶν ἔθνος γυναικῶν ἀνδροφόνων (Pind. Pyth.
iv. 252). Λήμνια ἔργα was a proverb for atrocity: cf. Aesch. Cho. 631
κακῶν δὲ πρεσβεύεται ('takes first place') τὸ Λήμνιον λόγῳ. Herod. vi.
138.

887. **ἄρδην,** 'utterly': as αἴρω means, (1) to lift up, (2) to take
away, so ἄρδην is used in the signification, (1) 'aloft': Soph. Aj. 1279
πηδῶντος ἄρδην Ἕκτορος τάφρων ὕπερ, (2) 'utterly' (take away, destroy):
Lat. *funditus*: Ion 1274 ἄρδην μ' ἂν ἐξέπεμψας εἰς Ἅιδου δόμους.

ἐξῴκισαν. ἐξοικίζειν means orig. to 'eject a person from his home,'
and this being equivalent to 'depopulate,' Eur. here uses it with the
direct accus. of the land so emptied: cf. supr. 812 n. He uses the word
infr. 948 in its proper sense.

888. **ὥς = οὕτως:** cf. supr. 441 n.

889. **τήνδ'**, pointing to one of her fellow-slaves, whom she addresses in the next line.

πέμψον ἀσφαλῶς, 'give safe-conduct to.'

891. **δή ποτε**, cf. supr. 484 τὴν ἄνασσαν δή ποτ' οὖσαν Ἰλίου, and n.

892. **σὸν οὐκ ἔλασσον ἢ κείνης χρέος**, cf. supr. 874 n. and Soph. Tr. 485 there quoted.

894. **ἐκείνης**, Hecuba. She puts herself in the place of the person delivering the message.

898. **καὶ γὰρ κ.τ.λ.**, 'for etc.' Ag. begins the sentence as though it were to run, 'for there is no chance of sailing at present: otherwise, if there were, I should not be able etc.' καὶ γὰρ introduces the double statement, εἰ μὲν ἦν—νῦν δέ, where the real point lies in the δὲ-sentence.

900. **νῦν δὲ**, 'as matters stand': a very frequent meaning: cf. L. and S. s. v. I. 3.

901. **ἥσυχον** is adverbial, and should be joined with μένειν: cf. Heracl. 477 γυναικὶ γὰρ σιγή τε καὶ τὸ σωφρονεῖν | κάλλιστον, εἴσω δ' ἥσυχον μένειν δόμων (and Elmsley's n.).

πλοῦν ὁρῶντας, 'on the look-out for a chance of sailing.' A very similar use of the verb is seen in Soph. Aj. 1165 σπεῦσον κοίλην κάπετόν τιν' (grave) ἰδεῖν τῷδε, where ἰδεῖν means to look about for and find: so Theocr. xv. 2 ὅρη δίφρον, Εὐνόα, αὐτᾷ.

903. Cf. fr. 1036 κακὸν γὰρ ἄνδρα χρὴ κακῶς πάσχειν ἀεί.

905. What may be regarded as the third act of the play closes at this point, and the chorus mark the interval between it and the last act, by singing an ode, in glyconic metre, descriptive of the fatal night, when, issuing from the wooden horse, the Grecian warriors opened the gates of Troy to their comrades, and making easy prey of its brave defenders, sunk in careless sleep after a day's rejoicing at the raising of the ten years' leaguer, avenged themselves in blood and fire for their long severance from home and friends. The ode is singularly beautiful, and it would be hard to parallel from ancient literature the picture of the husband, sleeping at last without fear of night alarms, his spear hanging unneeded, as he thinks, upon the wall, while his wife lingers looking χρυσέων ἐνόπτρων ἀτέρμονας εἰς αὐγάς, as she binds up her hair in preparation for a night of unbroken peaceful sleep. The contrast between that brief moment of happiness and security and the long years of misery and slavery before the captives, is drawn by a masterhand.

906. **λέξει**, passive: so regularly in trag.: cf. H. F. 582 ὁ καλλίνικος ὡς πάροιθε λέξομαι: Alc. 322: Soph. O. C. 1186. Similarly δηλώσεται,

Soph. O. C. 581 : τιμήσεται, Ant. 210 : φυλάξεται, Phil. 48. 'Thou
shalt no longer be spoken of as one among cities unsacked.' τῶν
ἀπορθήτων, sc. πόλεων. This was a boast of Athens, cf. Med. 826
ἱερᾶς χώρας ἀπορθήτου τε. Aesch. Pers. 350.

907. **νέφος**, cf. Phoen. 250 ἀμφὶ δὲ πτόλιν νέφος | ἀσπίδων πυκνὸν
φλέγει | σχῆμα φοινίου μάχης: Pind. Nem. x. 9 Οἰκλείδαν, πολέμοιο
νέφος: ix. 38 φόνου νεφέλαν: Isth. iii. 35 τραχεῖα νιφὰς πολέμοιο: Hom.
Il. xvii. 243 πολέμοιο νέφος περὶ πάντα καλύπτει. ἀμφί σε κρύπτει=
ἀμφικρύπτει σε: so 910 ἀπὸ—κέκαρσαι: 912 κατὰ—κέχρωσαι.

910. 'thou hast been shorn of thy circlet of towers': cf. Tro. 784
ὦ παῖ (Astyanax), βαῖνε πατρῴων | πύργων ἐπ' ἄκρας στεφάνας, ὅθι σοι |
πνεῦμα μεθεῖναι ψῆφος ἐκράνθη.

912. **κηλῖδα**, cognate accus.: 'hast been blackened with the foul
smoke's smirch most piteous.'

913. **ἐμβατεύσω**, 'shall I haunt thee': the word is specially used
of protecting deities: Soph. O. C. 678 ἵν' ὁ βακχιώτας ἀεὶ Διόνυσος
ἐμβατεύει. Aesch. Pers. 449, of Pan.

914. Cf. Virg. Aen. ii. 265 *invadunt urbem somno vinoque sepul-
tam :* | ......*tempus erat quo prima quies mortalibus aegris* | *incipit.*

915. **ἦμος** only used in this one passage by Eurip., though it is
found more frequently in Sophocles. It is one of the very many Ionic
words, which lingered on in Tragedy, after it had passed out of Attic
prose.. On the subject of such survivals, cf. Rutherford New Phryn.
pp. 1—31.

ἐκ, 'after.'

916. Whether σκίδναται or κίδναται is to be read '*anceps judicium,*'
says Porson. The word does not occur elsewhere in tragedy : σκεδάν-
νυμι is the Attic form.

μολπᾶν ἄπο and **θυσίαν καταπαύσας** are co-ordinate : 'after the
songs and sacrifice.'

920. **ξυστὸν δ' ἐπὶ πασσάλῳ** is parenthetic. Paley quotes Theo-
critus xxiv. 42 δαιδάλεον δ' ὥρμησε μετὰ ξίφος, ὅ οἱ ὕπερθε | κλιντῆρος
κεδρίνῳ περὶ πασσάλῳ αἰὲν ἄωρτο.

921. **ναύταν** is adject.: cf. supr. 406 n.

922. **Τροίαν** here of the Troad, not Troy-town: so often in the
Iliad: cf. iii. 74.

924. **μίτραισιν κ.τ.λ.** The μίτρα was an Eastern form of head-
dress, consisting of broad bands of bright colour, with lappets hanging
down over the side of the face. Herod. (i. 195) tells us that the
Babylonians confined their long hair with μίτραι: cf. Virg. Aen. iv.

216 *et nunc ille Paris cum semiviro comitatu | Maeonia mentum mitra crinemque madentem | subnixus, rapto potitur.*

ἀναδέτοις is ἅπ. λεγ. ἐρρυθμιζόμαν, 'was reducing to order' the wandering unruly tresses : a picturesque word.

925. **χρυσέων ἐνόπτρων.** The mention of mirrors is again probably a slight anachronism. Homer does not speak of them, and the earliest do not seem to date back farther than 500 B.C.: we frequently hear of silver and of bronze mirrors, but not of gold : so both here and in *Tro.* 1107 we may assume that the epithet has been chosen by the poet to heighten the picture of luxurious ease, and thereby accentuate the contrast.

926. **ἀτέρμονας εἰς αὐγάς,** 'looking into the fathomless bright depths,' to my thinking a perfect phrase. The fact that she is looking *into* the mirror seems to be an objection to Paley's view (quite apart from the question of taste), 'the light, which proceeding from a fixed point, viz. the mirror itself, is flashed back without any definite limit.' Mr Way, I am glad to see, is in substantial agreement with my rendering.

927. **ἐπιδέμνιος,** ἅπ. λεγ. For ἐπιδέμνιος πέσοιμι cf. supr. 797 ἀφῆκε πόντιον.

928. **πόλιν** : the πόλις strictly speaking was the Acropolis, or fortified height, round which the ἄστυ, or lower town, gathered : possibly the distinction should be observed here, as the Greeks would naturally make their entrance by the lower town (see next line κέλευσμα δ' ἦν κατ' ἄστυ κ.τ.λ.). Dr Schliemann asserted that there was no Acropolis at Troy, but the reference in *Od.* viii. 508 ἢ κατὰ πετράων βαλέειν (sc. the wooden horse) ἐρύσαντας ἐπ' ἄκρης, to say nothing of the epithets ἠνεμόεσσα and the like, is against him (cf. infr. 931 Ἰλιάδα σκοπιάν). Even if his view were correct, it would not affect this passage, as Eur. would assign to Troy the features usual in all old Greek towns.

930. **παῖδες Ἑλλάνων** : for this somewhat scriptural periphrasis, cf. Aesch. *Pers.* 402 (in the well-known description of Salamis) παρῆν ὁμοῦ κλύειν | πολλὴν βοήν, ὦ παῖδες Ἑλλήνων, ἴτε, | ἐλευθεροῦτε πατρίδ' κ.τ.λ. So Λυδῶν παῖδες, Her. i. 27.

934. **μονόπεπλος, Δωρὶς ὡς κόρα,** wearing only an under-shift, χιτώνιον, probably : references to the scanty dress of Spartan maidens (a sleeveless χιτών, not reaching to the knee, and open at one side) are frequent : cf. *Andr.* 596 sqq.

935. **προσίζουσ' οὐκ ἤνυσ',** 'nought it availed me that I sat me as

a suppliant' etc., lit. 'I accomplished nothing, sitting,' etc.: cf. Il. iv. 56 εἴ περ γὰρ φθονέω τε καὶ οὐκ εἰῶ διαπέρσαι, | οὐκ ἀνύω φθονέουσ', ἐπεὶ ἦ πολὺ φέρτερός ἐσσι.

936. Artemis favoured the Trojans in the war: cf. Il. v. 447 where Leto and Artemis ἰοχέαιρα tend the wounded Aeneas. She was worshipped as σώτειρα and παιδοτρόφος.

939. ἀποσκοποῦσ', 'turning earnest gaze upon': turning away from everything else (ἀπο-) to look at the city: ἀποβλέπειν is freq. in the same sense.

940. νόστιμον ναῦς ἐκ. πόδα, 'the ship hurried on its homeward way': κινεῖν πόδα, metaphorical.

942. ἀπεῖπον ἄλγει, 'faint am I for sorrow.' 'The aorist denotes a feeling, or an act expressive of it, which *began to be just before* the moment of speaking.' Hadley Gr. Gr. § 842. Cf. infr. 1276, ἀπέπτυσ': Soph. Aj. 536 ἐπῄνεσ' ἔργον καὶ πρόνοιαν ἣν ἔθου (and Jebb's note). The words are parenthetical: cf. supr. 920.

944. βούταν, cf. supr. 646.

945. αἰνόπαριν, 'Paris, author of ill': cf. Il. iii. 39 δύσπαρι, εἶδος ἄριστε, γυναιμανὲς ἠπεροπευτά: Alcman 50 (Welck.) δύσπαρις, αἰνόπαρις, κακὸν Ἑλλάδι βωτιανείρᾳ: Eur. Or. 1388 δυσελένα.

946. διδοῦσ' carries on the construction of the sentence begun at l. 937.

947. γᾶς ἐκ πατρίας ἀπώλεσεν, for γᾶς ἐξαπώλεσεν, 'drove ruined from': cf. Aesch. Ag. 528 καὶ σπέρμα πάσης ἐξαπόλλυται χθονός.

948. ἐξῴκισεν, cf. supr. 887 n. γάμος, οὐ γάμος κ.τ.λ. So Andr. 103 (of the same marriage) οὐ γάμον, ἀλλά τιν' ἄταν. On ἀλάστορος, cf. supr. 686 n.

951. ἄν, Helen. Notice the change of subject in the next line.

953. Polymestor, his two children and a retinue, which he dismisses at l. 981, appear upon the stage. This scene affords an opportunity for the display of that *irony*, which lies in the contrast 'between the thought which the speaker evidently designs to express, and that which his words properly signify' (i.e. to a person unconscious of his real meaning). For examples, see ll. 990, 995, 1000, 1021.

φιλτάτη δὲ σύ, he turns to Hecuba, after apostrophizing the dead Priam.

956. οὐκ ἔστιν οὐδὲν πιστὸν κ.τ.λ., 'nought is there, on which we may rely, neither good name, nor again that, though prospering now, we shall not fall on evil days.' To Hecuba and the chorus,

knowing Polymestor's real character, his opening words, οὐκ ἔστιν οὐδὲν πιστόν, are ironically significant.

958. **αὐτά**, human affairs generally. πάλιν τε καὶ πρόσω, 'backwards and forwards': usually πρόσω καὶ ὀπίσω.

959. **ἐντιθέντες** keeps up the metaphor of φύρουσι, which properly means to knead : ἐντιθ. then='put in as an ingredient.' ἀγνωσίᾳ, ignorance of what awaits us.

961. **προκόπτοντ'** : cf. Alc. 1079 τί δ' ἂν προκόπτοις, εἰ θέλοις ἀεὶ στένειν; Hipp. 23 : the word is properly used of pioneers cutting the way for an army.

ἐς πρόσθεν. On prepositions thus used with adverbs (e.g. εἰς ὅτε, εἰς ἀεί, εἰς αὐτίκα) cf. Rutherford New Phryn. pp. 117 sqq. The preposition εἰς with adverbs of time is found throughout Greek literature.

962. **μέμφει ἀπουσίας**, 'complain of my absence': cf. Hipp. 1402 τιμῆς ἐμέμφθη : Thuc. viii. 109. 2. The dative of the person (ἐμοὶ here) can be easily supplied. For the (causal) genitive, cf. Thompson Gr. Synt. § 101.

964. **ἀφικόμην—967 ἀφικόμην** : cf. supr. 527 n.

970. **αἰδώς μ' ἔχει**=αἰδοῦμαι, to which word the construction is unconsciously accommodated, and hence τυγχάνουσα not τυγχάνουσαν is written : ὀφθῆναί must be supplied : cf. supr. 812 n.: Cycl. 330 δοραῖσι θηρῶν σῶμα περιβαλὼν ἐμὸν | καὶ πῦρ ἀναίθων, χιόνος οὐδέν μοι μέλει : Hipp. 23 τὰ πολλὰ δὲ | πάλαι προκόψασ', οὐ πόνου πολλοῦ με δεῖ (=ῥᾳδίως ἐκτελῶ).

972. **ὀρθαῖς κόραις**, 'with unfaltering gaze': cf. I. A. 851 χαῖρ'· οὐ γὰρ ὀρθοῖς ὄμμασίν σ' ἔτ' εἰσορῶ. Lucan ix. 904 *lumine recto.*

973. **αὐτὸ**, my averted eyes. δύσνοιαν σέθεν, objective genitive.

974, 5. Weak lines : such maidenly restraint would not be expected from a woman of Hecuba's age and position. She will not directly face Polymestor, lest her expression should betray her, and put her enemy on his guard.

976. **καὶ θαῦμά γ' οὐδέν** : 'aye, nor is it matter for wonder': cf. Soph. O. T. 1319 καὶ θαῦμά γ' οὐδέν : 1132 κοὐδέν γε θαῦμα : Phil. 38 καὶ ταῦτά γ' ἄλλα θάλπεται ῥάκη, where Jebb notes that in instances like the present, the γε does not emphasize the immediately preceding word (as is more usual in this collocation of particles, καί...γε, e.g. Phil. 674 καὶ σέ γ' εἰσάξω), but helps καί to introduce a new fact. τίς χρεία σ' ἐμοῦ, sc. ἔχει : cf. Il. xi. 606 τί δέ σε χρεὼ ἐμεῖο ;

977. **ἐπέμψω** for μετεπέμψω, 'send *for*,' 'summon': cf. Soph.

O. C. 602 πῶς δῆτά σ' ἂν πεμψαίαθ', ὥστ' οἰκεῖν δίχα; 'how then should they fetch thee to them' etc.?

981. ἥδ' ἐρημία, lit. 'this isolation,' i.e. being unattended under these circumstances, with none but friends near (φίλη μὲν εἰ σύ κ.τ.λ.).

983. χρῆν, imperf.: cf. supr. 265 n. Notice χρῆν—984 χρή: σημαίνειν—999 σημανεῖς—1003 σημῆναι: and supr. 527 n.

986. πρῶτον μὲν εἰπὲ παῖδ', ὃν κ.τ.λ., εἰ ζῇ. On this prolepsis, by which a substantive belonging to a dependent clause is transferred to the principal clause, see Hadley Gr. Gr. § 878. Xen. Anab. iv. 4. 17 οἱ δὲ ἡρώτων αὐτὸν τὸ στράτευμα, ὁπόσον εἴη (it is very common in Xen., cf. Kühner's n. on Anab. i. 1. 5): Hom. Il. v. 85 Τυδείδην δ' οὐκ ἂν γνοίης, ποτέροισι μετείη.

989. τοὐκείνου μέρος, cf. supr. 874 n.: 892: 'as far as he is concerned.'

991. δεύτερον μαθεῖν, cf. 988 δεύτερον ἐρήσομαι.

992. We may presume that Polydorus had not seen his mother, since the day when he was sent from Troy to the guardianship of Polymestor, ten years before.

993. καὶ δεῦρό γε, cf. supr. 976 n. ὡς σὲ, 'to you': for ὡς, used only with persons, cf. Thompson Gr. Synt. § 255. Her son had indeed come to Hecuba.

995. Observe the irony of the line.

996. μηδ' ἔρα τῶν πλησίον, sc. τοῦ χρυσοῦ, 'do not covet the treasure of thy neighbours.'

997. ὀναίμην and ὄνασθαι are very common (especially ὀναίμην) in Attic Greek, but the indicative ὠνάμην belongs entirely to the late Greek. Rutherford New Phryn. p. 63.

'Far be it from me: but let me have profit of mine own.' It is just possible we should understand οὕτως before ὀναίμην, 'so (i.e. on these conditions, that I should not covet my neighbours' goods) may I' etc.; cf. Ar. Thesm. 469 καὐτὴ γὰρ ἔγωγ', οὕτως ὀναίμην τῶν τέκνων, | μισῶ τὸν ἄνδρ' ἐκεῖνον. The irony of ὀναίμην τοῦ παρόντος would be manifest to the audience, who were aware of Hecuba's intended vengeance.

1000. ὦ φιληθείς, cf. I. T. 983 ἀλλ' ὦ φιληθεῖσ'.

ἐμοὶ φιλεῖ, the dative of the agent after a passive verb is rare, except with perfect and pluperfect tenses: cf. Hadley Gr. Gr. § 769.

ἔστ'...χρυσοῦ κατώρυχες (1002): an example of the so-called *Schema Pindaricum*, in which a singular verb is joined with a masc. or fem. plural subject: the verb always stands first: cf. Plat. Gorg. 500 D ἔστι τούτω διττὼ τὼ βίω: Euthyd. 302 C ἔστι γὰρ ἔμοιγε καὶ βωμοί: Hes.

Theog. 825 ἦν ἑκατὸν κεφαλαί: Soph. Tr. 520 ἦν δ' ἀμφίπλεκτοι κλίμακες: Ion 1146 ἐνῆν τοιαίδ' ὑφαί: Pind. fr. 45. 16 τότε βάλλεται ἴων φόβαι, and Gildersleeve's n. on Ol. xi. 6. The use of the plural is, as it were, an afterthought in a sentence, which commenced with a singular verb.

1002. **κατώρυχες**, excavated chambers, such as that in which Antigone was immured: cf. Soph. Ant. 774 κρύψω (says Creon) πετρώδει ζῶσαν ἐν κατώρυχι.

1008. **'Αθάνας 'Ιλίας στέγαι.** Subterranean treasure-houses of the goddess: the so-called Treasury of Atreus at Mycenae was cut in the side of a hill, projecting but little above the level of the ground, and resembled no doubt a κατῶρυξ, such as is described as a treasure-house here, but as a tomb in Soph. quoted above. The domed building at Mycenae is now recognized as a tomb: the rich offerings buried along with a deceased chieftain would make tomb and treasure-house almost synonymous.

1015. 'But where?' asks Polymestor, 'this before us (αἴδ' corresponds to ταῖσδε in 1014) is the circuit of harbourage of the Greeks.' He points to the naval camp, the στέγαι, which form the background of the scene: cf. n. on 59 supra. It seems improbable to P. that the captives should be able to conceal treasure in the actual encampment of their lords.

1017. **ἀρσένων ἐρημία**, cf. Bacch. 875 (of the escaped hind) ἡδομένα βροτῶν ἐρημίαις. A guilty conscience makes Polymestor suspicious. ἐρημία, supr. 981, is used in a slightly different sense.

1020. **νεῶν λῦσαι πόδα οἴκαδε**, 'to loosen the sheets in the wind for a homeward voyage.' The πόδες were the ropes of the lower extremity of the sail: in supr. 940 the very similar expression νόστιμον ναῦς ἐκίνησεν πόδα seems to be metaphorical: cf. n. there. Also cf. supr. 98 n.

1021. **ὧν σε δεῖ**; cf. for the constr. Aesch. Prom. 86 αὐτὸν γάρ σε δεῖ Προμηθέως: H. F. 1170: Hipp. 490 οὐ λόγων εὐσχημόνων | δεῖ σ', ἀλλὰ τἀνδρός. The spectators again would recognize the bitter irony of these lines.

1025. **ἄντλον.** Elmsley on Heracl. 169 says that ἄντλος here = πέλαγος, 'by a misuse of language': I can find no parallel to such a meaning, while the use of ἀντλεῖν and the like, both literal and metaphorical, demands that ἄντλος should be the bilge-water, *sentina*, which gathers in the hold of a vessel, or else the hold of the vessel itself: the latter is the meaning in Od. xii. 410 ἱστὸς δ' ὀπίσω πέσεν, ὅπλα τε πάντα | εἰς ἄντλον κατέχυνθ', from which passage we can see that the ἄντλος was open: in Od. xv. 479 we have a case of a person meeting her death by falling into it, τὴν μὲν ἔπειτα γυναῖκα βάλ' Ἄρτεμις ἰοχέαιρα· | ἄντλῳ δ' ἐνδούπησε πεσοῦσ' ὡς εἰναλίη κήξ. Accordingly, although ἀλίμενον does not seem the most natural word perhaps to be applied to the ship's bilge, still taking it as = 'from which there is no escape,' we may translate, 'like to one falling into the bilge, whence is no escape, so shalt thou fall headlong from thy heart's desire, having wrought the destruction of thy life.' λέχριος is properly 'aslant'; cf. Med. 1168 (of Medea's victim) χροιὰν γὰρ ἀλλάξασα λεχρία πάλιν | χωρεῖ τρέμουσα κῶλα κ.τ.λ. ἐκπεσεῖ φίλ. καρδίας, 'thou shalt be cheated of thy cherished desire': cf. Thuc. viii. 81 ἵνα τῶν ὑπαρχουσῶν ἐλπίδων ἐκπίπτοιεν: and for καρδία in this sense, Soph. Ant. 1105 καρδίας τ' ἐξίσταμαι, 'I resign my cherished resolve.' Polymestor's cherished desire is the treasure, by the prospect of which Hecuba has decoyed him. Finally ἀμέρδω never = to lose, but always to take away, rob: so we must regard P. as sacrificing his life to his passion: some would translate, 'thou shalt lose dear life (καρδίας), thou, who hast taken away life (namely Polydorus)': nor is this impossible, though γε would then be expected with ἀμέρσας.

1029. Lit. 'for where liability to retributive justice and to the gods coincides, there is an overwhelming curse,' i.e. the man, on whom the wrath of both falls, is doomed. For συμπίτνει, cf. supr. 966, 846.

1032. ὁδοῦ τῆσδ' ἐλπίς, Way turns, 'it shall mock thee, thy way-faring's hope,' i.e. your hope of gain.

1034. ἀπολέμῳ, i.e. by a woman's hand. λείψεις βίον, the chorus do not of course know the precise nature of Hecuba's intended vengeance, and imagine death will be his penalty.

1035. The agonized cries of Polymestor are heard within the tent: in accordance with the practice of the Attic stage, scenes of violence are not enacted in the sight of the audience, though the cries of the victims are permitted to be heard: cf. Aesch. Ag. 1343, 1345 where the dying Agamemnon's voice is heard, ὤμοι, πέπληγμαι καιρίαν πληγὴν ἔσω...... ὤμοι μάλ' αὖθις, δευτέραν πεπληγμένος. In that passage, as here, the chorus divides into two groups, or ἡμιχόρια, the leaders of which speak on behalf of their companions. Compare too El. 1165: Aesch. Cho. 869: Soph. El. 1404.

1037. ὤμοι...σφαγῆς, cf. Thompson Gr. Synt. § 101, n. 1.

1039. ἀλλ' οὔτι μὴ φύγητε, 'assuredly ye shall not escape':

cf. Thompson Gr. Synt. § 302, who quotes many examples. (The beginner should read §§ 301, 302.)

1040. Cf. infr. 1174, where P. gives an account of what happened, ἅπαντ' ἐρευνῶν τοῖχον ὡς κυνηγέτης | βάλλων ἀράσσων : what the βέλος of the next line may be, is not a matter of much concern: it may have been the lance mentioned in 1155, or it may only be the hand itself (Paley): the scholiast apparently thought that P. *threw stones.*

1042. ἀκμή = καιρός, it is 'high time': cf. Aesch. Pers. 407 κοὐκέτ' ἦν μέλλειν ἀκμή: Soph. El. 1338 ἀπηλλάχθαι δ' ἀκμή.

1044. ἐκβάλλων πύλας, 'breaking open the doors': cf. Or. 1473 δόμων θύρετρα καὶ σταθμοὺς | μοχλοῖσιν ἐκβαλόντες.

1046. οὐ παῖδας ὄψει ζῶντας, a double taunt: 'you will not see them, since you are blind: nor alive, for they are dead.'

1047. ἡ γὰρ *mirantis est*: so infr. 1124. 'Hast thou indeed brought low the Thracian, and hast thou the upper hand of thy false friend?'

1050. τυφλῷ ποδί. Porson illustrates Eurip.'s fondness for this phrase from Phoen. 834, 1549, 1616, 1708. παραφόρῳ π., 'frenzied steps.'

1052. σὺν ταῖς ἀ. Τρ., 'with the help of,' as in the common phrase σὺν θεῷ. As regards the spelling, ξύν is the old Attic form, invariable in inscriptions up to about 416 B.C. (Rutherford, N. P. p. 24, n. 2): after that date, it rapidly gave way to σύν, but the preposition itself became rare, being supplanted by μετά with the genitive.

1055. ῥέοντι θυμῷ, 'raging with flood of fury': cf. Homer's description of Diomed, Il. v. 87 θῦνε γὰρ ἂμ πεδίον ποταμῷ πλήθοντι ἐοικὼς | χειμάρρῳ κ.τ.λ.: Ar. Eq. 526 εἶτα Κρατίνου μεμνημένος, ὃς πολλῷ ῥεύσας ποτ' ἐπαίνῳ | διὰ τῶν ἀφελῶν πεδίων ἔρρει.

1056. The rhythm of the following passage is mainly dochmiac, expressing strong excitement.

1057. πᾷ κέλσω; lit. 'into what harbour can I put?' For this metaphorical use, cf. Hipp. 140 θανάτου θέλουσαν | κέλσαι ποτὶ τέρμα δύστανον. Aesch. Prom. 183.

1058. Polymestor likens himself to a wild beast on the track of its quarry; groping his way with outstretched hands, his gait resembles that of a four-footed animal, but I think we need not go so far as the scholiast, and assume that he enters the stage on hands and feet: for the text, cf. crit. not. Lit. 'planting the tread of a four-footed beast of the mountains, following on their track (κατ' ἴχνος), in which direction (ποίαν ἐπὶ χεῖρα), this or that, am I to direct my shifting path (ἐξαλλάξω)?'

ὀρεστέρου, a poet. equivalent of ὀρεινός, as ἀγρότερος of ἄγριος.

1059. **ποίαν ἐπὶ χεῖρα,** 'in which direction?' cf. Cycl. 680 ποτέρας τῆς χειρός; and the common phrases ἐπὶ δεξιά and the like.

1061. **ἐξαλλάξω** implies a shifting or changing about: cf. Xen. Cyn. x. 7 ἵνα εἰς τὰς ἄρκυς ποιῆται τὸν δρόμον μὴ ἐξαλλάττων.

1062. **ἀνδροφόνους,** cf. supr. 886.

1064. **τάλαιναι,** 'audacious': so τλήμων, Soph. El. 439 εἰ μὴ τλημονεστάτη γυνὴ | πασῶν ἔβλαστε (Clytaemnestra), τάσδε δυσμενεῖς χοὰς | οὐκ ἄν ποθ', ὅν γ' ἔκτεινε, τῷδ' ἐπέστεφε.

1066. **ποῖ καί,** cf. supr. 515 n.: lit. 'in flight to which of the recesses,' i. e. 'whither have they fled, and are cowering in fear of me?'

ποῖ μυχῶν, like ποῦ γῆς; ποῦ φρενῶν; cf. Soph. El. 1174 ποῖ λόγων ἔλθω; Thompson Gr. Synt. p. 85. For the accus. after πτώσσω, cf. Il. xx. 426 οὐδ' ἄν ἔτι δὴν | ἀλλήλους πτώσσοιμεν. Od. xxii. 304: supr. 812 n.

1068. **τυφλὸν φέγγος,** 'the blinded light': cf. supr. 1035 τυφλοῦμαι φέγγος. For instances of *oxymoron*, cf. Thompson Gr. Synt. § 343.

1070. **κρυπτὰν βάσιν,** 'stealthy footsteps.'

1071. **πόδ' ἐπάξας,** lit. 'darting forth my foot against them,' i. e. rushing upon them. For the transitive force of ἐπάξας, cf. Soph. Aj. 40 καὶ πρὸς τί δυσλόγιστον ὧδ' ἦξεν χέρα; and Jebb's n. He quotes in support Or. 1429 αὔραν ἄσσων: Bacch. 145. Others take ἐπάξας as intrans., and compare βαίνειν πόδα, on which construction, cf. supr. 53 n.

1072. **σαρκῶν,** 'flesh.' In the older writers the plural is usual, the singular being employed of some one particular muscle, e. g. Od. xix. 450. For the sentiment, cf. Il. xxii. 346 (Achilles' speech to Hector) αἰ γάρ πως αὐτόν με μένος καὶ θυμὸς ἀνείη | ὤμ' ἀποταμνόμενον κρέα ἔδμεναι.

1074. **ἀρνύμενος λώβαν** must mean 'achieving their dishonour': ἄρνυμαι is a poet. word = win, gain (honour), and the mutilation (the special form of insult connoted by both λύμη and λώβη: infr. 1098) of his enemies P. regards as a prize.

1077. **βάκχαις "Αιδου,** 'hell's frenzied handmaids': cf. H. F. 1119 εἰ μηκέθ' "Αιδου βάκχος εἶ, φράσαιμεν ἄν. διαμοιρᾶσαι, supr. 716. The children are dead, but he fears lest, Pentheus-like, they be torn in pieces.

1079. **ἐκβολάν.** ἐκβάλλειν is used specially of children, cf. Ion 964 σοὶ δ' ἐς τί δόξ' εἰσῆλθεν ἐκβαλεῖν τέκνον; It was in the power of the father to say whether the child was to be reared or exposed: probably the ἀμφιδρόμια, or carrying of the child round the hearth on the seventh day after birth, was a token of the intention to rear the child as a member of the family. In Thebes only was the exposure of children forbidden. ἐκβολή here of course has not its strict meaning, but the casting out on the hillside of the Thracian's children suggests the analogous exposure, which was practised in Greece on new-born babes.

1081. **ναῦς ὅπως**, 'ship-like': cf. supr. 398: 'girding up my flax-woven robe, like a barque (brailing up its sails) with the ship-tackle, speeding to the lair of death, guardian of my children from despite.' The figure is somewhat quaint, and a violent change from the wild beast metaphor, which is kept up throughout, and to which κοίταν in the last line is still adapted.

1086. Cf. Aesch. Cho. 313 δράσαντι παθεῖν, τριγέρων μῦθος τάδε φωνεῖ.

1088. **ἰώ**, invoking aid: cf. Hipp. 884: Soph. Tr. 221: Phil. 736.

1089. **λογχοφόρον**. λόγχη was a cavalry lance, and therefore suited to the εὔιππον γένος of the Thracians. εὔιππον, cf. supr. 9 n.

1090. **Ἄρει κάτοχον**, 'possessed by,' 'subject to': cf. Soph. Tr. 978 ὕπνῳ κάτοχον.

1092. **ἀντῶ**, Aesch., Eurip., but never Soph.

1094. **ἢ οὐδείς**, ἢ coalesces with οὐ-.

1100. **ἀμπτάμενος ὑψιπέτης** should be taken together.

1101. Storms were associated with both these constellations, which are visible during the hottest period of the year, cf. Hes. Op. 607 εὖτ' ἂν δ' Ὠρίων καὶ Σείριος ἐς μέσον ἔλθῃ | οὐρανόν. The baleful influence of Sirius, the dog-star, was proverbial. Cf. Hom. Il. xxii. 25, where Achilles, bright and deadly, rushing over the plain, is likened to a star ὅς ῥά τ' ὀπώρης εἶσιν, ἀρίζηλοι δέ οἱ αὐγαί | φαίνονται πολλοῖσι μετ' ἀστράσι νυκτὸς ἀμολγῷ, | ὅν τε κύν' Ὠρίωνος ἐπίκλησιν καλέουσιν· | λαμπρότατος μὲν ὅ γ' ἐστί, κακὸν δέ τε σῆμα τέτυκται, | καί τε φέρει πολλὸν πυρετὸν δειλοῖσι βροτοῖσιν. Sirius was the dog of the hunter Orion.

1107. **ξυγγνώσθ'** = ξυγγνωστά ἐστί, cf. Med. 491 ξυγγνώστ' ἂν ἦν σοι, ib. 703: for the plur. cf. Hadley Gr. Gr. § 635. The chorus hint that suicide offers a ready and pardonable escape.

κρεῖσσον' ἢ φέρειν κακά, cf. Soph. O. T. 1293 τὸ γὰρ νόσημα μεῖζον ἢ φέρειν. The usual construction would be κρεῖσσον' ἢ ὡς or ἢ ὥστε: cf. Xen. An. iii. 5. 17 φοβοῦμαι μή τι μεῖζον ἢ ὥστε φέρειν δύνασθαι ξυμβῇ. κρεῖσσον' ἢ κατὰ with the accus. of a noun is a variation of this construction.

1109. Agamemnon appears on the scene, and, to judge from his elaborate opening, has 'conned his part.'

οὐ γὰρ ἥσυχος λέλακ', cf. supr. 1068 n. λέλακ', cf. supr. 678 n.

1110. πέτρας ὀρείας παῖς...Ἠχώ, 'Echo, child of the mountain rock': cf. the Irish *mac-alla*, son of the rock. I am not aware that Echo is personified by any poet before Euripides, who introduced her into his Andromeda (cf. fr. 118), and was laughed at for his pains by Aristophanes the following year (410 B.C.) in the Thesmophoriazusae: cf. 1008 sqq. where Mnesilochus, who has been bound by the women, is visited by Euripides in the character of Echo.

1112. ᾖσμεν, poet. form for ᾔδειμεν or ᾔδεμεν. Rutherford (N. P. p. 238) rejects in all cases the long penultimate, regarding ᾖσμεν etc. as the true Attic forms. If we had not known that Troy was fallen, this clamour gave us cause for terror in earnest, i.e. would easily have terrified us: the expression φόβον παρέσχεν is equivalent to a potential indicative with ἄν: cf. Goodwin Synt. of Gr. M. and T. § 432. This case is parallel to the use of ἔδει, ὤφελλον, ἐβουλόμην, ἔμελλον (without ἄν) and an infin., instead of a past indic. tense with ἄν of the verb in the infinitive: cf. Thuc. iii. 74 ἡ πόλις ἐκινδύνευσε πᾶσα διαφθαρῆναι, εἰ ἄνεμος ἐπεγένετο.

1119. ἄρα, with εἶχεν = 'as it appears.'

1121. 'Hath wrought me this ruin: ruin, nay, this more than ruin.'

1124. τί λέξεις; cf. supr. 511 n. ἦ γὰρ, cf. supr. 1047 n.

1127. οὗτος, τί πάσχεις; 'you there, what ails you?' is a colloquial equivalent: cf. Soph. Aj. 71 οὗτος, σὲ τὸν τὰς αἰχμαλωτίδας χέρας | δεσμοῖς ἀπευθύνοντα προσμολεῖν καλῶ. Alc. 773 οὗτος, τί σεμνὸν καὶ πεφροντικὸς βλέπεις; Frequently with σύ, e.g. infr. 1280: or with proper names, Soph. Aj. 89 ὦ οὗτος, Αἴας, δεύτερόν σε προσκαλῶ.

1128. μαργῶσαν, 'raging mad': this verb is found in the participle only, and is confined to the tragedians.

1129. τὸ βάρβαρον. Ag. means the absence of that self-restraint, which was so precious to the Greek: cf. supr. 327 n. 'Let uncivilized brute force and passion give way to a civilized method of settling disputes by argument and arbitrament': cf. Med. 536 πρῶτον μὲν Ἑλλάδ' ἀντὶ βαρβάρου χθονὸς | γαῖαν κατοικεῖς, καὶ δίκην ἐπίστασαι, | νόμοις τε χρῆσθαι μὴ πρὸς ἰσχύος κράτος.

1132. Euripides delighted, as no doubt an audience of his contemporaries delighted too, in the transference to the stage of the methods and modes of thought of the δικαστήρια: argument and counter-argument, skilful appeals to self-interest, prejudice and passion, represented under the forms of a rhetoric, specious at all times, even if somewhat forced, were echoes of their daily life greatly to the taste of the quick-witted men of Athens: to the less intellectually interested audiences of to-day, melodrama, with elaborate reproductions of the sights of a great city, administers a corresponding delight. Quintil. (Inst. x. 1. 68) says of Euripides, '*namque is et in sermone magis accedit oratorio generi, et sententiis densus, et in iis quae a sapientibus tradita sunt pene ipsis par, et in dicendo ac respondendo cuilibet eorum, qui fuerunt in foro diserti, comparandus.*' Cf. Ar. Ran. 774 (of Euripides' audience in Hades) οἱ δ' ἀκρόωμενοι | τῶν ἀντιλογιῶν καὶ λογισμῶν καὶ στροφῶν | ὑπερεμάνησαν, κἀνόμισαν σοφώτατον. It is noticeable that Polymestor's attack (1132—1182) and Hecuba's defence (1189 —1237) each take up 50 lines. For similar correspondences cf. Paley's preface to vol. ii. p. xvii.

1135. **ὕποπτος ὢν δὴ Τρωικῆς ἁλώσεως,** 'apprehensive, no doubt, of Troy's fall': ὕποπτος in this active sense is very rare; Thuc. uses τὸ ὕποπτον = 'suspicion,' i. 90: vi. 89. Similarly πιστός, Soph. O. C. 1031 ἀλλ' ἔσθ' ὅτῳ σὺ πιστὸς (relying) ὧν ἕδρας τάδε. (Cf. Jebb's n. ad loc. for further instances.)

1139. **Τροίαν** is more suited to ξυνοικίσῃ than to ἀθροίσῃ, which means to 'muster.' συνοίκισις was the uniting under a central power of scattered districts or tribes: cf. Thuc. ii. 15. 2 ἐπειδὴ δὲ Θησεὺς ἐβασίλευσε...καταλύσας τῶν ἄλλων πόλεων τά τε βουλευτήρια καὶ τὰς ἀρχὰς ἐς τὴν νῦν πόλιν οὖσαν ξυνῴκισε πάντας (of the συνοίκισις of Attica). Here the meaning is 'lest he should re-unite the scattered remnants of Troy, and muster its folk.' For the subj. after a secondary tense, cf. Goodwin, Synt. of Gr. M. and T. § 365. 'The subj. can also follow secondary tenses to retain the mood in which the object of the fear originally occurred to the mind': cf. Xen. Symp. ii. 11 οἱ θεώμενοι ἐφοβοῦντο μή τι πάθῃ.

1141. **ἄρειαν,** the construction lapses into the ordinary optative after a verb in a secondary tense.

1144. **ἐν ᾧπερ,** the antecedent is the idea conveyed in the sentence γείτοσιν δ' εἴη κακὸν Τρώων. Eurip. was in accord with Athenian feeling in making Polymestor ground his excuse ultimately on self-interest: for, if we may believe Thucydides, the average Athenian would admit no other spring of action as credible: cf. iii. 43. 2 μόνην τε πόλιν διὰ τὰς περινοίας εὖ ποιῆσαι ἐκ τοῦ προφανοῦς μὴ ἐξαπατήσαντα ἀδύνατον· ὁ γὰρ διδοὺς φανερῶς τι ἀγαθὸν ἀνθυποπτεύεται ἀφανῶς πῃ πλέον ἕξειν. These words are supposed to have been spoken about two years before the production of the Hecuba. This explains P.'s apparent incivility in hinting to Ag. that the Greeks were unwelcome neighbours.

1150. **κάμψας γόνυ,** cf. Soph. O. C. 19 οὗ κῶλα κάμψον τοῦδ' ἐπ' ἀξέστου πέτρου.

1153. **κερκίδ',** lit. = 'shuttle': here 'the production of the shuttle,' a robe: similar is the use of πόνος to denote what is 'produced by labour,' e.g. Or. 1570 ῥήξας παλαιὰ γεῖσα (coping), τεκτόνων πόνον. Aesch. Ag. 54 ὀρταλίχων πόνον (nestlings).

The Edones were an important Thracian tribe, who dwelt on the east or left bank of the Strymon: Amphipolis and Eion were in their territory. Here, as frequently in Greek and Latin poetry, the name is used to signify Thracian generally.

1154. **πέπλους.** This word signifies a long, full robe, and is rarely used except of women's garments: it is however found sometimes of the ample dress of βάρβαροι, cf. Aesch. Pers. 468. Soph. in the Trach. uses it four times of a man's robe, but Jebb (on 602) regards it as in these cases a 'general word for a stately garment.'

1155. **κάμακα,** properly a 'pole': for vines, Il. xviii. 563: of a spear-shaft, Aesch. Ag. 66: so here.

1156. **διπτ. στολ.,** i.e. both of spear and cloak.

1157. **ἐκπαγλούμεναι:** this verb, like μαργᾶν (supr. 1128), is only found in the participle; an Ionic survival, Rutherford N. P. p. 14.

1159. **γένοιντο.** 'A neuter plural subject denoting *persons* may have a verb in the plural.' Hadley Gr. Gr. § 604 a. It is noticeable that there is no caesura in this line.

διαδοχαῖς ἀμείβουσαι χεροῖν, lit. 'passing them on by successions of hands.'

1160. **πῶς δοκεῖς**; parenthetic: a colloquialism, not used either by Soph. or Aesch.: cf. Hipp. 446 τοῦτον λαβοῦσα, πῶς δοκεῖς; καθύβρισεν. I. A. 1590 κἂν τῷδε Κάλχας πῶς δοκεῖς; χαίρων ἔφη. Ar. Ach. 24. ἐκ, 'after.'

1162. **αἱ δὲ,** the corresponding αἱ μὲν must be understood before κεντοῦσι.

1163. **εἶχον,** 'held down.' He was on a κλίνη, or large couch. For the form of conditional sentence, εἰ ἐξανισταίην—εἶχον, cf. Hadley Gr. Gr. § 894.

1167. **οὐδὲν ἤνυον,** 'I could do nothing': cf. Andr. 1133 ἀλλ' οὐδὲν ἦνεν: Her. ix. 66 οὐδὲν ἤνυε. Poets prefer ἀνύω, prose writers ἀνύτω.

1168. **πῆμα πήματος πλέον,** 'outrage than all outrage worse,'

Way. The editors compare Aesch. Ag. 864 κακοῦ κάκιον ἄλλο πῆμα. πῆμα in apposition to the sense of δεῖν᾽ ἐξειργάσαντο.

1171. **κεντοῦσιν**, cf. supr. 1162.

1172. **ἐκ δὲ πηδήσας**=ἐκπηδήσας δέ. Tmesis is rare in Attic Greek, and is a survival from the time when prepositions were adverbs merely, defining or strengthening the force of case-endings, or modifying the meaning of verbs: cf. Thompson's Gr. Synt. § 249.

1173. **θήρ ὥς** recurs to the metaphor of supr. 1058. The wild beast turns upon the hounds, though in κύνας is further implied the reproach, which the word so often conveys in Homer, especially when used of women.

1174. **ὡς κυνηγέτης**. A good instance of Euripides' quickness of mind, which, while it leads him to metaphor, renders him incapable of sustaining a simile. The hunted quarry, turning on his pursuers, of the previous line, becomes the hunter of this: the θήρ becomes the κυνη-γέτης.

κυνηγέτης is the regular form in Prose, but κυναγός (like δαρός, ἕκατι, ὀπαδός and others quoted by Porson on Or. 26) is invariable in Poetry. The co-existence of these forms, says Rutherford (N. P. p. 496), shows that the Athenians at first accepted Doric forms relating to the arts of which the Dorians were the acknowledged masters, but subsequently brought these forms into harmony with the laws of their own language: but this dictum does not seem to account for all the instances, though the occurrence of both forms in Eur. proves the mixed character of tragic diction.

1175. **βάλλων ἀράσσων**, cf. supr. 1171 κεντοῦσιν αἱμάσσουσιν: 70 δείμασι φάσμασιν. The asyndeton expresses agitation.

σπεύδων χάριν τὴν σήν, 'busying myself in thy interests.' σπεύδων is intrans.; for χάριν, cf. supr. 874 l.

1177 sqq. It is from the consideration of detached invectives against women, like the present, without regard either to the context, or the character in whose mouth they are placed, that the unjust estimate, which brands Eurip. as a hater of the female sex, arises. To refute so baseless an estimate serious argument is not required: the mere statement that it was Eurip. who created Alcestis, Iphigenia, Macaria and Polyxena suffices. A critic who, in this play, would reject the evidence of Polyxena's character, and would prefer to base his view of the poet's meaning on the mad ravings of a barbarian, would not be entitled to a hearing. It is to Euripides' sympathy with women, to his recognition of their capacity both for good and ill, to his desire to open

a wider sphere of influence to that sex, of which even Pericles could say
it was the chiefest credit never to be spoken of, that we owe a gallery
of female characters, unsurpassed till Shakspere came.

1178. **εἴ τις γυναῖκας τῶν πρὶν εἴρηκεν κακῶς**, as, for instance,
Simonides of Amorgus, who classed women, according to their charac-
teristics, as partaking of the natures of the sow, the fox, the bitch, the
earth, the sea, the ass, the cat, the mare, the ape, in most uncompli-
mentary terms: though at last he admits the existence of a bee-like
class, whose virtues he celebrates unstintingly in a very beautiful passage
(vii. 83—93, Bergk's Anthol. Gr., ed. Hiller).

1179. **λέγων ἔστιν**, the so-called *Schema Chalcidiacum* is another
instance of old-Ionic survivals in tragic diction: cf. Her. iii. 99
ἀπαρνεόμενός ἐστι: ix. 51 ἐστὶ ἀπέχουσα: iii. 64 ἀπολωλεκὼς εἴη: Aesch.
Ag. 1178 ἔσται δεδορκώς: Eur. Cycl. 381 ἦτε πάσχοντες.

1180. **συντεμών**, sc. λόγον, which is easily supplied from λόγους,
1177: ἅπαντα ταῦτα is governed by φράσω. For συντέμνειν = 'cut an
account short,' cf. Tro. 441 ὡς δὲ συντέμω | ζῶν εἶσ' ἐς "Αιδην. Ar.
Thesm. 178.

1181. He speaks of them as though they were a breed of monsters.

1182. **ὁ ἀεὶ ξυντυχών**, cf. ὁ αἰεὶ βασιλεύων, 'the king for the time
being.' Thuc. iv. 68. 1 ἔπειτα δὲ καὶ τῶν Ἀθηναίων ἤδη ὁ ἀεὶ ἐντὸς
γιγνόμενος (each Athenian as he got inside) χωρεῖ ἐπὶ τὸ τεῖχος.
iii. 38. 5 δοῦλοι ὄντες τῶν ἀεὶ ἀτόπων (the paradox of the moment).

1183. 'Be not insolent, nor, by reason of thine own ill-experience,
condemn thus sweepingly the whole race of women': cf. fr. 658 ὅστις
δὲ πάσας συντιθεὶς ψέγει λόγῳ | γυναῖκας ἐξῆς, σκαιός ἐστι κοὐ σοφός · |
πολλῶν γὰρ οὐσῶν τὴν μὲν εὑρήσεις κακήν, | τὴν δ' ὥσπερ αὕτη λῆμ'
ἔχουσαν εὐγενές.

1187. Hecuba, after a brief prefatory address to Agamemnon,
deprecating the use of rhetoric in a bad cause, proceeds in lawyer-like
fashion to expose the weak points and improbabilities of Polymestor's
account.

οὐκ ἐχρῆν ἰσχύειν = εἰκότως οὐκ ἂν ἴσχυεν : so infr. 1189 ἔδει λέγειν
= εἰκότως ἂν ἔλεγεν: cf. Goodwin Synt. of Gr. M. and T. §§ 415,
416.

1188. This platitude, so frequently used by Eurip., is somewhat
inconsistent with Hecuba's words (supr. 817 sqq.), where she laments
her lack of πειθώ: but we must bear in mind that this speech is a
forensic display, and conforms to the rules of the courts, where a brief
προοίμιον, either to conciliate feeling in the speaker's favour, or to

minimise the effect of a powerful speech of an opponent, was usual: cf. a similar opening in Hipp. 983 sqq.

1189. Cf. Hipp. 928 χρῆν......δισσάς τε φωνὰς πάντας ἀνθρώπους ἔχειν, | τὴν μὲν δικαίαν, τὴν δ' ὅπως ἐτύγχανεν, | ὡς ἡ φρονοῦσα τἄδικ' ἐξηλέγχετο | πρὸς τῆς δικαίας, κοὐκ ἂν ἠπατώμεθα. εἴτε χρῆστ' ἔδρασε, sc. τις, which is easily supplied from ἀνθρώποισιν above: cf. Andr. 421 οἰκτρὰ γὰρ τὰ δυστυχῆ | βροτοῖς ἅπασι, κἂν θυραῖος ὢν κυρῇ.

1190. **σαθροὺς**, 'unsound.' The word is used of the false ring of a cracked vessel, and is therefore very appropriately applied to deceptive rhetoric, which ought not to have the ring of truth.

1191. **καὶ μὴ δύνασθαι τἄδικ' εὖ λέγειν ποτέ.** Cf. Thuc. iii. 42. 2 βουλόμενός τι αἰσχρὸν πεῖσαι, εὖ μὲν εἰπεῖν οὐκ ἂν ἡγεῖται περὶ τοῦ μὴ καλοῦ δύνασθαι.

1192. **οἱ τάδ' ἠκριβωκότες**, those who have reduced to a system the methods of giving fair names to foul deeds.

1193. The meaning is, 'they cannot keep up the appearance of honesty all through, but are found out and ruined.'

1195. **τὸ μὲν σὸν**, 'the share of my speech addressed directly to you.' **φροιμίοις**, 'at the outset.' προοίμιον was the technical name for the opening of a speech (προοιμιάσασθαι πρὸς εὔνοιαν says the handbook (τέχνη) of Theodectes: *exordiri ita ut eum qui audiat benevolum nobis faciamus et docilem et attentum*, Cic. de Or. ii. 19. 80). The other parts were the διήγησις, πίστεις, ἐπίλογος. Hecuba again turns to Agamemnon in the ἐπίλογος, l. 1232.

1197. **πόνον ἀπαλλάσσων διπλοῦν**, 'ridding them of the repetition of their labours,' i.e. a second expedition to Troy, in the event of its restoration by Polydorus: cf. supr. 1139.

1199. Was there any feeling in Athens that the Thracian alliance of 431 had been of but small advantage?

1201. **τίνα σπεύδων χάριν**, cf. supr. 1175 σπεύδων χάριν τὴν σήν. It may be an unintentional echo, or it may be scornful repetition: the emphasis added by καί (cf. supr. 515 n.) is in favour of the latter view.

1202. **κηδεύσων τινά**, 'with the hope of entering a Greek family by marriage?' κηδεύειν is to 'contract a marriage,' of the bridegroom usually (but cf. Med. 888, where in bitter irony Medea regards herself as κηδεύουσα, a marriage connection of, her rival, Jason's new wife), with special reference to the relations of his wife. Cf. Hipp. 634 κηδεύσας καλοῖς γαμβροῖσι, 'having married into a good family.' The verb here is transitive; lit. 'about to make some one a relation by marriage?'

1204. **σῆς**, emphatic. The subject to ἔμελλον is οἱ Ἕλληνες.

1205. **τίνα δοκεῖς πείσειν τάδε**; 'whom think you you will persuade of this?' For the double accus., cf. Soph. O. C. 797 ἀλλ' οἶδα γάρ σε ταῦτα μὴ πείθων, ἴθι.

1206. **εἰ βούλοιο τἀληθῆ λέγειν**, the apodosis understood is 'you would admit.'

1207. **κέρδη τὰ σά**, 'thy hope of gain': cf. Aesch. Eum. 704 κερδῶν ἄθικτον τοῦτο βουλευτήριον (of the court of Areopagus): Soph. Ant. 222 ἄνδρας τὸ κέρδος πολλάκις διώλεσεν.

1208. **ἐπεὶ δίδαξον**, 'for (if what I say is not true), tell me this, why etc.?' Cf. Soph. O. T. 390 ἐπεί, φέρ' εἰπέ, ποῦ σὺ μάντις εἶ σαφής; O. C. 969 ἐπεὶ δίδαξον...πῶς ἂν δικαίως κ.τ.λ.; El. 351.

The next two lines are almost a repetition of supr. 16—18.

1211. **τί δ'** repeats in a slightly different form the πῶς of l. 1208, the interrogative effect of which may be supposed to be dulled by the long sentence ὅτ' ἡσύχει—δόρυ. 'Why was it, I say (δέ)?'

χάριν θέσθαι, for the phrase, cf. El. 61 ἐξέβαλέ μ' οἴκων, χάριτα τιθεμένη πόσει: Ion 1104: Bacch. 721.

1215. **ἐσήμην'**, absolute, as frequently in Trag.: cf. Aesch. Ag. 497, 293 ἑκὰς δὲ φρυκτοῦ φῶς ἐπ' Εὐρίπου ῥοὰς | Μεσσαπίου φύλαξι σημαίνει μολόν. The latter passage probably suggested the word to Euripides, who regards Troy's burning city as the first of the chain of beacons, that spread the news of the triumph of the Greeks; 'and with its smoke the city gave the beacon-signal of its fall at the foeman's hand.'

1216. **κατέκτας**, a simple non-thematic aorist: cf. Monro Hom. Gr. § 13: Bacch. 1289 κατέκτας: Aesch. Eum. 460 κατέκτα (both in senarii): H. F. 424 ἔκτα (lyric): Soph. Tr. 38 ἔκτα, the only passage of Tragedy where this aorist of the simple verb occurs in senarii.

1218. **χρῆν σε δοῦναι φέροντα**, 'you ought to have taken and given etc.' i.e. during the siege of Troy.

1221. **ἀπεξενωμένοις**, cf. Soph. El. 777 φυγὰς ἀπεξενοῦτο.

1223. **τολμᾷς**, 'canst bring thyself.' Cf. Med. 590 ἥτις οὐδὲ νῦν | τολμᾷς μεθεῖναι καρδίας μέγαν χόλον. ἔχων καρτερεῖς, 'persistent in keeping': cf. I. T. 1395 οἱ δ' ἐκαρτέρουν | πρὸς κῦμα λακτίζοντες.

1224. **καὶ μήν**, introducing a fresh objection. τρέφων = εἰ ἔτρεφες: παῖδα is out of its place: τρέφων τὸν ἐμὸν παῖδα, ὥς σε χρῆν τρ. is the order.

1226. 'Tis in adversity the good man's friendship shines the clearest: prosperity of itself always (ἕκαστ'=in each instance) has friends.' These two lines explain and amplify καλὸν κλέος 1225.

1228. ὃ δ', Polydorus.

1230. νῦν δ', 'as matters stand now.'

οὔτε...τε, cf. Soph. O. C. 1397 οὔτε ταῖς παρελθούσαις ὁδοῖς | ξυνή-δομαί σου, νῦν τ' ἴθ' ὡς τάχος πάλιν : τε...οὔτε is not found.

1233. κακὸς φανεῖ, cf. supr. 1217 φανῇς κακός: supr. 527 n.

1234. εὐσεβῆ and πιστὸν correspond in meaning to ὅσιον and δίκαιον in the next line: for the distinction, cf. supr. 791 n.

1236. 'We shall say that thou hast delight in the wicked, being even such an one thyself.' By the use of τοιοῦτον Hecuba avoids calling her master κακός directly, and to this she alludes in the words δεσπ. δ' οὐ λοιδορῶ. So supr. 1233 she was careful to say κακὸς φανεῖ. There is a slightly generalizing force in the use of the plural δεσπότας, 'one who is in the position of my lord.'

1238. φεῦ φεῦ, expressing admiration: cf. Ar. Av. 1724 φεῦ φεῦ τῆς ὥρας, τοῦ κάλλους. Heracl. 535, 552.

1239. χρηστῶν ἀφορμὰς λόγων, 'a text for goodly discourse.' ἀφορμή is literally a 'starting-point.' For ἐνδίδωσ', cf. Ar. Eq. 847 λαβὴν (hold) γὰρ ἐνδέδωκας.

1243. οὔτ' ἐμὴν χάριν οὔτ' οὖν Ἀχαιῶν, 'neither for my sake, no, nor yet for that of the Greeks.' Cf. supr. 874 n.

1247. ῥᾴδιον, 'a light matter': cf. Hipp. 1441 μακρὰν δὲ λείπεις ῥαδίως ὁμιλίαν.

1249. μὴ ἀδικεῖν: for the synizesis, cf. Hipp. 997 φίλοις τε χρῆσθαι μὴ ἀδικεῖν πειρωμένοις. Cf. Hadley Gr. Gr. § 42, Jebb on Soph. O. T. 555.

πῶς φύγω; cf. Thompson Gr. Synt. § 132 c.

1252. γυναικός, the genit. is due to the comparative idea contained in ἡσσώμενος.

1253. ὑφέξω δίκην τοῖς κακίοσιν, 'shall be held accountable to my inferiors,' Hecuba, to wit, who is a slave: cf. Or. 1649 δίκην ὑπόσχες αἵματος μητροκτόνου | Εὐμενίσι τρισσαῖς.

1254. εἴπερ, 'if, as is the case,' i.e. 'since.'

1256. 'What then of me?' lit. 'what do you think I should do?'

παιδός, for the genit. cf. Thompson Gr. Synt. § 101.

1258. γάρ. 'Yes, for should I not rejoice at taking vengeance on you?'

1260. This line takes up the construction of l. 1258.

1261. μὲν οὖν corrects a previous statement as wrong or inadequate. Latin *immo vero.* Here ναυστολήσῃ is the word corrected, κρύψῃ being substituted for it. ἐκ καρχησίων, 'from the mast-head': so called from its likeness to the cup of the same name. It was used as a look-out: cf. Rich's Dictionary of Antiq. s. v.

1263. Lit. 'thyself shalt ascend on thy feet by the mast.'

1265. Ovid's account is somewhat different (Met. xiii. 565 sqq.), *clade sui Thracum gens irritata tyranni | Troada* (i.e. Hecuba) *telorum lapidumque incessere iactu | coepit. at haec missum rauco cum murmure saxum | morsibus insequitur, rictuque in verba parato | latravit, conata loqui. locus extat, et ex re | nomen habet.* Cicero says (Tusc. iii. 26) *Hecubam autem putant propter animi acerbitatem quandam et rabiem fingi in canem esse conversam.*

πύρσ' ἔχ. δέργ., 'with glaring bloodshot eyes.'

1267. The worship of Dionysus is closely connected in tradition with Thrace. It was in Thrace that King Lycurgus strove to bar the god's progress from Asia Greece-wards, paying for his impiety by a cruel death: in Thrace too, among the peaks of Rhodope, Dionysus had an oracle, to which reference is made in the next line (cf. Herod. vii. 111). The god was worshipped under the name of Sabazios (Ar. Vesp. 9, where the schol. notes Σαβάζιον δὲ τὸν Διόνυσον οἱ Θρᾷκες καλοῦσιν).

For the dat. Θρηξί, cf. Or. 363 ὁ ναυτίλοισι μάντις.

1269. γάρ, 'no, for had he done so, never wouldst thou etc.'

1270. 'Shall I die, or shall I live to accomplish the days of my life as I am (i.e. a slave)?' This seems to me the best interpretation of the line. Irregularly, but quite intelligibly, θανοῦσα is put for θανοῦμαι, being attracted by ζῶσα, although the finite verb ἐκπλήσω (βίον) is not exactly suited to it. ἐνθάδε, 'in my present position,' i.e. a slave.

1272. 'Wilt thou say a name called after my changed shape, or what?' ἢ τί is parenthetic.

1273. Κυνὸς σῆμα, a promontory on the eastern coast of the Thracian Chersonese: cf. Thuc. viii. 102. τέκμαρ, 'a sign,' i.e. a landmark.

1276. ἀπέπτυσ', cf. supr. 942 n. αὐτῷ ταῦτα κ.τ.λ., equivalent to 'may your prognostications recoil on yourself': cf. Cycl. 270 A. κακῶς παῖδες ἀπόλοινθ'...B. αὐτὸς ἔχε.

1277. ἡ τοῦδ' ἄλοχος, Clytaemnestra. οἰκουρὸς πικρά, 'home-guardian to his sorrow': the meaning is that Clytaemnestra's govern-ment of Agamemnon's house during his absence was to be fatal to him, by reason of her connection with Aegisthus, and the consequent plot to murder her husband. For the phrase, cf. Hipp. 787 πικρὸν τόδ' οἰκούρημα δεσπόταις ἐμοῖς.

1278. **μήπω μανείη.** '*μήπω verecunde in votis pro μήποτε dicebant.*' Pflugk. Cf. Soph. El. 403 μήπω νοῦ τοσόνδ᾽ εἴην κενή. Heracl. 359.

Τυνδαρὶς παῖς, Clytaemnestra. It was to the madness of another Tyndarid, Helen, that the war and all its misery was due.

1280. **οὗτος σύ,** cf. supr. 1127 n. Agamemnon's anger is roused at the impertinence, as he regards it, of the frenzied Thracian. μαίνει echoes Hecuba's μανείη of 1278.

1281. **φόνια λουτρά** refers to the bath in which Agamemnon was slain by Aegisthus and Clytaemnestra: cf. Aesch. Ag. 1129.

Those who had lost the power of seeing external objects were supposed to become endowed with extraordinary capacity for penetrating with the eye of the mind into the mysteries of the gods' will and of the future. Possibly for this reason, possibly too as a king of Thrace, the country whence had come the early seers, Orpheus Linus and the rest, the gift of prophecy is here given to the blind barbarian, whose general character, one is forced to admit, does not qualify him eminently to act as the mouthpiece of the gods. It is noticeable that in the Heracleidae Euripides gives a similar power to a similar character, Eurystheus, just before his death.

1283. 'Will ye not check his tongue?' to the attendants.

1284. **ἐγκλήετ᾽,** sc. τὸ στόμα.

1285. **νήσων,** genit. depending on που. Thompson Gr. Synt. p. 85.

ἐκβαλεῖτε, exposure on a desert island was no uncommon penalty: cf. Od. iii. 270 δὴ τότε τὸν μὲν ἀοιδὸν ἄγων ἐς νῆσον ἐρήμην | κάλλιπεν οἰωνοῖσιν ἔλωρ καὶ κύρμα γενέσθαι. The 'marooning' of Philoctetes naturally suggests itself as an instance of the use to which small rocky islands may be put: a use which recommended itself to the Romans at a later date, who found the Aegean a suitable retreat for many whose residence at Rome was regarded as undesirable: '*aude aliquid brevibus Gyaris vel carcere dignum,* | *si vis esse aliquid*' is Juvenal's cynical remark, i. 73 (where Prof. Mayor's note will satisfy the most curious).

1286. **καὶ** intensifies the force of λίαν.

1287. **'Εκάβη, σὺ δ᾽,** cf. supr. 372 n.

1290. Cf. the last lines of Seneca's Troades, *repetite celeri maria captivae gradu,* | *iam vela puppis laxat et classis movet.*

1291. **εὖ δὲ τὰν δόμοις ἔχοντ᾽ ἴδοιμεν.** Notice the irony of these lines.

1294. **δεσποσύνων μόχθων,** cf. supr. 362 sqq. The captives pass from one scene of wretchedness to the experiences of another, yet untried: so one act in life's dreary tragedy closes.

NOTES ON THE TEXT.

THE MSS of Euripides may be divided into two families, representing two separate recensions : the first, to which the oldest extant MSS belong, contained 8 plays : Hecuba, Orestes, Phoenissae, Andromache, Hippolytus, Medea, Alcestis, Troades : also Rhesus, a play of doubtful authorship, once commonly ascribed to Euripides. No MSS which we have, with two exceptions, contain all the eight, the Troades being most frequently omitted. The following table will make this clear :

A.	Marcianus 471	contains	Hec. Or. Phoen. Andr. Hipp.
B.	Vaticanus 909	,,	Hec. Or. Phoen. Andr. Hipp. Med. Alc. Tro. (Rhes.)
C.	Hauniensis	,,	Hec. Or. Phoen. Andr. Hipp. Med. Alc. Tro. (Rhes.)
E.	Parisinus 2712	,,	Hec. Or. Phoen. Andr. Hipp. Med.
F.	Marcianus 468	,,	Hec. Or. Phoen. Med.
a.	Parisinus 2713	,,	Hec. Phoen. Andr. Hipp. Med. Alc.
b.	Florentinus (Vossii)	,,	Hec. Phoen. Andr. Hipp. Med. Alc. Tro. (Rhes.)
c.	Florentinus xxxi. 10	,,	Hec. Or. Phoen. Andr. Hipp. Med. Alc. (Rhes.).
d.	Florentinus xxxi. 15	,,	Andr. Hipp. Med. Alc.

A is our best MS : it is of the xii century, and contains marginal scholia and interlinear glosses, and has been extensively corrected in green ink by a later hand. It is preserved in S. Mark's library at Venice. Besides the five plays of Eurip. it contains the works of the geographer Dionysius Periegetes.

B is of the xii or xiii century : the leaves containing Hec. 212—256, 712—1069 have been lost. It contains scholia and glosses and has been corrected by two hands at least, and is in the Vatican library at Rome.

C, at Copenhagen, is of small value, especially in Hec. Or. Phoen. It seems to be a corrupted copy of B.

E is of the xiii century, and contains Sophocles and Aristophanes, as well as the six plays of Euripides. Where the ink has faded it has been restored by a later hand, often well. It has very few scholia and glosses.

F, a manuscript of the xiii century, contains, besides Euripides, three plays of Aeschylus, six plays of Sophocles and the works of Oppian, and has suffered badly from ignorant annotators. It, like A, is in S. Mark's library at Venice.

The next four MSS Kirchhoff thinks are copies of a codex of the same class as the above, edited and emended by a Byzantine scholar of the xiii century according to the standards and canons of his time.

a, elegantly written but considerably damaged. It contains a life of Euripides, some remarks of Hephaestion on metre, and some lines on the Hecuba by Tzetzes. Prinz says that in the Hec. Or. Phoen. it is very close to A, and therefore of weight. Unfortunately lines 1—522 of the Hecuba are missing in the original, and have been supplied by later worthless hands. It is of the xiii century.

b is now lost, but once belonged to Isaac Voss, who has left a list of its variants. It is of little value.

c is a moth-eaten MS of the xiv century, and contains Sophocles' plays as well.

d, also of the xiv century, is in bad condition, and contains six comedies of Aristophanes as well as the four plays of Euripides.

A compendium for school use was made by a Byzantine scholar, containing Hec. Or. Phoen., and was very extensively used in the xiv and xv century; copies of it are preserved in large numbers : sometimes all three plays are found together, sometimes copies of the separate plays. These editions frequently have copious notes, but are of no independent value.

We now come to the second family of MSS, representing a different recension. MSS of this class contained the eighteen (or, counting the Rhesus, nineteen) extant plays of Euripides. Unfortunately we have only two copies of this edition.

L, Florentinus xxxii. 2, a MS of the xiv century, containing six plays of Sophocles, Hesiod, and all Euripides' extant plays except the Troades.

G and P together contain all the plays. They formed one MS, but by some chance the book was divided, and G was only discovered recently. P contains Andr. Med. Supp. Ion Iph. Aul. Iph. T. Hipp. Alc. Tro. Bacch. Cycl. (Rhes.) Heracl. (1—1003): also Soph. Ant.

OC. Tr. Phil. G contains Heracl. (1003—end) Herc. Hel. El. Hec. Or. Phoen. together with Soph. Aj. El. OT. The MS was probably of the xiv century.

The value of these MSS consists in the fact that, though themselves of not very early date, they are derived from an archetype older than the xiii century. This archetype itself had suffered from the hands of correctors and scholars, but as representing a different and independent recension of the text, it has provided us with a valuable means of checking the other edition, its very errors even sometimes serving to direct us to the true reading. A manuscript in the British Museum (Harleianus 5743) gives us fragments of the Alc., the Troades and Rhesus in this edition : and to the same family belongs the MS, from which the author of the Christus Patiens made his compilations. It seems to have contained Hec. Or. Hipp. Med. Tro. Bacch. (Rhes.).

13. ἥ. MSS ἥν, but the rule is ἥ *eram*, ἥν *erat*, at any rate for Aesch. Soph. and Eur.'s earlier plays.

76. The corruption in this line is of early date. In most MSS we find ἥν περὶ παιδός. ....δι' ὀνείρων | εἶδον γὰρ φοβερὰν ὄψιν ἔμαθον ἐδάην. The writer of G endeavoured to make sense by adding εἶδον after ὀνείρων, and beginning a new sentence with εἶδον γάρ. The source of error lies in the εἶδον γὰρ, which was wrongly inserted here, having caught the copyist's eye in l. 90 infr. ὄψιν was either added as object to εἶδον, or was written against φοβερὰν to show to what noun the adjective referred : finally ἔμαθον was an interlinear gloss, explanatory of the rare word ἐδάην.

80. ἄγκυρ' ἀμῶν: so Meineke for ἄγκυρά τ' ἐμῶν. The rare word ἀμῶν was not understood by the copyist, who corrected, as he thought, ἄγκυρα μῶν into ἄγκυρά [τ' ἐ]μῶν. Other editors correct ἄγκυρ' ἔτ' ἐμῶν, but *facili lectioni praestat ardua.*

91. ἀνοίκτως. Porson for ἀνάγκᾳ | οἰκτρῶς.

164. δαίμων νῷν. All the best MSS have δαιμόνων, which is not metrical. Musgrave proposed the reading in the text. Porson, thinking that a quotation in Dionysius, de compositione verborum (v. 105), illustrating the solemn effect of spondaic rhythm, refers to this passage, would read ποίαν ἢ ταύταν ἢ κεἰ'αν | στείχω ; ποίαν δῆθ' ὁρμάσω ; | ποῦ μοί τις θεῶν | ἢ δαίμων ἐστὶν ἀρωγός ;

224. ἐπέστη. I keep the reading of the MSS, though Nauck's ἐπέσται is generally accepted. ἐπιστάτης ἐπέσται is a jingle of sound merely, while ἐπιστάτης ἐπέστη is akin to such phrases as δραμεῖν δρόμον

H. E.   8 and the like. Eur. is not careful to avoid unmeaning assonance, but it seems gratuitous to import it.

231. **κἄγωγ' ἄρ'**, L. Dindorf for κἀγὼ γάρ. For the force of ἄρα, cf. n. in commentary.

οὔ με χρῆν. MSS οὔ μ' ἐχρῆν. Cf. n. in commentary on 265.

246—250. The order in the text is that of the Byzantine editors : the MSS give 246, 249, 250, 247, 248. Wecklein would reject 247, 248 as a dittography of 245, 246.

274. **καὶ τῆσδε γραίας.** Valckenaer for καὶ τῆσδε γεραιᾶς of the MSS: the latter is possible metrically; cf. supr. 63, where γεραιᾶς is an anapaest.

279. **ταύτῃ γέγηθα κἀπιλήθομαι κακῶν**, an importation from Or. 66, followed here till rejected by Hartung.

293. **λέγῃς.** Muretus for MSS λέγῃ.

312. **ὄλωλε.** E has ἄπεστι.

328. **τοὺς φίλους.** Prinz needlessly proposes τοὺς φθιτούς. The meaning of the text is, 'regard as friends those who are friends indeed,' i.e. benefactors. Prinz's alteration gives only a weak repetition of the next clause.

332. **πέφυκ' ἀεί.** G, and so Stobaeus quotes: πεφυκέναι is the reading of most of the MSS, though πέφυκ' ἀεί is sometimes given as a variant.

367. **ἐλευθέρων.** Blomfield for MSS ἐλεύθερον.

378. Omitted by Nauck.

397. G has κεκτημένη, which leads Prinz to adopt a conjecture (made in 1865) οὐ γὰρ οἶσθα δεσπότας κεκτημένη ; This is very probable.

416. **με χρῆν.** MSS. μ' ἐχρῆν. Cf. supr. 231 crit. n.

425. **ἀθλία.** Markland for MSS ἀθλίας. A however gives ἀθλίου.

432. **κάρᾳ πέπλους.** Kirchhoff for MSS κάρα πέπλοις.

441—443 are rejected by most editors, on very insufficient grounds, as it seems to me : see n. in commentary.

467. **θεᾶς ναίουσ'** is Nauck's brilliant emendation for Ἀθαναίας.

469. The reading is doubtful. A has ἄρα, B ἄρματα corrected to ἄρματι. Paley reads ζεύξομαι ἄρματι πώλους | ἐν δαιδαλέαισι κ.τ.λ. and infr. 478 τυφομένα δορίληπτος | ὑπ' Ἀργείων κ.τ.λ., but with little support from good MSS.

481. The ordinary punctuation is λιποῦσ' Ἀσίαν Εὐρώπας θεράπναν, ἀλλάξασ' Ἅιδα θαλάμους. This is translated 'having left Asia the slave of Europe, etc.' This kind of personification does not seem to me to be in Euripides' style, and his use of the word θεράπνα (cf. n. in commentary) is against such an interpretation.

490. Nauck would expel this line.

528. **αἴρει** is recovered from *a*, which is a valuable MS from 523 onward. ἔρρει is the vulgate.

535. **μου.** The later MSS give μοι.

555, 6. The two following lines are rejected by nearly all editors. οἱ δ', ὡς τάχιστ' ἤκουσαν ὑστάτην ὄπα, | μεθῆκαν, οὔπερ καὶ μέγιστον ἦν κράτος.

559. A has λαγόνας, and one or two other good MSS ; the rest have λαγόνος : Brunck proposed μέσας for the vulgate μέσον.

569. **εὐσχήμως.** With much hesitation I leave this barbarous looking adverb in the text. (The adj. seems to appear first in Dio Cassius : it is quoted in Etym. M.) A gives εὐσήμως : *a* εὐσχήμως, and so ELG. Pliny (Ep. iv. 11) quotes εὐσχήμων, which Prinz accepts.

578. **οὐ πέπλον οὐδὲ κόσμον.** As supr. 574 mention was made of leaves and logs only, the remarkable taste of an ingenious scholar emends the reading of the MSS, which surely needs no defence, to οὐ πέταλον οὐδὲ κορμόν.

580. MSS **λέγων**, which Reiske retained, reading εὐτεκνωτάτην τέ σε. λέγων has been corrected to λέγον in A*a*, which is found also in other MSS. The omission of the augment, though not common, occurs sometimes in long ῥήσεις, and as Talthybius was immediately before repeating the comments of the crowd, it seems natural to refer τοιάδε to their remarks : if this is so, we should read λέγον.

595. **ἄνθρωποι.** Hermann for MSS ἀνθρώποις.

620. **τ', εὐτεκνώτατε** G. Other MSS κεὐτεκνώτατε : cf. n. in commentary.

624. **πλουσίοισι.** I have written this for πλουσίοις ἐν. The sense is 'we are puffed up, some of us by our wealth, others by our reputation among our fellow-citizens.' ὀγκοῦσθαι is used with the dative, or sometimes with ἐπί : never with ἐν, which seems to have been introduced into this line through a mistaken idea of its parallelism with the next, the structure of which is quite different.

626. Reiske's conjecture **τὰ δ' οὐδὲν ἀλλ' ἤ** is very tempting.

665. **ὑπερ** AEL, ἄπο BG. ὑπερ would be more likely to be corrupted than ἄπο, as its use here is somewhat unusual : cf. n. in commentary.

742. **προσθείμεθ' ἄν** AE. προσθείμεθα other MSS.

758. Probably a line has fallen out after this verse. If this view is correct, Hecuba and Agamemnon speak in couplets from 752, where she turns to address him, to 761, where they commence a dialogue in

single lines. In A*a* 756—758 are missing: in F they have been added by a second hand in the margin, and are also found (in the original hand) after 779. Kirchhoff's theory is that the archetype was written in pages of 20 lines, and that 755 ended a page (as it does in A): then by the copyist's error the next four lines, 756—758 and a fourth line now lost, were omitted, but added at the bottom of the next page, thus accounting for their insertion in F after 779, and that the fourth line, being at the very bottom of the page, got worn away and so entirely lost.

793—797 have been rejected either wholly or in part by most editors. I have retained them and believe them to be defensible. For the interpretation cf. n. in commentary.

820. **τί** A*a*. · **πῶς** other MSS.

821. **γὰρ ὄντες** AL. τοσοῦτοι or τοσοίδε other MSS.

831, 832. Two verses, the many variants in which make it probable that they are not genuine, follow here. Prinz gives them as follows:

ἐκ τοῦ σκότου γὰρ τῶν τε νυκτέρων βροτοῖς | φίλτρων μεγίστη γίγνεται βροτοῖς χάρις.

847. **τῆς ἀνάγκης.** The MSS have τὰς ἀνάγκας, which I have with some hesitation altered. The accus. was probably due to the feeling that an object to διώρισαν was required. None of the explanations of the ordinary text seem satisfactory.

850. **ἔγωγε** LG: other MSS give ἐγὼ σὲ.

859. **δ' ἐμοί.** Elmsley for MSS δέ σοι.

947. **ἀπώλεσεν.** There seems no need for ἀπούρισεν or ἀπήλασεν: see instances of ἐξαπόλλυμι in n. in commentary.

950. **οἰζύς.** Porson corrected the MSS ὄϊζύς.

953. Nauck would expel this line.

967. **ἀφικόμην.** Prinz's conjecture ἐφεσπόμην is unnecessary. Instances of careless writing, such as the repetition of ἀφικόμην here after its use above 964, are frequent in Euripides: see n. in commentary on supr. 527.

970—975. Suspected lines. Porson condemned 971, though the irregularity of construction is easily paralleled. Dindorf rejects all six lines: Hartung, with whom I incline to agree, the three lines 973—975. They are singularly weak, and have the appearance of an unintelligent adscript.

1000. **ἔστ', ὦ.** Hermann for MSS ἔστω.

1013. Some read **πέπλων ἔντος ἢ κρύψασ' ἔχεις;** The alternative offered by ἤ seems better.

1026. **ἐκπεσεῖ.** Hermann for MSS ἐκπέσῃ. If the latter is retained, we must place a comma only at δίκην : but the construction is then very harsh.

φίλων κερδέων is Herwerden's attractive conjecture for φίλας καρδίας.

1030. **οὔ.** Hemsterhuis for MSS οὐ.

συμπίτνει is the form given by our best MS A; the other MSS and the corrector of A give συμπιτνεῖ. πιτνῶ is generally banished from the texts.

1042. **ἐπεσπέσωμεν.** Possibly we should read ἐπεσπαίσωμεν : cf. supr. 116, and n. in commentary.

1055. **ῥέοντι :** others read ζέοντι.

1058. I have changed the punctuation of this passage : for the interpretation cf. n. in commentary. The usual punctuation is τετρά-ποδος βάσιν θηρὸς ὀρεστέρου | τιθέμενος ἐπὶ χεῖρα κατ᾽ ἴχνος; ποίαν | ἢ ταύταν ἢ τάνδ᾽ | ἐξαλλάξω, τὰς | ἀνδροφόνους κ.τ.λ., to interpret which is difficult.

1074. Perhaps we should read ἀρνύμενος λώβας λύμας τ᾽ ἀντίποιν᾽ ἐμᾶς : comparing supr. 213, and infr. 1098. ἀρνύμενος λώβαν is very harsh : for the usual interpretation, cf. n. in commentary. ἀρν. ἀντίποινα on the contrary is a natural expression.

1087. **δαίμων ἔδωκεν ὅστις ἐστί σοι βαρύς,** which had been in-serted here from 723, by a copyist probably who did not see that ἐστί is to be supplied in l. 1086, was rejected by Hermann.

1100. **αἰθέρ᾽** is found in the MSS before ἀμπτάμενος, though a scholiast marks it as superfluous : it was no doubt a gloss on οὐράνιον μέλαθρον.

1101. **ὑψιπέτης,** the reading of L, I have adopted : it should be taken closely with ἀμπτάμενος. ὑψιπετὲς (which L. and S. render 'fallen from heaven') is the usual reading : the former is of course connected with πέτεσθαι, the latter with πεσεῖν.

1151. **χειρὸς.** Milton for MSS χεῖρες.

1153. **θάκους.** Hermann for MSS θάκουν.

1174. Rejected by Prinz.

1185, 1186. Dindorf rejects these lines, and is followed by most editors. I see no reason for excision. The verses are quoted by Stobaeus, so that if spurious they must have been inserted 700 years before the date of our earliest MS. The fact that the chorus, infr. 1238, speak two verses only might be regarded as *contributory* evidence of their importation, but to start from it, as Paley does, is surely rash. None of the conjectures of Hermann, Nauck and others are satisfactory :

accordingly I have printed an emendation of my own. The MSS give πολλαὶ γὰρ ἡμῶν, αἱ μέν εἰσ' ἐπίφθονοι, | αἱ δ' εἰς ἀριθμὸν τῶν κακῶν πεφύκαμεν, the sense of which is manifestly worse than weak, to say nothing of the harshness of the syntax. I have written πολλαὶ γὰρ ἐσμέν· αἱ μέν εἰσ' ἐπίφθονοι, | αἱ δ' εἰς ἀριθμὸν οὐ κακῶν πεφύκαμεν. The concession naturally comes first (αἱ μέν εἰσ' ἐπίφθονοι), while the use of the *third* person dissociates the speaker from the class, who after all are spoken of as ἐπίφθονοι only, i.e. exposed to bad feeling: the vindication naturally comes last, and is equally naturally in the first person, while οὐ κακῶν seems to me the very expression wanted here, conveying an idea of proper self-esteem with studied moderation: cf. I. A. 498 where Menelaus says ἀνδρὸς οὐ κακοῦ τρόποι | τοιοίδε in a very similar spirit: so too fr. 218 κόσμος δὲ σιγῆς στέφανος ἀνδρὸς οὐ κακοῦ· Soph. Aj. 550 ὦ παῖ, γένοιο πατρὸς εὐτυχέστερος, | τὰ δ' ἄλλ' ὅμοιος, καὶ γένοι' ἂν οὐ κακός. The omission of αἱ μέν in A (the only variation in the MSS) may be merely a slip of the copyist, or may have been subsequent to the corruption of ἐσμέν into ἡμῶν (a natural corruption enough, owing to the following subdivision αἱ μέν...αἱ δέ).

1197. φὴς is better than φῆσ', as the use of 'Αγαμέμνονος in the next line shows that Hecuba is here addressing Polymestor, not Agamemnon.

1199. Hermann's conjectures πρῶτα ποῦ ποτ' with the interrogation at γένος, and in 1201 οὑτὰν (the MSS give οὗτ', which Dindorf corrected to οὐδ' found in the text) seem probable.

GREEK INDEX.

ENGLISH INDEX.

www.ingramcontent.com/pod-product-compliance
Ingram Content Group UK Ltd.
Pitfield, Milton Keynes, MK11 3LW, UK
UKHW042146280225
455719UK00001B/138